THE AUTOCADET'S GUIDE TO VISUAL LISP

Optimize and customize your AutoCAD design environment

Bill Kramer

Routledge
Taylor & Francis Group

NEW YORK AND LONDON

First published 2002 by CMP Books

This edition published 2015 by Focal Press

Published 2023 by Routledge
605 Third Avenue, New York, NY 10017
4 Park Square, Milton Park, Abingdon, Oxon OX14 4RN

Routledge is an imprint of the Taylor & Francis Group, an informa business

ISBN 13: 978-1-57820-089-4 (pbk)

Cover art: Damien Castaneda

Table of Contents

Introduction

AutoCADet: A person who uses AutoCAD directly or indirectly to create or analyze graphic images and is in possession of one or more of the following traits: wants to learn; has an interest in improving the way AutoCAD works; is a visionary AutoCAD user; is willing to try new approaches to solving problems; or just loves to play with computers.

With Visual LISP, AutoCADets can expand AutoCAD into new realms and create expert commands that enhance the productivity and quality of their work.

This book provides a general introduction to Visual LISP. In each chapter, you learn several concepts regarding a specific aspect of the language and then follow examples to reinforce those concepts. The examples are taken from real working applications. The idea is to teach you how to develop utilities that you can then use to create more complex programs. LISP is a building-block language in that you construct blocks of working code and then use them to build even more.

You do not have to be a programmer to understand this book. However, if you do know another computer language, some of the material will be familiar. In either case, list processing and the techniques for manipulating lists of data will probably be new topics. I recommend that you take your time reading each section and grasping the concepts. For more details, use AutoCAD's online help system, which provides even more examples.

The book begins with an introduction to the language and the environment. Then you dig into the nuts and bolts of Visual LISP, such as data types, basic programs, and converting data to different formats. Next, you learn about user interfaces and activities involving the operator. And finally, you look at the interfaces available in Visual LISP, with an overview of using ActiveX objects and files.

A CD with all the examples from the text plus some extras is provided with this book. The examples in the book have fewer comments than the listings on the CD. In this way, you can concentrate on the code itself while reading the book, and then review and use the functions on the CD without having to reference the text to find out how something is working.

As you embark into learning the Visual LISP, you will find out about its strong traditions and long history in both AutoCAD and computer science as a whole. I have been programming AutoCAD for a long time and enjoy the constant learning process that it involves. I hope you will as well.

Acknowledgments

I would like to acknowledge the following people who played a part in this work. Some were directly involved, such as my good friend Phil Kreiker of Looking Glass Microproducts, who provided the technical edits for the book, and Susan Pink of Techright, who converted my musings into something you can actually read. These two played important roles in making this book a success, and I thank them for their efforts. I would also like to thank the many programmers who have contributed to AutoCAD and Visual LISP — you did a fantastic job producing an extraordinary suite of products. Thanks to the technical support staff for the AutoCAD Developer's Group, especially for answering several questions that came up while writing this book. I can't forget to mention the wonderful people at CMP who provided me with another opportunity to write about a subject I truly enjoy. And last but not least, I thank my family, who stand behind my sometimes odd pursuits.

CHAPTER 1

The Big Picture

When using a tool, it can be helpful to know where it originated, so this chapter begins with a brief history of Visual LISP. Next, you learn about the AutoCAD family of programming options — blocks and menus; scripts and DIESEL; Visual LISP, ObjectARX, and Visual Basic — so that you can understand why some think Visual LISP is the best choice for most AutoCAD customizations. The chapter concludes with some advice on getting started programming in Visual LISP.

The History of Visual LISP

Visual LISP is derived from the LISP language, which was defined back in the late 1950s at the Massachusetts Institute of Technology (MIT). LISP was an experiment in reducing the time required to define a problem to the computer. The underlying idea was that future computers would be significantly faster and capable of handling vast amounts of data as well as processor instructions. Therefore, longer processing time and increased resource usage would not matter, but the cost of the people needed to define problems would. (This vision was extraordinary when you consider that it was made during the 1950s, when the few computers that were in existence had little processing power and disk space by today's standards.) The experiment was a modest success. Meanwhile, advances were being made with private industry tools such as FORTRAN from IBM. Because LISP required a lot more computing power than most people had at their disposal and because it was the result of university work with no company standing behind it, the language remained an idle curiosity taught to computer scientists.

LISP versus other languages

LISP differed from other languages in several ways. First, most programming languages convert source code to assembler or the machine language of the processor. LISP, however, is *evaluated,* which means each line of a program is read and processed as it is supplied to the computer. Although this approach is much slower during program execution, it gives a program the capability to change itself during execution. That meant LISP programs could be adapted in ways other programming languages could not.

The second way that LISP differed from other programming languages was in its syntax. Computer languages had two basic formats: machine language or algebraic. Machine language formats contained an operation followed by a single value or a memory reference to a value. Algebraic formats appeared more like written formulas of numbers and variable values. LISP combined the two formats by having an operation followed by any number of values, references, or other statements. This syntax form is often called prefix, notation.

LISP's prefix notation led to the use of another distinguishing feature of LISP: parentheses. The various logical parts of a LISP program are separated by parentheses. Each statement in LISP starts with an open parenthesis followed by the operation. If the operation includes *arguments* (variable values and references), they follow the operation name, separated by spaces. A closing parenthesis marks the end of the statement. The complete statement, including the parentheses, is called an *expression*. A key item to keep in mind about expressions is that they always return a value.

The parentheses get interesting when you consider that you can have expressions inside expressions. (This is why some people say that LISP means Lost In Stupid Parentheses.) For example, the following expressions produce the same answer, but one takes a bit longer to read:

```
C = A * (B - 2.0) + B
(setq C (+ (* A (- B 2.0)) B))
```

The first example is how the expression might appear in Visual Basic, C++, or FORTRAN. The second expression is how it appears in LISP. To read the second expression, go to the innermost parentheses, (- B 2.0), which says, "B minus 2." The operation is first, followed by the variables, values, and expressions. After computing the result, go out another level of parentheses to where that value is multiplied by the value of A. Then go out another level to where B is added to the result.

Although this approach is difficult to read, it makes good programming sense. When you provide a program expression, the computer does two things: evaluates the expression and then computes the instructions. When evaluating, the computer reads the entire expression and checks to make sure it can recognize the outermost components. All it checks at first is that you have a valid expression — matching parentheses and an operation followed by values or expressions. Then it looks at the first operation. This tells the *evaluator* (the program running in the computer that accepts your program input in LISP) what to expect next in the way of parameters or operands.

For example, if the expression starts with (+, the evaluator expects to find at least one number following the plus operation. The evaluator puts that operation request on the system stack and examines the arguments. (A *stack* is a storage strategy that works like a stack of plates: the first thing stored is the last thing used.) If an argument starts with a parenthesis character, it is evaluated and the result is saved on the stack with the operation that started the process. If the next input item is a value, it is used directly. This process continues until the closing parenthesis is encountered. At this point, the data is available for the operation to take place.

Don't worry if you didn't follow all that; I discuss this concept again later in the book. For now, note that the LISP syntax allowed the computer to quickly handle program code as an evaluator.

LISP to Visual LISP

Because of LISP's memory requirements, it was not a popular programming language for the development of commercial products through the 1960s and 1970s. However, the fact that LISP had an evaluator driving the execution of programs that could change as needed was useful in a variety of application environments, including artificial intelligence, adaptive systems, and robotics.

During the 1970s and 1980s, LISP was ported to smaller and smaller computers as they became available at universities and colleges. One of these versions, written in C and called XLISP, was posted on CompuServe in the High-Level Languages forum. (CompuServe was an extensive computer network service where you could trade files and messages.) A systems programmer from Autodesk retrieved the file, which was quickly integrated into AutoCAD.

Over the next year, Autodesk continued to refine LISP, producing a powerful language called AutoLISP. The earliest releases of AutoLISP were simple versions of what is now Visual LISP. The basics of LISP were provided along with a minimal capability to interface with the user and the AutoCAD command processor. You could write a program that accepted input from the user and then drew new geometry; this in itself was powerful.

In later releases of AutoLISP, programmers could read and write data to the current drawing. This feature created a boom of new applications as engineers and architects learned the language and began to exploit the programming powers of AutoCAD.

Autodesk then released the ADS (Autodesk Development System) library, which enabled C programs to communicate with AutoLISP. ADS was followed by ObjectARX, which could do everything ADS did and more. Autodesk stated that in the future everything would be accomplished with ObjectARX — and to many this appeared to be AutoLISP's death call.

Shortly after ADS was first available, a group of European developers began using a new programming tool: a replacement for AutoLISP that became known as the European Compiler. This compiler created FAS files from LSP files, resulting in programs that were not only reported to run four times faster but were also encrypted, which helped prevent piracy of AutoLISP-based applications. But the European Compiler didn't catch on immediately, especially in the United States, because it wasn't from Autodesk and it didn't appear that Autodesk would endorse it.

Undeterred, the developers of the AutoLISP compiler continued to improve it and came out with a version called Vital LISP that was packaged more as a software utility product. Vital LISP was a vast improvement over AutoLISP. Vital LISP took advantage of ObjectARX, opening the way for expansion and improvement. Virtually all of the system-level utilities that developers found lacking in AutoLISP were provided in Vital LISP. Plus Vital LISP came with a text editor optimized for LISP program entry.

Autodesk purchased the Vital LISP technology, improved it with the introduction of more than 800 functions, and repackaged it as Visual LISP. At this time, Visual Basic for Applications (VBA) was introduced into AutoCAD. This stifled the rumors that Autodesk was phasing out AutoLISP.

The result of this evolution is a powerful programming language that requires a long time to master but also enables you to begin writing simple programs in a short time.

Programming Choices in AutoCAD

AutoCAD is expensive, and some may argue that it should not need customization. But AutoCAD is powerful because it can be customized. Out of the box, AutoCAD is a great drawing tool. Graphic design and editing are easy after you learn the basics.

If you create drawings that are variations of each other, you can save complete or partial drawings and then reload and edit them. But consider the time-savings if you could automate that task.

For example, suppose that you frequently create drawings that contain circles representing attachment points for a fixture. You want to show only the holes, not the fixture. You insert the fixture, use the through-hole locations in that drawing to locate new circle centers, and then remove the fixture block. Compared to drawing the circles one at a time from other parameters, this is a great timesaver. Now consider what would happen if you wrote a program that accomplished the same task in just a few seconds. The time you'd save would quickly add up and easily justify the time you would spend creating the program.

In your own work with AutoCAD, can you identify a repetitious task — something that is time consuming but requires skill rather than a lot of thought? If so, you have identified the perfect candidate for automation.

For larger installations, automating AutoCAD can turn into a full-time job. For smaller places, automation is a way to stay ahead of the competition as well as keep the job fresh and exciting.

AutoCAD can be customized in many ways to meet the needs of designers and engineers. Each customization tool has strengths and weaknesses that are not easy to identify at a glance. Some relate to you directly. Do you already know a programming language or two? Do you know how to run AutoCAD? Do you have the time to program in addition to your other job-related tasks? Following is a quick look at each of the programming options in AutoCAD.

Blocks and menus

Blocks and menus are easy to program and are often an AutoCAD operator's first step in customizing AutoCAD. Properly constructed, block libraries can save you a lot of time when you are creating drawings that have many similar components. When combined with a menu system, block libraries can become extensive.

Menus are the primary interface for the AutoCAD operator and an important part of the user's computer environment. Menus are easy to manipulate, which is why they are one of the first programming tasks that AutoCAD operators perform. If you haven't yet customized the AutoCAD menu and created blocks, give it a try. What you learn in this book will compliment that skill nicely.

Scripts and DIESEL

Blocks are not the only tools AutoCAD operators use. A sequence of commands that you repeat frequently can be *scripted* and placed in a menu. For example, if you frequently copy and then rotate a sequence of geometry, you can turn those tasks into a script. A *script file*.

Scripting is available in two ways. You can create an SCR (script) file, which is a text file containing AutoCAD commands that you can create using a text editor or AutoCAD's scripting tools.

Scripts have been very useful for plotter operations, and you can still find them in many sites. As AutoCAD's user interface evolved, however, scripts because more difficult to maintain because dialog boxes sometimes changed the sequence of commands. (AutoCAD commands that contain a dialog box often also have command-line versions as well. For example, the LAYER command displays a layer dialog box. To prevent the dialog box from appearing, you add a hyphen before the command, as in -LAYER.

Using DIESEL (Direct Interpretively Evaluated String Expression Language), you can define variables and use them in your menu design. This enables you to control more of the AutoCAD environment and command execution sequence. Scripts and DIESEL are powerful tools when programming menus.

Visual LISP

Visual LISP is a powerful programming language that you can use to automate complex sequences of AutoCAD commands, perform calculations, and much more. Visual LISP, which was derived from AutoLISP, is a full-featured programming language, supporting variables, expressions, loops, conditionals, and more. You can use Visual LISP to communicate with other systems through ActiveX as well as control almost all elements of the AutoCAD system.

Visual LISP persists today despite newer tools such as Visual Basic mainly because the legacy of AutoLISP has provided a large library of useful programs and examples that can be used to create even more powerful tools in AutoCAD.

ObjectARX

ObjectARX is a set of C++ libraries for building dynamic link libraries (DLLs) that you integrate directly into AutoCAD. ObjectARX is useful for adding new commands and functions to AutoCAD, but its complexity makes it difficult for beginning programmers to use.
ObjectARX provides a tool for adding functions (called external subroutines) to the Visual LISP environment. That means you can expand Visual LISP with new commands suitable for your application. For some applications, this is the best solution to follow.

For each new release of AutoCAD, ObjectARX applications must be rebuilt and ObjectARX modules may have to be adapted. For example, AutoCAD 2000 introduced the addition of multiple documents, which were not supported in AutoCAD Release 14. This meant that ObjectARX applications had to be reprogrammed to take into account the existence of multiple open documents. The MDI (Multiple Document Interface) change also had an effect on Visual LISP and Visual Basic, but not to the same degree that it did with ObjectARX-based applications.

Visual Basic

You can use Visual Basic to run AutoCAD. In addition, a variation of Visual Basic called VBA (Visual Basic for Applications) is supplied with AutoCAD. VBA uses the same object interfaces as Visual Basic but it starts in AutoCAD. VB and VBA are powerful programming environments that rely on the ActiveX *exposure* (a method of accessing subroutines and variables) of other products to allow you to tie together the various features of applications such as databases and word processors with AutoCAD.

Visual Basic is an attractive solution for programming AutoCAD because it is easy to learn the Visual Basic programming environment. A dialog box editor provided with the package makes the creation of sophisticated dialog boxes a breeze. However, not all applications in AutoCAD revolve around a dialog box, and Visual Basic is cumbersome as a command enhancement tool.

Making a choice

This section provides some factors you should consider when deciding how to program AutoCAD. The foremost factor is what you already know about AutoCAD and computers.

If you know Visual Basic, that might be the logical place to start. But there are roadblocks if you want to create commands that AutoCAD operators can use with ease. For example, getting toolbar and tablet selections to blend with your Visual Basic applications can be challenging.

If you know AutoCAD, Visual LISP is the better solution. You probably have access to many programs that work with older versions of AutoCAD. At the very least, a search of the Web will turn up a lot of Visual LISP applications that you can adapt. (Note, however, that you might find someone else's style of programming confusing.)

Those who know C++ may find ObjectARX an interesting approach to customizing AutoCAD. You may be able to successfully build an ObjectARX application due to the tightness it enjoys with AutoCAD, but you will find that operators expect flexibility. Before digging into ObjectARX, you should understand how AutoCAD users actually use the system and how drawings are structured. Creating a few drawings under the watchful eye of an experienced AutoCAD operator can go a long way towards learning the proper processes.

AutoCAD can be customized at multiple levels. And when you are selecting an interface language, the level from which you are designing the integration of AutoCAD with another process is important. A database system with an ActiveX interface can be tied to AutoCAD using the Visual Basic options (VB or VBA). Visual LISP can also talk to the ActiveX system and includes other database integration options using SQL. C++ supports ActiveX as well as many other database tools that may be an important part of the application you are creating. The idea of database integration may be important to the application, but keep in mind that sometimes you can mix the application environment as well. That is, you could use C++ for the portions of the application that need to talk to the database and link them to Visual LISP as external functions.

Another issue is related to the level of operator integration. If the application is intended for operators, it should be command based. The command can then be typed or placed in a menu for selection by the operator. Only Visual LISP and ObjectARX provide this feature, although you can write a Visual LISP command function that launches a VBA macro. As mentioned, they can be intermixed.

I think Visual LISP provides the easiest way to develop user interfaces and presents the best tools for the creation of operator-level commands. ObjectARX provides the tools needed to take Visual LISP further or deeper into another environment.

Sometimes the integration of a task is controlled by a source outside AutoCAD. In those cases, you can use an ActiveX solution (using Visual Basic) or a variation of ObjectARX called Object-DBX. These types of integration are rare but can be powerful tools for using AutoCAD in an automated environment. For example, you can build an application that automatically reads drawings and processes them into NC/CNC code for a machine tool. Visual Basic and ObjectARX (DBX) provide tools to run AutoCAD automatically without an operator. Writing these types of programs can be a challenge, and you must anticipate all the places where AutoCAD can get fouled up due to bad input.

Back to the question of which option is best. Because you are reading this book, you are probably an AutoCAD operator and are comfortable with the command system. You probably want to know how to make your work with AutoCAD more productive. AutoLISP and Visual LISP were written for AutoCAD operators to enhance their environment beyond just menus. Visual LISP is not hard to learn, and before long you will be writing fantastic utilities that enhance your productivity.

Getting started

An application starts with an idea. Perhaps you want to improve your usage of AutoCAD by transforming boring repetitive tasks into a few keystrokes. Maybe you want to link various tasks that share graphical data to automatically draw something or perform a calculation. If you don't know what you want the computer to do for you, the examples in this book, which are taken from real-world applications, might spark some ideas.

In the initial stages of learning to program AutoCAD, choose easy tasks to automate. I recommend starting with a few simple AutoCAD command functions, such as COPY and ROTATE, combined with other logic. In fact, you use just that example in the next chapter, where you explore the Visual LISP Integrated Development Environment, or VLIDE.

CHAPTER 2

The Visual LISP IDE

The Visual in Visual LISP comes from its development environment. Before Visual LISP and its IDE (Integrated Development Environment), AutoLISP developers had to use text editors or word processors, which know nothing about LISP syntax and requirements. Testing involved loading the files into AutoCAD to see whether they worked. Debugging tools were left to the invention of the programmer. To improve this situation, independent developers created tools, one of which evolved into Visual LISP.

The Visual LISP IDE (VLIDE) consists of a set of tools that exist in a window separate from AutoCAD's main window. This separate window contains multiple child windows that help you manage source files and projects as well as test programs. The term visual is used because the windows use colors and icons so that you can navigate quickly from one task to another.

A variety of tools are provided in the IDE, including parentheses matching, automatic indentation, color-coding of source text, dialog box previews, a function search utility, and symbol tracking. Programmers are the users in an IDE, so all its tools are designed to make their job more productive.

Because you will be using the VLIDE to create new programs, it is important that you know the basics of how to use it from the onset. You start by becoming familiar with the various windows, toolbars, and terms in the VLIDE. Then you look into the basic operations involved when developing programs: creating files, editing files, testing programs, and hunting down syntax errors.
Note, however, that a single chapter cannot handle all the features in the VLIDE. This chapter introduces the concepts and provides a foundation for using the tool. By the end of the chapter, you will be able to start the VLIDE, load a program file into the editor, perform basic syntax checks, and test the program.

Finding Your Way Around the IDE

The Visual LISP Integrated Development Environment consists of a group of windows in which you enter, run, test, and debug programs. The IDE is a major step forward from the basic text editors used to enter and edit programs. Table 2.1 lists the various windows that can appear in the Visual LISP IDE.

Table 2.1 VLIDE windows.

IDE Window	Description
Apropos	Finds matching keywords for internal symbols. With more than 800 internal functions in Visual LISP, this search utility is helpful even for experts.
Console	Loads and runs program files and functions from the $ prompt. When you run a program in the Console window, it behaves similarly to one run from the AutoCAD command line. You can minimize this window.
Error Trace	Displays error-related information such as a failed expression. Use it with the Trace Stack window to get a program working correctly.
LSP and DCL File Editors	Appears when you create or load a text file. These color text editor windows know about LISP and DCL formats, keywords, and structures. You will spend most of the time in the VLIDE in the LSP or DCL window, entering and editing program text.
Project	Lists the various files included in a project. Double-click an entry in the list to display the associated file in a text editor window. You can move this window outside the main VLIDE window to leave more room for the code windows.
Symbol Service	Displays the current binding (value) of symbols. Use it to set the flags for various symbols when debugging an application. You must close this window before using any other windows in the VLIDE.
Trace	Traces the activity of the Visual LISP environment. Referenced only when something is seriously wrong in the system. You can minimize this window.
Trace Stack	Displays the basic contents of the stack while the evaluator is running. (The stack is where the calling sequence of a program is stored during execution.) You use this window when you are debugging a program.
Watch	Displays the binding of symbols and other information while the program is running. You view this window when you set a breakpoint to see the contents of the symbol being watched.

Starting the IDE

You can start the Visual LISP IDE in AutoCAD 2000 (or higher) in several ways. In the command-entry method, you type the following on the AutoCAD command line:

```
VLISP
```
or
```
VLIDE
```

The other way to start the IDE is using the AutoCAD menu; choose Tools > AutoLISP > Visual LISP Editor.

When the IDE starts, the last project loaded is displayed, as if you had walked away from it for a minute. You don't have to reload the project and its associated files to begin working on the code.

If you are starting Visual LISP for the first time, however, you see a screen containing the Trace and Console windows, as shown in Figure 2.1.

If the Visual LISP IDE did not load, something is wrong with your installation of AutoCAD. Visual LISP is installed as part of the standard installation of AutoCAD 2000. You may need to install the program again, selecting the standard options to enable Visual LISP. Note that you must have the full AutoCAD 2000 implementation. Visual LISP is not available for the AutoCAD LT versions, and only an initial version was available for AutoCAD Release 14.

Figure 2.1   The opening window in the VLIDE.

Exiting and reentering the IDE

In this section, you briefly explore how to switch from the VLIDE to AutoCAD itself. When writing LISP programs for AutoCAD, it is not uncommon to have to return to the AutoCAD drawing editor to review command sequences, test a program that involves interactive graphics, or just load a drawing at someone's request.

To exit the VLIDE, click the Close icon (labeled in Figure 2.1) or choose File > Exit. Either method closes the current project, giving you the opportunity to save any files you have modified. Control of the computer is then returned to the AutoCAD drawing editor. VLIDE is no longer running, but Visual LISP is still available from the AutoCAD command line for running your functions and expressions. You typically exit the VLIDE when you have finished programming for a while.

The usual way to use the VLIDE with AutoCAD is to switch between the two, without exiting the VLIDE. You can jump into AutoCAD to do something, and then return to the VLIDE to continue programming. You can accomplish this in several ways: click the Activate AutoCAD icon on the View toolbar, choose Window > Activate AutoCAD, or click the AutoCAD application in the Windows taskbar (which is normally at the bottom of the Windows desktop).

Note that the taskbar also contains an entry titled Visual LISP for AutoCAD. When started inside AutoCAD, the VLIDE becomes another Window application that is running. You can switch between the AutoCAD drawing window and Visual LISP at any time by simply clicking AutoCAD or Visual LISP in the Windows taskbar. When you start the Visual LISP IDE, you should see the normal Windows cursor, which is an arrow or a text-editing symbol. If you see an icon like the one in Figure 2.2, Visual LISP is busy running a function and the IDE is not available for text editing. To get back to the normal Windows cursor, return to AutoCAD and cancel or finish running the Visual LISP expression.

Figure 2.2   The Visual LISP busy cursor.

Navigating the Console window

As stated, the Visual LISP IDE consists of a set of windows that are all related to the purpose of writing applications in Visual LISP. The VLIDE is a multiple document interface (MDI), which means it contains multiple windows inside a master window. The master window for the application contains child windows in much the same way that the Windows desktop contains application windows. To switch from one window to the other, just click inside the window.

When you select Visual LISP from the Windows taskbar, the master window is reactivated, and the last child window active when it was closed or abandoned is the active window. The Console and Trace windows are always present in the master window. Other windows appear as needed. Figure 2.3 shows the VLIDE with the Console window and one source code window open. The Trace window is minimized in this figure.

The primary child window of the VLIDE is the Visual LISP Console. The Console cannot be destroyed or closed but in can be minimized. Any expressions you type in the Console window are evaluated immediately.

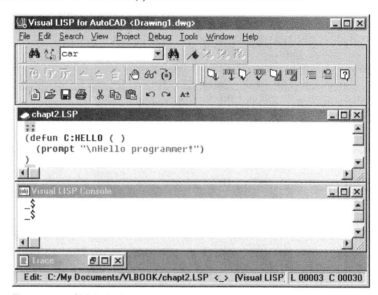

Figure 2.3   Child windows in the master window.

The Console is most useful when testing or setting up variables as you run functions. Simply type the name of the variable and press Enter, and its current value appears. You can also establish the variable values before running a function using the (SETQ) expression. For example, type the following LISP expression at the Console window's _$ prompt.

```
(setq A 2)
```

Press the Enter key, and the value 2 appears on the next line, as shown in Figure 2.4. Now type

Figure 2.4   An expression in the Console window.

the letter A and press the Enter key. The value 2 appears again.

You can use the Console window to seed values in variables before running a test. You can use it also to launch functions that you're developing, allowing you to create small modules and then glue them together into larger applications. When a function is evaluated, its results are posted in the Console window.

The Console window is for the developer — not for the user of the LISP routines you write. Ideally, the typical user never sees any part of the VLIDE.

Another window in the VLIDE that remains at all times is the Trace window. Basically, this window is where you can see what is going on inside the VLIDE program. For the most part, this information is about the version of Visual LISP and is not that important to application development, so it's usually minimized.

Navigating the text editor

In this section, you'll move deeper in the VLIDE by creating a simple program file. Starting a new program in the IDE is simple — after all, the IDE is primarily a text editor for program source files. Choose File > New file (or click the New file icon on the Standard toolbar). The text editor window appears, as shown in Figure 2.5.

When a text editor window is active, you can start typing Visual LISP code right into the text file. Unlike in the Console window, the text editor window has no prompt and the text you type is not run or evaluated. However, the IDE does check the code as you enter it and provides some features to assist you in programming.

Figure 2.5   An empty text editor window.

Typing your first program

The first program presented in most programming book is the simple Hello program. Listing 2.1 shows the code required for the Hello program in Visual LISP.

Listing 2.1   The Hello program.

```
(defun HELLO ()
    (prompt "\nHello programmer!")
)
```

To enter your first program in Visual LISP, follow these steps:

1. Start a new file in the VLIDE.

2. Type the program in Listing 2.1. Note how the parentheses and other items are colored as you enter them.

3. Move the cursor to the start of the program and click. Now press Ctrl+right bracket (]). The cursor should jump to the ending parenthesis. If it does not, check your typing against Listing 2.1 and make the necessary corrections.

4. Choose Tools > Load Text in Editor (or press Ctrl+Alt+E). This loads your program into Visual LISP so that you can test it in the Console window.

5. Type HELLO at the $ prompt in the Console window. The system returns information about the HELLO symbol, telling you that the HELLO symbol is a user subroutine or function (type USUBR).

6. Run the program by typing (HELLO), including the parentheses. The Console window displays NIL, which is the result of the function.

Note that the program didn't display "Hello programmer!" In Visual LISP, all functions return a result. If there is nothing to return, as is the case in the (HELLO) example, NIL is the result. You find out more about symbols in later chapters. For now, it is important to understand that you have defined a symbol named HELLO that is of the type USUBR (user subroutine).

Now type the HELLO symbol at the AutoCAD command prompt. You're told that it is an unknown command and that you can find out about the commands by typing help. This difference demonstrates how the IDE talks to the programmer but the command system of AutoCAD talks to the operator.

Now type (HELLO) at the AutoCAD command prompt. The string Hello programmer! appears, followed by NIL. The result of running the subroutine is to print a message in the AutoCAD text window and return nothing.

After typing and testing the program, you may want to save it. To do so, choose File > Save. The default directory for saving a new Visual LISP file is the current directory. When first learning to program, it is a good idea to create a temporary directory inside AutoCAD's program directory for files. In the File Open dialog box, click the New folder icon (it looks like a folder with a bright spot at the top) and define one of your choice in which to save the HELLO function.

To load the HELLO program in Visual LISP, choose File > Open File and then select the source (LSP) file. The file appears in a text window. Press Ctrl+Alt+E to load the contents of the text window into the Console for running and testing. (Later in the chapter, you learn two other ways to load a program.)

Color coding and other formatting

As you enter code, note the color-coding applied to the various elements. By default, parentheses are shown in red, reserved words are blue, comments have a gray background, and text constants inside quotes are magenta. Color-coding helps you keep the components of a program straight and aids in finding typographic errors during program entry.

The purpose of the IDE is to make you more productive, so you should use the color system to your advantage. If you don't like the default colors presented in the VLIDE, you can change them. Choose Tools > Window Attributes > Configure Current. A dialog box appears, allowing you to change the colors of the various items in the Visual LISP editor. Following is what these items mean:

:LEX-PAREN	Parentheses
:LEX-SYM	Reserved words
:LEX-COMM1	Comments
:LEX-STR	ext inside quotes

When you type program text, the IDE indents it to create source files that are easier to read. You can control how much the IDE will indent each new expression entry as well as where it will place closing parentheses by default by choosing Tools > Environment options > Visual LISP Format options. You can use these format options also to change existing source code to match you own preferences. First define the format options desired. Next, choose Tools and then choose either Format Code in Editor or Format Code in Selection. The selected code area is converted to the format options defined. Having the capability to import code from other sources into your own desired format makes building a library of useful tools easy.

Visual LISP Files

Visual LISP source files have the LSP extension. In addition to Visual LISP files, you will also be working with Dialog Control Language (DCL) files, compiled programs (FAS), and packaged products (VLX). Most of the time, you will be editing LSP source files in the VLIDE. When you supply program modules to your users, you can elect to compile them so that they load and run faster. Another feature of compiling your programs is that no one but you can change the program's operation.

When you edit and save source files, the last file saved is backed up. That file has the same name as the LSP source file but with the _LS extension. Should you make a horrible error, you can restore to the previously saved version of the file by renaming the _LS file to LSP. The same is true with DCL source files.

Loading and testing LSP source files allows you to create applications more quickly because you do not have to compile them for testing. You can load a saved LSP file into memory in several ways:

• Access the APPLOAD command in the Autocad menu (Tools > Load application).

• Use the (LOAD) expression at the AutoCAD command line, in a menu, or in the VLIDE Console window.

• Open the file in a text editor window and press Ctrl+Alt+E.

LSP files are the source code of your programs. When you are finished with the program and want to share it with others, you compile the LSP source files into FAS files.

Like LSP files, FAS files can be loaded by using the (LOAD) expression in Visual LISP at the command line or in the Console window or by using the APPLOAD command in AutoCAD. FAS files are smaller than the original LSP source files and cannot be loaded into the text editor, but they will load faster into the system. FAS files consist of a simplified language that is processed by the computer more quickly than the longer source code, which is full of comments and extra spaces for readability.

An application can use multiple FAS or LSP files. However, if you will be mixing compiled files, it is a good idea to create a project. A project glues the various modules into one unit so that symbol references are consistent between all FAS and LSP files. Projects are created by adding source files or compiled FAS files to a named project list. Changes to the various components are tracked and the project can be updated with a make operation, in which only those items that have changed are compiled and linked. The output of a make operation is a VLX file. The VLX file combines all FAS and LSP (and DCL) files into a single, larger file.

If you are building a complex application with many function names, link the FAS and DCL files into a single VLX file. A VLX is a compiled project bundled or packaged into a single unit, making it easier to supply to users. Distributing your application as a VLX file has several advantages. The greatest advantage is that you have your own memory and symbol space for your application. This means you can write a function that uses a simple name, such as (get_data), and know that other programmers can also use that function name in their own applications without any effect to your version of it. In this case, the function is private to your own memory. You can selectively expose functions (make them available to users).

With Visual LISP, you should "think big but start small." Start with LSP programming. It will evolve on its own into FAS-style programming, which will in turn move you into VLX files. The remainder of this book focuses on LSP-style programming and does not explore the FAS and VLX aspects of Visual LISP.

VLIDE Toolbars

When you first start the VLIDE, you are presented with a series of icons, or tools, grouped in toolbars. To find out a bit more about an icon, move the mouse pointer over it. A small window appears, identifying the icon. Many icons duplicate menu options.

You can turn the various toolbars on and off. This feature is helpful when you need more screen space, such as when you are using the smaller screen of a laptop computer.

This section lists every icon on the Visual LISP toolbars and explains how you might make use of them while working in Visual LISP. Several icons are also described in more detail later in the chapter.

The Standard toolbar

The Standard toolbar, shown in Figure 2.6, contains many common icons found in other Windows products. All but the Complete word icon are standard icons used in Windows.

The Complete word icon is found in editor environments that use a dictionary of reserve words. This function helps you complete the word you are typing. For example, if you type (DE and then click the Complete word icon, the word DEFUN is placed where you were typing. Try it again, but this time do not include the letter E. A long list of all reserve words beginning with the letter D is displayed in an Apropos window. You can then scroll through the list, highlight a function, and click the Help button (in the Tools toolbar) to learn more about that function. Apropos is helpful when you are first

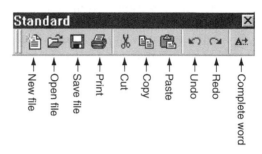

Figure 2.6   Standard toolbar icons.

learning Visual LISP or when you are using an unfamiliar function.

The Search toolbar

The Search toolbar, shown in Figure 2.7, is another toolbar full of standard features found in most Windows-based text editor products. The Find and Replace features are the most frequently used icons in this toolbar. There is also a quick search, in which you type a string in the window area provided and then click the Find toolbar string icon.

The remaining icons in the Search toolbar deal with bookmarks. You use bookmarks to mark your place in source code when working with large files. As you jump from one section of code to the next, comparing items such as symbol name spellings and parameter lists, you can set a bookmark to make it easy to return to a particular location. If you have a large volume of code in a single text file, the bookmark features are very helpful. (However, I recommend that you split a large source file into smaller, easier-to-manage chunks and use the project manager in the VLIDE to help you keep track of everything.)

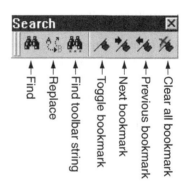

Figure 2.7   Icons in the Search toolbar.

The Tools toolbar

The Tools toolbar, shown in Figure 2.8, contains powerful edit and testing features. For example, when you are writing a program and want to test it, you can load the entire contents of the editor window or just a selection of it into the Console window. The first two icons in the Tools toolbar load the entire editor window or only the highlighted code, respectively.

By loading only a section of your code into the Console window, you can test small elements of your application. The normal procedure is to set up some symbol values that are needed in the test code. Follow these steps:

1. At the _$ prompt in the Console window, type (SETQ) and the values you need to set.

2. Move to the text editor window and highlight the code to test.

3. Click the Load selection icon, and then view the results in the Console window.

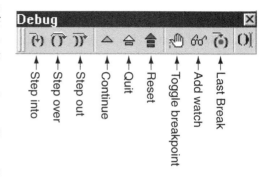

Figure 2.8   Icons in the Tools toolbar.

You can use some other debugging tools at the same time; you find out about them shortly.

You use the next two icons in the Tools toolbar when checking your code. Like the previous two, these icons are for the entire active window or the highlighted code. You can use the Check edit window icon to see whether the file will load into the Console window properly. In most cases, you use the Check selection icon to find unbalanced parentheses in sections of code. These tools assume you are an experienced LISP programmer and know what you are looking for and what the messages mean. One cool feature is that when you check a file and there is a problem, all you need to do is double-click the message in the Console window and the code section where the problem was found is highlighted.

You use the next pair of tools to format the code. Formatting is helpful when you need to debugsomeone else's code. You can run the code through the format operation and standardize the indentation and other aspects of the source code. In addition, when you see code at the wrong level of indentation, is usually means the code has a missing parenthesis or unbalanced parentheses. Once again, you must know how to read code and work with Visual LISP to get the most of this feature. It will make your code more presentable, but it will not correct it without your help.

You use the last pair of icons to comment your code. You can select a block of code and comment it out do that it doesn't run when loaded. Use the Uncomment block icon to turn the code back on again when you have finished testing. The basic idea is to switch portions of your program on and off while you are testing it.

The commenting feature is handy if you develop large-scale applications because you can disable large sections of code quickly for testing. For example, suppose your application performs many calculations and then draws something. You can test the drawing portion of the application by commenting out the math section, setting variables to the results needed from the calculations, and then running just the drawing component. Later, as you develop the math section, you can keep the testing parameters handy should you ever decide to change the drawing portion and want to quickly test just that part.

The Debug toolbar

The icons in the Debug toolbar, shown in Figure 2.9, are tempting, but using them requires practice. If you have used another visual-type editor, you should have no problem learning the tools provided with Visual LISP.

The greatest debugging tool in Visual LISP is the breakpoint, which stops the execution of your program in mid-stride so that you can look at the contents of the variables and watch the program run one step at a time. When the system reaches a breakpoint while evaluating your program, it stops, displays the Watch window contents along with your source code indicating where in the program the execution is currently located, and waits

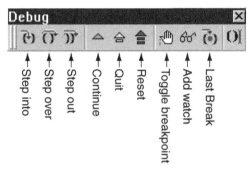

Figure 2.9   Icons in the Debug toolbar.

for your signal to continue. (For more on setting breakpoints, see the upcoming section, "Using the IDE to Debug Programs.")

You use the Debug toolbar icons to set breakpoints and to step through the program after you are running in debugging mode. Note that most of these icons are turned off until you start to run some code through the evaluator in Visual LISP's Console window.

The first three icons in the Debug toolbar are for moving in and around expressions in the program. You can step into the next expression, step over it, or step out of the current function altogether. This allows you to watch the execution of your program from the breakpoint onward as each expression is evaluated. And this is where the Watch window becomes a handy tool. Activate the Watch window by selecting the Add watch icon. Type the name of any symbol in your program, and the current value of that symbol is displayed in the Watch window while your program runs.

The three arrow icons in the toolbar control what to do when the program reaches a breakpoint. Use them to continue to the next designated breakpoint, exit the current test run, or reset the run. Note that when you are stepping through a program using the first three icons in the Debug toolbar, you are creating temporary breakpoints. The three arrows (green, yellow, and red) are displayed while you are stepping through the parentheses.

The Last break icon shows you the last breakpoint in your program while it is running. When at a breakpoint, you can set more breakpoints later in the program and then click this icon to quickly return to the last breakpoint that was active when performing the test run.

The last icon cannot be selected. It simply indicates where in the code you have stopped for the breakpoint, either before or after the expression. (You can set a breakpoint both before and after an expression is evaluated so that you can check the values in the program.)

The View toolbar

The View toolbar, shown in Figure 2.10, displays the various window components of the VLIDE and enables you to switch between AutoCAD and VLIDE. To activate one of the windows, just click the appropriate icon. These icons allow you to quickly navigate your way around the various features of the Visual LISP system.

Loading a Program into AutoCAD

As mentioned, programs are stored and edited as LSP files and compiled into FAS or VLX files for distribution. No matter what format a program is in, you can load it into AutoCAD for testing by using the (LOAD) expression at the command line or in a menu entry.

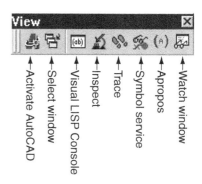

Suppose that you create a simple program called (TEST) and store it in a file named MYTEST.LSP using the VLIDE text editor. At the AutoCAD command line, you could type (LOAD "MYTEST"), parentheses and all, and the source file will load into memory and be ready to run. Type (TEST) at the command line and the function runs.

The (LOAD) expression can be used with a menu, as in the following example.

Figure 2.10   Icons in the View toolbar.

```
[My Test]^C^C^C^P(IF (NULL TEST) (LOAD "MYTEST"))(TEST)
```

After the menu label, the menu command sequence starts by canceling any open command in AutoCAD. The open parenthesis starts the Visual LISP evaluator in AutoCAD. The IF means the expression is a conditional test. The TEST symbol is tested to see whether it has a null value. Because the function is named TEST, the symbol will not have a null value after the function has been loaded. If the test for null indicates that the function must be loaded, the (LOAD) expression loads the MYTEST.LSP source file from the current search path. The closing parentheses terminate the (LOAD) and (IF) expressions. The (TEST) function is started after the conditional expression is finished.

Another way to load Visual LISP program is to use the APPLOAD command in AutoCAD. APPLOAD allows you to build a list of LSP, FAS, VLX, ARX, and other AutoCAD customization files to be loaded quickly each time you start AutoCAD. When developing and testing your applications, use APPLOAD to create a list of the function files to be loaded for the tests. This will allow you to reload the file set quickly each time you start a fresh drawing for a clean test.

APPLOAD presents an imposing dialog box at first glance, as shown in Figure 2.11, but it is easy to use. The primary component is the capability to add a function load to the Startup Suite, which is the list of files to load each time you open or create an AutoCAD drawing.

Using the IDE to Debug Programs

After you get your programs loaded and begin to run them, you may encounter problems. Visual LISP provides a variety of tools to assist you in tracking down and correcting these problems. Programmers call this tracking and correction process debugging.

The two most common areas where beginning and experienced programmers alike run afoul in Visual LISP involve parentheses imbalance and unanticipated changes in symbols or variables. Visual LISP provides excellent tools for tracking down both problems, as you find out in this section.

Finding parentheses imbalance

One of the most common problem when programming Visual LISP is parentheses imbalance. VLIDE provides several tools to help prevent your logic from getting Lost In Several Parentheses. The first tool is available when you type code in the text editor. Each time you enter a

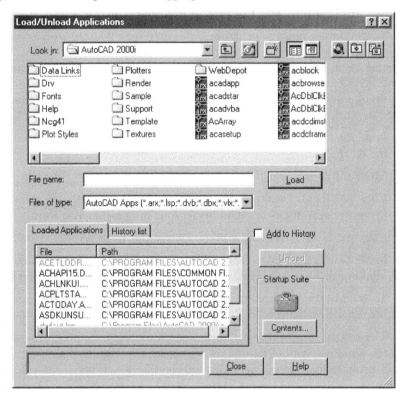

Figure 2.11 APPLOAD command dialog box.

closing parenthesis, the balancing open parenthesis is briefly shown and then the cursor returns to the entry point following the close. (At first I found this feature disturbing because I type relatively fast. But after working with the VLIDE for a few hours, I found it to be a useful feature because it showed the structure of my program while I was typing the code.) The automatic display of the balancing open parenthesis might indicate missing or extra parentheses that need to be corrected in the program source code.

The VLIDE has a second way to help you find parentheses imbalance. You can quickly locate missing or extra parentheses in the editor using the Ctrl and bracket keys. Press Ctrl+left bracket ([) to move the cursor to the start of the nearest expression. Press Ctrl+right bracket (]) to move the cursor to the end of the nearest expression. By jumping back and forth through a series of expressions, you can locate a missing or extra parenthesis quickly.

You can use the parentheses balance feature also to cut-and-paste sections of code. Press Ctrl+left brace ({) to move forward or Ctrl+right brace (}) to move backwards in the source file, selecting the text in between. You can then use the standard Windows-style cut, copy, and paste commands (Ctrl+X, Ctrl+C, and Ctrl+V, respectively) as desired.

Using breakpoints and the Watch window

A *breakpoint* is a point in program code where you want to stop execution so that you can see the values of variables or check to see how your program is progressing. When your program reaches a breakpoint, execution stops and you can enter the VLIDE to see the contents of the Watch window.

Breakpoints are turned on and off in the source code. To set a breakpoint, you first need some code to work with in the editor. Follow these steps:

1. Load the "Hello" function in the editor by typing it in a new window in the IDE or by opening the on the CD.

2. Move the cursor near the open parenthesis in the (PROMPT) expression.

3. Click the Toggle breakpoint icon (labeled in Figure 2.9). The parenthesis is highlighted in red. (You can set as many breakpoints in your program as you want.)

4. Click the Load active edit window icon in the Tools toolbar (labeled in Figure 2.8).

5. In the Console window, type (HELLO). The function's source code is displayed with the cursor blinking at the toggle location. In addition, all icons in the Debug toolbar are now available.

6. To remove the breakpoint, simply position the cursor at the breakpoint and click the Toggle breakpoint icon again.

The second step in using a bookmark is to run your program and add symbol names to the Watch window. Symbol names are Visual LISP variables that can represent different data while your program is running. Symbols representing functions are not normally viewed in the Watch window.

To add a symbol to the Watch window, click the Add watch icon (labeled in Figure 2.9). A small dialog box asks you what symbol you want to watch. Type the name of the variable you want to track. Alternatively, you can highlight the name of a variable in the source code, and then click the Add watch icon. (You can add more symbols to the Watch window by clicking the Add watch icon again and supplying the symbol names.) At each breakpoint, the values of the selected symbols are shown in the window. You can show all symbols, including program and data lists.

Breakpoints and the Watch window are a powerful combination for finding errant steps in your programs. You can watch your programs run in the computer by using several other tools in the VLIDE, such as stepping through code in debug mode. As you work with the IDE, you will find more treasures that can improve your programming productivity.

Summary

This chapter introduced the VLIDE, or Visual LISP Integrated Development Environment. More than just a pretty text editor, the VLIDE is a powerful tool for creating advanced applications using Visual LISP. Combining multiple text editor windows, a Watch window, breakpoints, tracing, parentheses balancing, print formatting, and more in a single environment for programmers is the greatest step forward that the AutoCAD-based LISP system has ever taken.

The chapter introduced also the various files that are manipulated in Visual LISP: LSP (source) files, FAS (compiled) files, VLX (project) files, and DCL (dialog control language) files. You saw how to load and test these programs in both AutoCAD and the VLIDE.

A lot of information was presented about the VLIDE so that you will have a basic understanding of this tool before you begin writing anything significant in Visual LISP. The usefulness of some features may not become clear until later in the book. Visual LISP is a deep and complex language, yet it is easy to learn and use productively. Years of enjoyment and accomplishment are awaiting you as you master this wonderful component of the AutoCAD system.

CHAPTER 3

The Essence of Visual LISP

The LISP programming language appeared on computers in the 1950s and has undergone many changes in its lifetime. Visual LISP is an adaptation of the original LISP and is one of the most widely used versions in the world. Some basic concepts underlying Visual LISP make it unique in the world of programming. These concepts range from powerful ones that can be exploited by talented programmers to those that are simply odd in relation to other languages

This chapter looks at the concepts underlying the LISP language. Of key importance is the evaluator and how it works. The discussion continues with a look at how symbols are used in a program. You finish the chapter by looking at special symbol treatments such as the creation of commands and how to recover from errors in your program.

Although some information in this chapter is advanced, it is presented early in the book to provide an overview of the environment. You might want to review this chapter from time to time just to make sure you are getting the most out of Visual LISP.

The Evaluator

Your exploration of the essence of Visual LISP starts with the evaluator. All program code is written with the evaluator in mind. This is partly why the syntax appears odd, especially for programmers who know other computer languages.

The evaluator follows some basic rules:

- If you give the evaluator a number, it returns the number. In fact, if you give the evaluator any single item, such as a quoted string of characters, that item is returned as a result.

- If you give the evaluator a symbol name, it returns the content, or binding, of the symbol. For example, if you are using the TMP symbol to represent a temporary result in a computation and you give the evaluator the TMP symbol name, the value that TMP points to is returned.

- If you give the evaluator a list (an ordered set of symbols and lists), the first element of the list is checked to see whether it is a recognized function name. If the first member is a function, that function is evaluated, with the remainder of the list considered the parameters to the function. If the first member is not a function, the contents of the list are evaluated and returned.

The two basic types of functions are those that exist in Visual LISP and those you can define. The functions that exist in Visual LISP are called subrs (pronounced "sub-ers"). You can add more subrs through the ObjectARX system. Some Visual LISP functions are loaded as ObjectARX modules when you need them. (Not all are loaded initially because some are called only when programming specific types of interfaces, such as ActiveX.)

Reading expressions

A list in which the first member is a subr or a function recognized by the evaluator is considered a form in traditional LISP lingo and an expression in Visual LISP. This is different than most other computer programming languages, in which program and data formats are clearly delineated, and can be a stumbling block for people learning LISP after mastering another language such as BASIC, FORTRAN, or PASCAL. In LISP, functions are defined as expressions that contain expressions. That is, a function is a list that contains sublists. Thus, every function is a list but not every list is a function.

In LISP, lists are represented with surrounding parentheses. When you read a LISP program, you look for open parentheses. An open parenthesis character signifies the beginning of a list. If you encounter another open parenthesis before a matching closing parenthesis, the list is nested. That is, one or more lists are inside the list. When programming in LISP, programs are structured as nested lists, where each nested list is an expression.

This might seem to be an odd way to represent a problem to the computer but it is a simple structure that the computer can anticipate and work with to solve problems. It does, however, require that you think a bit differently than you do when using other languages.

Immediately following the open parentheses are the names of the functions or subrs to be run. Following the name of the function is another function, a constant value, or a symbol reference to be evaluated and passed to the function. The values of the symbol reference, constant, or function result are passed to the function as arguments.

To see how this scheme works, we'll perform a basic operation. Suppose that you want the computer to solve a numeric expression, computing the sum of 1 plus 2. In the algebraic form most of us were taught in school, this problem is expressed as 1+2. The plus sign (+) stands for addition; in this statement, you are asking for the addition of the numbers on either side of the plus sign. A human reading this expression has no problem understanding the statement. A computer, however, reads only one character at a time and is expected to react accordingly.

Think about the 1+2 statement from a computer's standpoint. The first character encountered is 1. What is the computer expected to do? The logical solution is to tell it to read ahead until it finds something telling it what to do with this number. In the meantime, the computer needs to store the value 1 until it is used in some way.

When LISP was first created, computer memory was at a premium, so it didn't make sense to store a number until the computer could determine what to do with it. One alternative was to use prefix, or Polish, notation. In prefix notation, you state what you are going to do first, and then you state what you will use for the desired operation. For example, the expression to sum 1 and 2 in prefix notation is + 1 2. The primary advantage of prefix notation is that the computer can be prepared to perform the necessary work. Then it needs only to accept the values to produce the result. It's not quite like that, but you can see the simplification clearly if you consider programming something more complex, such as a quadratic equation.

The (+ 1 2) expression is a valid Visual LISP expression that you can type at the AutoCAD command prompt or the _$ prompt in the Visual LISP `Console` window.

For example, suppose you are drawing something that involves a right triangle. You know that the longest distance along the triangle (the hypotenuse) is 6.75 and the angle from the X-axis relative to some other point is 15 degrees. If you start a line at 1.5, 1.75, you can use Visual LISP to find the location of the next point.

```
(POLAR (LIST 1.5 1.75 0.0) (/ Pi 12.0) 6.75)
```

This may look like gibberish now, but after you become accustomed to working with Visual LISP, you will be able to read it easily. This code tells the system to create a new point calculated as a polar expression from point (1.5, 1.75) at an angle of `Pi` (3.14159...) radians divided by 12 for a distance of 6.75. `Pi` equals 180 degrees, and the `Pi` over 12 value is 15 degrees.

To accomplish the same thing using only AutoCAD commands, you would have to draw a construction line from the known point (1.5, 175) using the notation @6.75<15 for the to point. Then you would draw a line from 10,15 to the end point. Last, you would erase the construction line.

The (POLAR) example just shown demonstrates several things about LISP. Look closely at the expression and go to the innermost parentheses pairs. There are two nested lists. The first defines a list of numbers. In Visual LISP, a list of two or three numbers can denote a point. The first number (1.5) is the X-ordinate, the second (1.75) is the Y-ordinate, and the third (0.0) is the Z-ordinate. Lists are easy to manipulate, as you will learn later in this book, and point lists are the easiest of all. Plus, several functions are designed just for points (such as the POLAR function).

Another thing you can learn from this example is that Visual LISP uses radians and not degrees for angles. Radians work better in computer calculations. In the example, you must make an adjustment in the presentation of the problem to Visual LISP and convert the angle values in degrees to radians. To convert degrees to radians, multiple the degrees value by `Pi` and divide the result by 180. The final result is the angle in radians. `Pi` is stored in Visual LISP as a constant available for applications immediately. This value is precise and should not be replaced with some other value because that will affect the precision of the overall system.

The last thing this example shows us is that Visual LISP is ready at all times in AutoCAD. Visual LISP comes to action when you type an open parenthesis. In the example, an open parenthesis is followed by the POLAR function (an internal function in Visual LISP). This function returns the result from a polar coordinate point shift given a base point in X, Y format along with an angle (in radians) and a distance. The result was returned to the LINE command, which had been waiting for a point. AutoCAD and Visual LISP work well together.

An open parenthesis starts the evaluator in Visual LISP. The evaluator waits until it has a close parenthesis before running the code. Therefore, in the example function, the value of `Pi` divided by 12 was calculated first because there is an open and close pair of parentheses. The computation happens before the POLAR function runs so that values are available to POLAR.

Assigning values to symbols

Symbols are the names by which you reference various components of a program. Some symbols are already defined in Visual LISP, such as Pi and POLAR.

In the context of Visual LISP, everything is a symbol. When a symbol is used to hold a value, it is called a variable symbol or just a variable. When a symbol is used to hold a function definition list, it is called a function. Symbols that reference internal functions in Visual LISP are called subrs.

You can set symbols (names you created) to numbers and other values in a program by using the (SETQ) function, which is a combination of the (SET) and (QUOTE) functions. (SETQ) accepts pairs of symbols with expressions. After a symbol has been set to a value as the result of a SETQ-based expression, you can use the symbol name to get that value instead of repeating the entire expression again. (Again, when used in this way, a symbol is often called a variable because it represents a variable value for your program.) For example, suppose that you want to use the value of Pi divided by 12 in several computations. You would start by devising a symbol name for 15 degrees, such as D15. The (SETQ D15 (/ Pi 12.0)) expression sets the value of Pi divided by 12 to the D15 symbol. You can then use that value in another expression by just referencing the symbol (variable) name.

The POLAR command used previously can be revised as (POLAR (LIST 1.5 1.75 0.0) D15 6.75), as long as you set D15 before its use.

(SETQ) works with pairs, allowing you to set up more than one symbol (variable) reference at one time. Suppose that the point (1.5, 1.75) will be used in your program, and you want to create a point list variable to hold this value. Any value may be assigned to any symbol. Unlike other programming languages that require you to define the data type and then set the value, in LISP you accomplish everything by setting the value directly. The following expression establishes two symbols, PT and D15, to have the values of a point list (1.5, 1.75, 0.0) and a constant (Pi divided by 12), respectively.

```
(SETQ PT (LIST 1.5 1.75 0.0) D15 (/ Pi 12.0))
```

At first, LISP is difficult to read because of the parentheses and prefix notation, which are also what make it succinct. To see just how succinct the LISP language is, consider the same code written in BASIC.

```
Dim PT(0 to 2) As Double
Dim D15 As Double
D15 = 3.14159254 / 12#
PT(0) = 1.5: PT(1) = 1.75: PT(2) = 0#
```

Visual BASIC and Visual Basic for Applications do not contain a value of Pi. One trick you can use is to multiple 4 by the arctangent of 1. This will yield an accurate value for Pi in BASIC. Visual LISP, on the other hand, already has the Pi constant computed to the maximum accuracy of the machine. Visual LISP also does not require that you declare the type of data you will be using ahead of time. Space is allocated on an as-needed basis, so you need fewer lines of code.

Brevity of coding, however, comes with a price: readability suffers. As a result, make sure that you include comments in your code. (Comments are notes explaining what you are doing.) In

Visual LISP, a comment is any text that follows a semicolon (unless that semicolon is inside a string) out to the end of the physical line. In addition, any text appearing between the character sequences ; | and | ; is an inline or multiple-line comment.

Physical versus logical code lines

Visual LISP has two types of code lines: logical lines and physical lines. A logical line of code is a complete expression — that is, something enclosed in parentheses, such as the statement (+ 1 2). Logical lines of code may contain other logical lines of code. A function is a logical line of code that contains one or more logical lines of code. Think of logical lines of code as the components or steps in a program.

Logical lines of code are entered as physical lines of code in the text editor. You can use any number of physical lines of code to represent a logical line. Physical lines end with a carriage return (the Enter key). Logical lines end with the balancing parenthesis to the open parenthesis at the start of the logical line.

The logical line of code (+ 1 2) could be entered over four physical lines, as in the following.

```
(+
   1
   2
)
```

You can add a comment to any physical line of code by entering text between a semicolon (;) and the end of the physical line. All text after the semicolon is considered a comment and is ignored by the evaluator when it runs. When you view code in the VLIDE, the comments appear as highlighted text.

Reserved functions in LISP

LISP's evaluator accepts expressions and returns a result. The primary tools for this are subrs or reserved functions in LISP. A subr is a function that is known by Visual LISP when it first starts. You can think of subrs as symbols that are already assigned and should not be changed.

When a subr appears at the front of a list, that list is considered a form and can be evaluated. The values following the subr are arguments. The (+ 1 2) expression has the + subr and two arguments, 1. and 2. When you type the closing parenthesis and a white space, the expression is evaluated, resulting in the answer, 3. A white space is the Enter key, the spacebar, the Tab key, or a comment.

If you type the (1 2 3) expression in LISP, it returns the list (1 2 3). If you type the expression in the evaluator at the AutoCAD command prompt, you get an error because the first member of the list is 1, it should be a function or subr name.

All expressions return an answer

A key factor in programming LISP applications is that all expressions, including functions and subrs, return an answer. Where a particular answer goes is up to you, the programmer. In most cases, the result of a function or subr is used as an argument to another function or subr. The fact that everything is expected to return an answer is a key feature to the brevity of coding in LISP. This feature can be used to nest expressions inside other expressions, making the code brief but also difficult to read.

The fact that all functions and subrs return an answer is an important feature in the programming of Visual LISP applications. If you have never programmed before, you will find the technique straightforward. Each element of a problem is broken down into steps, and those steps are further broken down to form a program. Each element inside a single step returns its answer to the step it is a part of, and this continues throughout the application. After you become familiar with the thinking process, it is easy to create advanced programs. Experienced programmers might be accustomed to breaking things down into modules, only some of which return answers. The remaining modules simply use or establish values in variables and do not return a result.

In programming Visual LISP, the result of a function is called the direct result, or effect. A well-behaved function uses only the values supplied to it as parameters and returns data as a direct effect. For many applications, it is difficult to write functions that always behave well. Later in the chapter, you look at how Visual LISP stores variables and functions in the computer.

Evaluate now or later?

In most cases, a program is evaluated to produce a result. But sometimes you do not want something evaluated right away. You might be building a complex list of data and need to keep that data from being interpreted as program code.

The QUOTE subr is used to inform the evaluator that you do not want to evaluate the expression or symbol; you merely want to use it as-is. For example, the expression (QUOTE (1 2 3)) returns a list of data (1 2 3). It does not try to evaluate the list; doing so would result in an error because 1 is not a function or subr name. The QUOTE subr results in the data being passed back directly from the evaluator. Thus, the (QUOTE (+ 1 2)) expression results in the list (+ 1 2).

If you want to force the evaluation of a symbolic expression, use the EVAL subr. The (EVAL (QUOTE (+ 1 2))) expression results in the value 3. That is a silly example, because you could just enter (+ 1 2) to get the same result with a lot less typing. But it does illustrate how you can take a list of data returned by the QUOTE subr and treat it like a program by supplying it to the EVAL subr. It is unlikely you will need to write code that uses this advanced capability of LISP, but it is handy every so often, and some of examples later in this book make use of this dynamic power in the system.

Atoms and Lists

Before you go too much deeper into LISP subrs and functions, you need to understand the types of data you may be manipulating. LISP data is either an atom or a list. Making this definition even simpler is the notion that an atom is anything that does not have parentheses, except the NIL symbol or value. NIL is an empty list and is usually not shown with parentheses. NIL is the atomic value nothing, or empty. You use NIL also to represent the value false when working with true-false logic in a LISP program. Anything that is not NIL is true.

Visual LISP contains several atomic data types, such as number and text atoms. You perform arithmetic-type operations on numbers, but not with text. The atomic types help keep your variables in order. Plus, you can test the types during program execution, giving you tremendous control over the environment your program runs in.

Table 3.1 describes the specific atomic types in Visual LISP. Because Visual LISP is intended for use in the AutoCAD environment, some elements are specific to AutoCAD and do not exist in other LISP environments.

Table 3.1 Data types.

Data type	Description
INT	Integer. A whole number ranging from –2,147,483,648 to 2,147,483,647. Integers are useful in counting and in controlling loops. An integer cannot contain a decimal point.
REAL	Real; also known as a double-precision real number. A number with a decimal point. Real numbers can be quite large or quite small, with up to 14 significant digits. If you need to count very large numbers or perform numerical work that may involve fractions or decimals, you use reals.
STR	String. Text characters stored together form a string. Strings can be from zero characters up to as many characters as can fit in memory. Strings are always are surrounded by double quotation marks.
ENAME	Entity name. An entity reference in AutoCAD. The entity name of an object is a direct pointer to the entity object in memory. Entity names change from one drawing edit session to the next.
PICKSET	Pick set; also known as a selection set. A group of entity names. Pick sets are commonly used in programs when working with a group of objects, such as all the lines in a drawing or all entity objects on a particular layer.
FILE	File handle. An integer used to represent an open file.
SYM	Symbol. A reference name that can be used to denote data of any type, including lists. By itself, a symbol is a set of characters.
SUBR, USUBR, EXRXSUBR	Subr, user-defined subr, and ObjectARX-defined subr. A reference name to a function, either internal to Visual LISP or the result of a load or FAS compile.
VLA-object	VLA object. An ActiveX object.
VARIANT, SAFEARRAY	Variant and safe array. ActiveX data elements typically intended for VBA. A *variant* is a general-purpose data container. A safe array is a fixed collection of data.

The data types in Table 3.1 are the basic data elements you will encounter in Visual LISP. The last remaining data type is the list, which from a programming point of view is anything between parentheses. In Visual LISP, the list data type holds both data and programs. Programs are defined using a list structure, in which each element in the list is a logical line of code (expression).

Working with Symbols

You can create or define symbols in Visual LISP in two ways. One method defines a symbol that will hold data to be used by your program. The other method references your program function definition. Note that most LISP programmers use the term variable name instead of symbol.

Defining symbols with SET

To define a data-oriented symbol, you use the SET subr, which has two arguments: a symbol reference and a value. The SET subr stores the value in the computer, where it can be retrieved at a later time by using the symbol name. For example, the following LISP code sets the A symbol, or variable, to the value of integer 100.

```
(SET (QUOTE A) 100)
```

The QUOTE subr causes the evaluator to not evaluate the A symbol. This is what you want because you are putting data into A, not retrieving it. Instead of evaluating A, the expression uses the A symbol as an argument to the SET subr. The value 100, on the other hand, is evaluated and results in the value 100. This value is stored in the system using a reference symbol A.

Before you go any deeper into how symbols are stored and retrieved, you should learn a shorthand way of telling the evaluator, "Don't evaluate the symbol, use it." Instead of typing the QUOTE expression inside the SET expression, you can use the single quote mark, as in the following.

```
(SET 'A 100)
```

When you type the single quote mark, the evaluator expands the expression to include the parentheses and QUOTE subr. Thus, do not be surprised if QUOTE appears when you step through your code at runtime using the debugging tools.

Although the single quote mark is fine in most circumstances, when evaluated it expands the code by adding the QUOTE expression. This adds to the time required to service the code in the evaluator and takes up more space in the computer's memory. When LISP was developed, neither of these traits was desirable. As a result, a new SUBR called SETQ was created to reduce the simple expression even further to (SETQ A 100).

SETQ is a combination of SET and QUOTE. In most cases, you use SETQ to establish variable values to be used later in your program. The following sequence of expressions shows how variable symbols are used in programming. First, the A symbol is set to integer value 1, which is also returned as the result of the expression.

```
(SETQ A 1)
```

Then the B symbol is set to integer value 10, which is also returned as the result of the expression.

```
(SETQ B 10)
```

Finally, the C symbol is set to the value resulting from adding the values in A and B. If the previous expressions had been evaluated just before this expression, the result returned from the expression would be 11.

```
(SETQ C (+ A B))
```

If you look at the last expression more closely, you can see that it is actually two expressions. The first expression is (+ A B). When the evaluator is given this expression, it evaluates A first. The A symbol has been set to a value of 1 in a previous expression. That value is tucked away and the evaluator continues by getting the value in B, which is 10. The result, 11, is stored using the C symbol reference.

SETQ expressions that appear in a sequence one after another can be combined into a single expression. This results in slightly faster execution because the evaluator does not have to work with each individual expression. It also results in less typing when defining an expression or a complex series of expressions. You could present the previous sequence to the evaluator as the following single expression.

```
(SETQ A 1 B 10 C (+ A B))
```

Symbols and values must appear in pairs. The preceding expression pairs A with 1, B with 10, and C with the result of adding A and B. And because the last assignment made was the result of adding A and B, 11 is the result.

SETQ creates symbols that are associated with values. You could use SETQ also to create symbols related to symbols and other expressions. This is where LISP is powerful compared to other languages. Suppose that you want to set up a variable symbol that references another symbol, such as the A symbol.

```
(SETQ D 'A)
```

The quote mark before A tells the evaluator to only return the symbol, not evaluate it. At the completion of this expression, the D symbol contains the A symbol. If you check D, it returns a value of A — not the value of A, just the symbol. To get the value, you would have to further evaluate the symbol, as in (EVAL D). This sort of programming is not used for most applications and is mentioned simply to let you know that it is available.

Defining symbols with DEFUN

The second subr for defining symbols is DEFUN. Symbols defined using DEFUN are user-defined functions and can be used just like internal subrs. Plus, you can define functions that act like commands for AutoCAD operators.

When defining a function, you must supply three components, as shown in the syntax of the DEFUN expression.

```
(DEFUN <name> (<parameter list>) <expressions> )
```

The first component is the symbol name by which your function will be referenced. The name should be unique because if you use the name of another function, the original function is no longer available, its symbol having been replaced with your new definition. Sometimes, however, you want to replace the definition of a given function (one of your own functions or, rarely, a function internal to Visual LISP), such as when testing new developments. When you want to replace an earlier test version, just use DEFUN and define it again.

The second part of the DEFUN expression is the parameter list. The symbols in the parameter list house values that you need to supply to the function from the calling routine. Any changes made to these symbol values remain inside the function. I get back to this shortly. If there are no parameters, you must provide an empty list, represented by an open and closing pair of parentheses.

The third component of a function definition consists of the expressions that make up the function.

Throughout the remainder of this book, you will be creating functions of various types that will be used to create even more functions. With this building-block approach, you can build complex applications. Next, you take a closer look at naming a function.

Naming symbols

A function name is a symbol, so function names follow the rules for all symbol names in the Visual LISP environment. A symbol name can consist of characters or a combination of characters and numbers, but it cannot consist of only numbers. The following are valid symbol names: ABC, ABC1, 1A2, 2Pi, *PiR2, and Pi*R2. You can use any characters except the space, tab, apostrophe (single quote), double quote, period, semicolon, and parentheses characters. (These characters are used for other purposes in Visual LISP.)

Symbol names are not case sensitive. For example, the following symbols are the same: abc, aBc, and ABC. The evaluator convert the input into uppercase. In addition, symbol names can be of any length.

Symbol names should convey a meaning that is useful to those reading the program. For example, if you have a function that calculates the area of a circle, you might name your symbols RADIUS and AREA. Using mixed uppercase and lowercase for symbol names might make the code easier to read. The following expressions are the same.

```
(SETQ Area (* 2.0 Pi Radius))
(SETQ AREA (* 2.0 Pi RADIUS))
(SETQ area (* 2.0 Pi radius))
(SETQ AREA (* 2.0 Pi RADIUS))
```

Symbol names can aid in a program's legibility as much as comments.

When defining a function name, you can create a new command by adding C: at the front of the symbol. For example, suppose that you want to create a command for AutoCAD named FIDGIT. The symbol name used for the function in Visual LISP would be C:FIDGIT. (The C: stands for command function; it has nothing to do with a drive letter on your hard disk.)

If you want the symbol name to replace an AutoCAD standard command, you should undefine the command before defining the symbol name. To undefine a command name, you use the UNDEFINE command in AutoCAD. When undefined, the local language version of that command is no longer available. The global name must be used to invoke the original command. This feature is provided so that you can disable components of AutoCAD or replace its commands with your function definitions.

To illustrate, the expressions in Listing 3.1 undefine the LINE command and replace it with a bogus command.

Listing 3.1   Replacing the LINE command.

```
(COMMAND "_UNDEFINE" "LINE")
(DEFUN C:LINE ()
   (PROMPT "\nLINE command not available!"))
```

When the two expressions in Listing 3.1 are evaluated at the AutoCAD command prompt and you are using the English version of AutoCAD, the LINE command is replaced with the prompt message. Note that to use the LINE command, you must prefix it with an underscore, as seen in the "_UNDEFINE" command. The underscore at the start of a command allows the English-language version of the command name to be recognized in localized (non-English) versions of AutoCAD.

To run the original command, even if it is undefined, you include a period at the start of the command. For example, if you wanted to draw lines after the expressions in Listing 3.1 are evaluated, you could type .LINE and the normal LINE command would begin.

In Listing 3.1, the LINE command remains undefined until you either redefine it or start another drawing, at which time the expressions must be run again to disable the command. The redefinition is lost because the C:LINE symbol is known only in the drawing space in which it was created. I talk about spaces as they apply to symbols and functions in several places in this book. Here, however, you learn the concepts behind the scope of symbols within a single space.

Symbol Scope

The scope of a symbol, or variable, is where it can be seen. If you change a given symbol, you most likely expect to retrieve it at a later time. Should that symbol no longer be available or have a value that has been changed due to another routine running, your program is suffering from a scope-related error.

Tracking the scope of a symbol in Visual LISP is simple. Symbols are defined as either local or global in relation to a function. A symbol is local if it appears in the parameter list of the function. If the symbol appears before a slash in the parameter list, it has an initial value supplied by the calling function. When the symbol appears after the slash, its initial value is NIL. A symbol is considered global otherwise.

A local symbol can be seen only inside the function and by functions called inside that function. After the function is finished, the symbol is no longer set to the value inside the function and reverts to the value it had before the function was called.

Table 3.2 summarizes the differences between global and local symbols as well as bound symbols.

Note that a symbol can be local to a given function in which another function is invoked or called. If the symbol in the called function is also local (it is found in the parameter list) and that

Table 3.2 Symbols in a function.

Variable type	Scope	Usage	Description
Global variable	Available everywhere in an application	Holds calculated values that might be useful elsewhere.	A symbol is global with respect to a function if it does not appear in the parameter list of the function.
Local variable	Available only in a function	Holds temporary variables or null variable symbols. The value is NIL when the function starts.	A symbol is local with respect to a function if it appears in the parameter list of the function following the slash character.
Bound variable	Available only in a function	Holds passed parameter values. Only the value is passed, not the reference.	A symbol is bound to a function if it appears in the parameter list of the function before the slash character.

symbol is set or changed to some value, two versions of the symbol exist at once: the current value in the internal function and the saved value in the calling function. When the called function is finished, the symbol once again has the saved value, and the reference created when the called function was evaluated is gone.

Symbol scope is managed through the use of the stack, an important component in LISP that is responsible for many things. For now, I will simplify the stack and describe it only as it relates to symbols. Figure 3.1 shows a simple stack diagram. Items are placed on the stack from the top and removed in reverse order. That is, the first one on is the last one off. (And the last one on is the first one off.)

Each stack element contains two pieces of information: the symbol name and the value associated with that symbol. Symbols and values are stacked in memory as they are used or defined. This allows two different entries to exist in the memory of the computer with the same name. When you access the stack to look for the value associated with a given name, you get the value of the entry most recently placed on the stack.

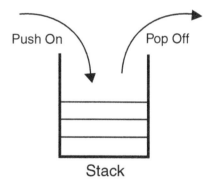

Figure 3.1   Stack storage.

Symbol scope examples

The simple example in Listing 3.2 will help illustrate symbol scope. The A1 function in the listing does four things. First, it sets the value 1 into the A symbol. A appears in the parameter list of the A1 function after the slash character (/), meaning that it starts with an initial value of nothing, or NIL. Second, the A1 function prints the value stored in the A symbol. This results in the number appearing at the command prompt or console in Visual LISP.

Third, the A1 function calls the A10 function. (The function definition for A10 is shown in Listing 3.3.) Note that to call a function that has no parameters (arguments), you use the symbol name

Listing 3.2   Defining the A1 function.

```
(DEFUN A1 ( / A)
   (SETQ A 1)
   (PRINT A)
   (A10)
   (PRINT A)
)
```

surrounded by parentheses. The (A10) expression starts the A10 function and waits for it to return a result. (This nesting of functions is how you develop complex programs, as you will explore in the next chapter.) After the A10 function is finished and returns control to A1, the A1 function performs the fourth operation, which is printing the value of A.

Listing 3.3   Defining the A10 function.

```
(DEFUN A10 ( / A)
   (SETQ A 10)
   (print A)
   (A100)
   (PRINT A)
)
```

The A10 function in Listing 3.3 is essentially the same as the A1 function. The A symbol is defined as a parameter to the function following the slash, which means that it has a NIL value at the start of this function. As the A10 function begins to evaluate the first occurrence of the (print A) expression, after being called from A1 function, the LISP stack of symbols contains two entries that are both named A. The lower entry (the first one on the stack) has a value of 1. The upper entry has a value of 10. Using the "last in, first out" rule, the (print A) expression uses the value associated with the last entry on the stack, 10.

The next step in the A10 function is to call the A100 function, which is shown in Listing 3.4.

Listing 3.4   Defining the A100 function.

```
(defun A100 ( / A)
   (setq A 100)
   (print A)
)
```

The definition of A100 follows the same lines as the definitions of A1 and A10. A symbol named

A is defined in the parameter list following a slash. As the (print) expression is evaluated, three entries are on the stack with the value A.

Now, if you typed all three of these functions in an editor window of the VLIDE, loaded the three into the console for testing, and typed the (A1) expression, the following output would appear.

```
$ (A1)
1
10
100
10
1
```

Of special note is the value of A printed in the second (print A) expression inside the A1 and A10 functions. After calling the A100 function, the value of A inside the A10 function remains 10. The same situation is observed in the A1 function, where A has a value of 1.

After the (A1) expression has been evaluated, check the value of the A symbol. It should be NIL or whatever other value you may have set it to earlier.

The example just shown is plain and simple. The A symbol is used over and over in each of the functions. But what happens if the parameter list is changed so that A is not present? Listing 3.5 revises the function definitions for A1, A10, and A100 without A as a member of the parameter list.

Listing 3.5   Defining A1, A10, and A100 without local variables.

```
(defun A1 ( ) (setq A 1) (print A) (A10) (print A))
(defun A10 ( ) (setq A 10) (print A) (A100) (print A))
(defun A100 ( ) (setq A 100) (print A))
```

If these functions are typed and evaluated by entering the (A1) expression, the resulting output is different.

```
$ (A1)
1
10
100
100
100
```

The A symbol was changed to 100 at the deepest level of the nested functions, inside A100. Because A was not in the parameter list, the change was reflected to the next higher level. A was not in the parameter list of any of the functions; if you check its value, you will find that it is now 100.

If a symbol name appears in the parameter list, it will be found on the stack. If the symbol name does not appear in a parameter list, as in the preceding example, it is stored in another memory location known as the heap. The *heap* is where you place symbols that can be accessed by all other functions in your application. In the preceding example, the A symbol was not defined in the parameter list of any function. As a result, whenever the symbol is accessed, the value and location from the heap are retrieved.

In Listing 3.6, I change the sample functions one last time, putting the A symbol back in the parameter list of the A1 and A10 functions, but not in A100.

Listing 3.6   Local scope example.

```
(defun A1 ( / A) (setq A 1) (print A) (A10) (print A))
(defun A10 ( / A) (setq A 10) (print A) (A100) (print A))
(defun A100 ( ) (setq A 100) (print A))
```

Load and run this set of expressions.

```
$ (A1)
1
10
100
100
1
```

Trace down to the deepest nesting inside the A100 function. The A symbol is set to the value of 100. The evaluator searches for the A symbol to see whether it had a location already set aside for it, starting with the stack. At that instant, two members on the stack answer by the name of A. The last one in is retrieved (it has the value of 10), and the value is replaced.

A100 then prints the value in A (which is 100) and returns to A10. The A symbol is retrieved from the stack, where there are still two values. The most recent, from the parameter list declaration of A10, is retrieved with the value 100, which is printed.

A10 then finishes and control is returned to A1. As A10 finishes, it clears the stack of the A parameter it had defined. Now the stack has only one member for A, the original value of 1 set earlier in the A1 function evaluation.

These basic examples show how the parameter list keeps your symbols in order. When you program applications, it is important to keep in mind where your symbols are stored and what value they might contain. Symbols used for variables can change in value during the evaluation of a series of nested expressions, and it is easy to lose track of the details.

You should use a standard naming scheme to help differentiate between temporary variable names and those needed elsewhere in the application. (For example, I use the name TMP for a temporary variable. If I need more than one, I call the next one TMP2, and so on.)

If your program shares the memory of Visual LISP with other programs, your variables might change during the evaluation of those other routines. At the same time, you might end up changing a variable used by another program, rendering it useless. For now, suffice it to say that you should avoid putting variables on the global heap and should store them on the stack during execution. That means putting them in a parameter list somewhere in your application.

Naming scheme

All my programs follow a naming strategy that Autodesk recommends for developers wanting to publish their work as part of the Developer Network. The first part of the strategy involves defining a set of five or so unique characters. All global symbols, both variables and function names, use these same symbols as a prefix.

Suppose that you are creating an application for designing widgets, so you use WIDGT as the prefix. Your function names follow the prefix with an underscore character, and your variables follow the prefix with a colon. You then complete the name with a meaningful string, following the rules for naming variables. As long as no one else has written an application named WIDGT, your application should not interfere with any others.

The naming standard for symbols applies to symbols stored on the heap. For variables stored on the stack during runtime, names can be anything you want in your application. This shortens the coding requirements and makes for more elegant error-recovery options.

My applications typically start by retrieving global heap values stored using the prefix characters. These variables are then moved into local variables for easier manipulation and easier recovery from any problems. The application then runs using the local variable references. Before the application ends, the local variables are placed back in the global variables for later reference. Another place to store variables is in an AutoCAD entity using extended data or attributes. Yet another option is to define an Xrecord object. As you can see, the topic of using variables is an important topic to get a handle on.

Returning Results

I have one last thing to note about functions and variables. Remember that all functions return a value. For example, in the A1, A10, and A100 example function set, (PRINT A) returns a value to the console, printing the result of 1 twice at the command prompt. You can avoid the direct return to the command prompt in Visual LISP by adding a (PRIN1) or (PRINC) expression at the end of the function. Most of the examples in this book take advantage of the "silent exit" provided by (PRIN1) when a command function is involved.

Sometimes a function returns more than just a single result or returns a result that is difficult to express as a data list or single value. In these cases, you can program the function to change global values. This is what happened in Listing 3.6, where the A100 function changed the A symbol, which was global with respect to A100 but local with respect to the parent function, A10. When a function changes the value of a variable that is global with respect to the function, the function is said to have a *side effect*.

Side effects can be desirable. For example, suppose you have a function that handles all input from the operator and sets a series of variables from that input. The function then returns a true or false result indicating whether or not valid input was received. In this case, the desirable side effect is the setting of variables when the input is valid. Side effects in applications can also be the source of problems that are difficult to trace. Unintended side effects occur whenever a variable assigned a value in a function is not included in the function's parameter list.

Inspecting Symbols

When creating applications, you will often find yourself needing to check the values, or binding, of various symbols. There are two times when you will need to do this the most: to check global variables after running a program and to check local variables while the program is running. After running the application, you may want to check the global variable bindings to see whether they are what you expect them to be. This is accomplished by typing the name of the symbol at the console (at the _$ prompt in Visual LISP) or by typing an exclamation point (!) followed by the symbol name at the AutoCAD command prompt.

At the console in Visual LISP, the sequence appears as follows.

```
_$ (setq A 100)
100
_$ A
100
_$
```

At the AutoCAD command line, the same result is obtained by typing the following.

```
Command: (setq A 100)
100
Command: !A
100
Command:
```

The only difference is the addition of the exclamation point at the AutoCAD command prompt. The result is the same. The value for the symbol stored in the Visual LISP heap is displayed.

When using local variables or when you want to watch the value of a symbol while the program is running, you must use the Watch window in Visual LISP and run the application from inside the console. The Watch window works with breakpoints you set. This requires that you prepare the program and environment before the test run. (For details on setting breakpoints, refer to Chapter 2.)

The first step is to set the breakpoints where you want to stop evaluation and check the values of the symbols in question. Locate the cursor at the open or close parenthesis of the expression where you want to stop. Then select the Toggle breakpoint icon (labeled in Figure 2.9 in Chapter 2). The parenthesis changes color to indicate that a breakpoint has been established at that location. You can set as many breakpoints as you want in your program code.

To add a symbol to the Watch window, click the Add watch icon (labeled in Figure 2.9). A small dialog box asks you what symbol you want to watch. This is a powerful tool when debugging an application of virtually any size.

You can add symbols names while at a breakpoint when running the function. The Watch window updates at each breakpoint with the current bindings of the symbols you have requested for display. You can add and remove symbols from the Watch window during runtime as well. This feature is especially useful when trying to track down problems in advanced applications.

Another debugging tactic available when at a breakpoint is to enter expressions in the Console window. This feature enables you to test various expressions using the data available, right then, from the stack and the heap, and then break out of the program to adjust the code and run the test again. The debug facilities in Visual LISP are several quantum leaps ahead of the original AutoLISP as well as other program editor systems for LISP development with AutoCAD.

When you load and evaluate a program with breakpoints, the Visual LISP source code is shown where the break is taking place. The Watch window is also displayed if you have activated it previously. If it is not active, choose the View menu in the Visual LISP window and then choose Watch window.

Move to the next breakpoint by clicking the green arrow icon on the Debug toolbar. To exit the evaluation and return to the editor to make changes, click the red arrow icon. A little practice with the Watch window and breakpoints will reveal the power they give you when testing your applications.

Recovering from Errors

While talking about debugging, it is a good time to bring up the subject of how a program can gracefully recover from an error. Even though you may have tested your program thoroughly, errors will occur. You need to set up a path for the system to follow when a problem occurs in the evaluation of your application. To do this, you use the *ERROR* symbol as a function in your program code.

Visual LISP starts the *ERROR* function when an error occurs in the evaluation of the code. The type of error is supplied as a string argument to the function. You have the opportunity to save your global variables from the local variables because the function is running within the scope of the function that caused the error. To save values stored in local variables, simply use SETQ to move them to global variable names. When doing this, use great care because the error trap has been tripped once and won't be tripped again even if an error occurs in your recovery operations.

When programming an error-recovery trap, do not try to communicate with the operator using input statements. Instead, save the variables you want to save, restore any system variables you may have changed, and return control to the system. You may want to send a message on exit telling the operator what went wrong or how to restart your application.

An example of an error trap is presented in Listing 3.7. This error trap resets a few AutoCAD system variables and, if the error was not the result of a function cancel request, updates some global variables. The error trap is related to a fictional function where many of the variables are established.

Listing 3.7   Error trapping.

```
(DEFUN *error* (MSG)
  (SETVAR "CMDECHO" 1) ;Line 1
  (IF (AND SAVED_TEXTSIZE ;Line 2
          (= (TYPE SAVED_TEXTSIZE) 'REAL))
     (SETVAR "TEXTSIZE" SAVED_TEXTSIZE)) ;Line 3
  (IF (NOT (WCMATCH (STRCASE MSG)  ;Line 4
                 "*CANCEL*"))
    (SETQ USER_USERNAME INPUTNAME)) ;Line 5
)
```

The line containing the Line 1 comment is an expression that shows the SETVAR subr in action. SETVAR is used in Visual LISP just like the SETVAR command in AutoCAD. The function has two arguments: the name of the system variable as a string and the value to be used. The type of data presented as the value will vary depending on the system variable being changed. Line 1 sets an integer flag for the CMDECHO system variable. CMDECHO is frequently turned off (value of 0) while Visual LISP programs are running. This function turns CMDECHO back on again.

SETVAR appears again in Line 3, but this time with a real number argument for the value to be set into the text height system variable. Before using the value supplied as a variable in Line 3, it is tested in Line 2 to see that it is proper. Line 2 is a combination of two tests and starts with the IF subr. Following the IF subr is a test or predicate expression. A predicate expression checks to see whether something is true or false. In LISP, anything that is false is NIL, and anything that is not NIL is considered to be true. The predicate in Line 2 is an AND combination.

The combination in Line 2 is an AND expression, so both tests must evaluate to true for the combination to be considered true. The first test is whether the SAVED_TEXTSIZE symbol evaluates to a non-NIL value, and the second test is whether SAVED_TEXTSIZE is a real number. In this example, the SAVED_TEXTSIZE, USER_USERNAME, and INPUTNAME symbols are assumed to have come from the parent function that is making use of the *ERROR* function.

Presenting the evaluator with just the symbol name is a way to test the symbol to see whether it has a value. The evaluator returns the current value, or binding, of that symbol when used in this context. If the binding is NIL, the test is false. If the binding is not NIL, the test is true and the second test in the AND expression takes place. By nesting predicates in this way, you can define complex problems with a few lines of code.

Skipping to line 4, you can see another test expression. In this expression, MSG, which is the message string parameter supplied to the function when the error handler was tripped, is tested to see whether it contains the "CANCEL" string. When "CANCEL" is found in the string, it means that the operator pressed the Escape key to end the current activities. Beginning at the innermost parenthesis pair, the (STRCASE MSG) expression converts to uppercase every character in the MSG string. The resulting string is returned to the (WCMATCH <result string> "*CANCEL*") expression. The WCMATCH subr is a powerful tool for comparing strings, a frequent task when your application involves user input or dimensions. WCMATCH (for wildcard match) is similar to many wild-card-based comparisons. The asterisk character (*) is a wildcard character that matches any character or set of characters. This function returns true if the characters CANCEL are found in the message string.

In this error trap, you want to check whether the user pressed the Escape key to cancel the process. In this case, you should not save your temporary variables in global memory. But if the user did not press Escape, you could save the input value in the global variable. Thus, line 4 contains a NOT expression that reverses the answer for the WCMATCH expression. In other words, you are interested in knowing whether the message string does not contain the word CANCEL.

If the message does not indicate a cancel, the INPUTNAME variable is saved in the USER_USERNAME global variable in line 5. The INPUTNAME variable is assumed to exist as part of the fictional application. If INPUTNAME does not have a binding, the USER_USERNAME variable is set to NIL.

This function restores system variables and saves global variables for your application. That is all is it is expected to do under most circumstances. However, sometimes an error trap function must work with other error trap functions. After all, they all use the same *ERROR* symbol name (if they share the document variable space). One way to avoid serious conflicts is to preserve the *ERROR* symbol before defining your own in an application. Another way is to define the *ERROR* symbol as a local variable at the onset of your program, and then run the DEFUN expression inside your program module, as shown in Listing 3.8.

Listing 3.8   Replacing the *ERROR* function.

```
(SETQ ERRORSAVE *ERROR*)
(DEFUN *ERROR* (Msg)
    ... your error trap function ...
    ... end error trap by setting *ERROR* to ErrorSave
    (SETQ *ERROR* ERRORSAVE)
)
```

The (SETQ *ERROR* ERRORSAVE) expression must appear also at the end of the application because it will most likely not always terminate through the error trap. If you are careful in the usage of the symbol and the preservation of preexisting error traps, your program should get along fine with others in the system.

There are better ways to work with the *ERROR* trapping system in Visual LISP if your goal is to distribute software or provide for a larger user base. One of the best ways is to use the namespace aspect of a compiled Visual LISP application. That way, you know the *ERROR* trap routing was through your program and only your program. You can learn more about compiled Visual LISP applications in the online help system in the Visual LISP IDE.

Example: Returning Current AutoCAD Settings

Thus far in this chapter, I have discussed in general terms the essential power that lies in Visual LISP. In this section, you run an application that shows the power of Visual LISP in terms of defining problems to the computer. That is, you see an example that actually does something that might be considered useful.

The (C:HELLO) function, starting with Listing 3.9, demonstrates many of the concepts you have explored in this chapter. This version of (C:HELLO), which is more useful than the one presented in Chapter 2, displays the settings of the current AutoCAD session. The user or the programmer control these settings in a list of items. The list contains system variable names as well as the symbol names of functions to run to obtain an answer about the drawing or system environment.

Listing 3.9   Defining a data list.

```
(SETQ SETTINGSQUERY
    '(("CLAYER" "Current layer")
      ("TEXTSTYLE" "Current text style")
      ("DIMSTYLE" "Current dim style")
      ("TEXTSIZE" "Current Text Size")
      ((E_COUNTER NIL) "Number of entities")
      ((E_Counter "LINE") "Number of Lines")
      ((E_COUNTER "INSERT") "Number of block inserts")
      ("TDINDWG" "Time in Drawing")))
```

This is a complex example, involving features of Visual LISP that might be unfamiliar to those just learning the language, such as list processing and the use of programs as data. The report generated by the next function is driven by the contents of the SETTINGSQUERY data list, which is a nested list. The SETQ expression assigns the entire list to the SETTINGSQUERY symbol. The single quote mark at the beginning of the nested list definition means that nothing in the list is evaluated as the assignment is made.

Each sublist in SettingsQuery contains two pieces of data: the first piece of data is either a string or a list, and the second is always a string. Each list entry represents an element of data that you want to extract from the AutoCAD system. If the first data piece is a string, it is expected to be the name of an AutoCAD system variable. If the first data piece is a list, the list is evaluated. The result of the list evaluation or the system variable retrieval is displayed following the string value, which is the second piece of data in each list item.

Sample output from a simple test drawing follows. After the function set is loaded into memory, the (C:HELLO) command function runs. Changing the data list modifies the output.

```
Command: HELLO
Current layer = 0
Current text style = Standard
Current dim style = Standard
Current Text Size = 0.200
Number of entities = 12
Number of Lines = 4
Number of block inserts = 2
Time in Drawing = 0.012
```

Listing 3.10 shows the (C:HELLO) function definition. (Note that the listing on the CD contains more comments and additional prompts to the operator at the beginning of the function.) The (FOREACH) expression is the heart of the routine. Given a list of data, an expression based on (FOREACH) takes each element out of the list and moves it to another symbol reference. Within the (FOREACH) expression are more expressions to be evaluated using the list member data.

Look towards the bottom of the listing for the closing parenthesis on the same line as the END FOREACH comment. This is the closing parenthesis for the entire FOREACH expression. As you can see, FOREACH makes up most of the function. What that means is that inside this function, you are working with each individual list element in the SETTINGSQUERY data list. The first time the function runs, the ITEM symbol contains the first element in the data list. The second time, the ITEM symbol contains the second element in the data list. The FOREACH expression sequence repeats for each element in the data list.

The FOREACH expression is called a loop. The program loops through the expressions in the FOREACH expression for each member of the list argument. Loops and iterations are important parts of programming logic, repeating tasks over and over until a solution is reached.

Inside the FOREACH loop expression, the ITEM and SETTINGSQUERY symbols are presented as arguments. ITEM is a local symbol that will house each of the elements in SETTINGSQUERY one at a time. Because each element of SETTINGSQUERY is a list, ITEM will be a list. SETTINGSQUERY is a nested list, and thus each element is expected to be a list itself.

The next expression in the program is a conditional (COND). The COND and IF statements are both conditionals and provide the tools by which LISP can make decisions. They are used in a program when you want to test the condition or setting of something. Based on the condition, the program executes specific code and skips other sections of code. The IF conditional expression is used when there is one test with up to two possible branches to follow. COND is used when more tests are needed, as in the example program.

This program is testing to see whether the first element in ITEM is a string or a list. The element could also be a number or some other atomic data type that the program does not support. Thus, the program could take one of three possible branches.

Listing 3.10 Defining the HELLO function.

```
(DEFUN C:HELLO ( / TMP ITEM)
  ; Loop through the SettingsQuery data list
  (FOREACH ITEM SETTINGSQUERY
    (COND ;Test first element in Item
      ; Is it a string?
      ((= (TYPE (CAR ITEM)) 'STR)
        (SETQ TMP (GETVAR (CAR ITEM))))
      ;Is it a list (expression)?
      ((LISTP (CAR ITEM))
        (SETQ TMP (EVAL (CAR ITEM))))
      ;Otherwise we don't know what it is.
      (T
        (PROMPT "\nInvalid object in Item - ")
        (PRINC ITEM) ;show user what it was
        (SETQ TMP NIL) ;no further output
      )
    ) ;END COND
    ; Check to see whether TMP has a binding
    (IF TMP
      (PROGN
        (PROMPT
          (STRCAT
              "\n" ;New line of output
              (CADR ITEM) ;Descriptive text
              " = " ;Equal sign and spaces
          ))
      (PRINC TMP)))
  ) ;END FOREACH
  (PRINC) ;Quiet exit from function
)
```

The first test is to see whether the type of data in the first element of the ITEM list is a string. The test expression contains several nested expressions that manipulate the data. Starting at the innermost parenthesis pair, the (CAR ITEM) expression extracts the first data element in the ITEM list. The result of the expression is passed up to the next level, which is (TYPE (...)), where (...) is the expression just evaluated. The TYPE expression returns a symbol representing the type of data provided as an argument. TYPE returns 'STR for a string, 'INT for an integer, NIL for nil, and so on. In this example, you are retrieving the type of data for comparison. If the value is a string, you want to act accordingly.

The result of the (TYPE (...)) expression is returned to (= (...) 'STR), which is a test expression. A test expression returns one of two values. If the test fails, the result is NIL. If the test passes, the result is the T symbol, which stands for true. In LISP, anything that equals NIL is false, and all other things are true. Thus, this test returns T if the type of data found in the first element of the ITEM list is a string.

When a true result is found, the expressions in the parentheses for the test are evaluated. Note that the = expression has two open parentheses. The expressions that are found before the matching close are associated with the test expression inside the COND expression. When a string is found as the first element in the ITEM list, the program is supposed to retrieve the AutoCAD system variable related to the name. (Visual LISP excels at accessing the AutoCAD environment.) GETVAR returns the value of an AutoCAD system variable given the name. The result of the GETVAR function is placed in the TMP symbol.

GETVAR returns a variety of data types, ranging from strings to numbers to data lists. SETQ does not care about the type of data and simply puts it in the TMP symbol for later reference. GETVAR provides access to all system variables in AutoCAD, including many that are not normally seen by operators, such as the serial number of the AutoCAD package ("_PKSER").

The SETQ expression is the only expression associated with the string data type comparison. A closing parenthesis mates with the open parenthesis found at the start of the equality test. Following the closing parenthesis is another test expression, which checks to see whether the first element in ITEM is a list.

You can test to see whether a variable references a list in two ways. You can use the LISTP expression to see whether an item is of type LIST. The only problem is that something with a value of NIL also evaluates as being a LIST. (This has to do with the nature of lists, which you explore in later chapters.) The other way to test whether a symbol has a binding to a list is to use the TYPE expression. TYPE returns LIST if the item in question is a list. If the item is NIL, the value returned from TYPE is NIL as well.

The second test in the COND expression checks whether the first member of the ITEM sublist is a list. If it is, it is assumed to be a form. That is, it can be evaluated to produce a result. In LISP, the evaluator can be invoked inside a program and presented with an expression or symbol to produce a result. This is accomplished using the EVAL subr. When given a symbol, EVAL returns the value, or binding, of that symbol. When given a list, EVAL tries to evaluate it as an expression. This means the first element in the list must be a function name or an internal subr from Visual LISP; otherwise, there will be a problem.

In the example function, the EVAL expression argument is the value of the first element in the ITEM list. The result is stored in the TMP symbol using SETQ. The data in ITEM is the name (and any required arguments) to a function call you have defined. Refer back to Listing 3.9, to the SETTINGSQUERY values that contain the name E_COUNTER. This is the name of your own function, which is shown in Listing 3.11.

The call to E_COUNTER has been stored as a list that has yet to be evaluated, in other words, a part of a program stored as data. This is perfectly normal in LISP, unlike in many other programming languages. (This feature in LISP brings up some interesting possibilities, such as programs that change themselves as they run.)

Returning to the example function, you reach the last test for the COND expression. A T is located in place of a test expression. T is true and thus the test is always true. When used at the end of a COND expression like this, the T is sometimes called "otherwise" because of the way you read the program to yourself. The example function logical could be read as:

> On the condition that the first element in the list is a string, get the system variable. If the first element in the list is a list, evaluate it. Otherwise, post an error message to the operator and do not output anything.

At the completion of the COND expression, the function tests the TMP symbol to see whether it has a binding. The (IF TMP ...) expression simply checks the TMP symbol; if it is not NIL, the expression following the test is evaluated. Remember that the difference between IF and COND is that IF offers one or two branches. The COND expression offers any number of optional branches. There is another subtle difference that you will explore next.

The IF expression consists of a test followed by a single expression that is evaluated when the test is true. Following that expression is space for an optional expression that is evaluated if the test is false. If the optional expression does not exist, program control skips the expression following the IF test. The IF expression appears in one of the following two forms.

```
(IF <test> (then-expression))
(IF <test> (then-expression) (else-expression))
```

The <test> can be a symbol name or an expression. When the value is NIL, the test is false. When the value is non-NIL, the test is true.

When you need more than one expression in an IF statement clause, use the PROGN expression. PROGN allows you to group a set of expressions into one expression, satisfying the single expression requirement. Another alternative is to define a function and simply use the function call in the statement. I discuss test expressions (called predicates) and the use of conditions in Chapter 7. For now, note that the example function uses an IF statement that contains one expression for the THEN case using the PROGN subr.

In the THEN expression of the example, a string is output showing the descriptive text and the value in TMP. Two expressions are contained in PROGN. The first is a PROMPT in which the string in the second element of the ITEM list is displayed followed by an equal sign. The second expression is another type of print statement called PRINC. PRINC outputs the value of an expression and, if given a symbol, outputs the value associated with that symbol. Thus, PRINC can handle any data type, whether it is a real number, an integer, a string, or a list. PROMPT can work with only strings, which is why you could not simply add the TMP value to the PROMPT string.

Inside the PROMPT expression is the STRCAT string concatenation subr. STRCAT takes any number of strings and runs them into a single, larger string. In this example, three strings are combined. The first is the character combination \n, which is a new line character constant in Visual LISP. (When used in a prompt statement, the output begins on a new line. Without it, PROMPT outputs the string immediately following the previous output, with no space or new line inserted.)

The second string combined in the STRCAT expression is the result of another expression, CADR. CADR similar to the CAR subr except it returns the second element of the data list. CAR and CADR type statements in Visual LISP will make more sense after you explore the composite primitives. For now, just remember that CAR gets the first member of a list and CADR gets the second member.

The last string added in the STRCAT expression is the = constant, which is added to separate the descriptive text from the output of the data in the TMP symbol. These three strings are combined in STRCAT and returned to the PROMPT expression, which sends the characters to the command window in AutoCAD.

This concludes the example function, with the exception of the E_COUNTER utility function that was used as part of the example data list. E_COUNTER is shown in Listing 3.11 for reference. I describe how functions like it work later (in Chapter 13), after you explore the entity-handling features in Visual LISP.

Listing 3.11 Counting entities of a particular type in a drawing.

```
(DEFUN E_COUNTER (ETYPE / SS1)
  (IF (OR (NULL ETYPE)
          (= ETYPE ""))
    (SETQ ETYPE "*"))
  (SETQ SS1 (SSGET "X" (LIST (CONS 0 ETYPE))))
  (IF SS1 (RTOS (SSLENGTH SS1) 2 0) "0")
)
```

Summary

You covered a lot of ground in this chapter. Starting with an overview of how Visual LISP works, you found out the concepts behind the evaluator, what symbols are all about, and how to define functions. The example demonstrated list processing and the use of program code as data while showing off the power inherent in the language.

Visual LISP is unlike most other computer programming languages. If you work with other languages, you will know that you have mastered Visual LISP when in your other code, everything is a function and returns a value to be used by a calling function that in turn sends a value back. Perhaps the only drawback to Visual LISP is the enormous library of functions that are available for a variety of application-related tasks. With more than 800 functions, many of which remain to be documented, it is easy to overlook one or two that may be important for your current work.

If the concepts behind list processing unnerved you, do not worry. Lots of Visual LISP programs are written with a distinctive accent from other languages. The program in this chapter, for example, could have been written more quickly as a series of outputs for a small list of items. FORTRAN, C, Basic, or Pascal programmers might be more comfortable avoiding lists until some basic concepts are understood, such as the fact that lists are a lot like arrays and structures, two powerful storage strategies design to optimize the repeating nature of the computer. You cannot avoid data lists, however, when it comes to geometry, because points are stored as lists of three numbers.

CHAPTER 4

Working with Strings

The most common type of data you will use when writing programs is the string type, which consists of a string of characters. Strings can carry an assortment of data, most of which is coming in from or going out to the user. Input and output is a key element of any program. In this chapter, you explore how strings are stored, created, joined, torn apart, and converted.

Storing Strings

Visual LISP treats all strings as equals. Whether a string is empty or many characters long, the operations remain the same.

To create a string constant, you simply supply a string between quotation marks (") in the appropriate place in the program. Your string can be any length, although you might want to keep it within reasonable limits for printing. Strings are created also by when they are read from a file, input by the operator, obtained from dialog boxes, or the result of a conversion from another data type.

To save a string, you use a SETQ expression and giving the string a symbol name. Strings are stored on the stack or the heap, depending on where the symbol is defined. It is a good idea to keep strings from growing too large to minimize the amount of stack or heap space used. If your program is running out of memory, you probably have too many strings in use. There are two recurring themes to memory problems and strings.

It may be that the stack is overflowing (a stack overflow error is produced in Visual LISP), in which case you are most likely using large strings in a function that is being called frequently or recursively. Those strings should be moved to the heap or to a function that is higher in scope so that they are not stored on the stack each time the function is called.

Another issue often related to poor string management is a significant slowdown in performance after running a process for a while. If this occurs, the heap is probably storing strings that are not being used anymore and are just taking up space. You should free up the symbols by setting them to NIL. The next time Visual LISP manages heap memory, it will make use of the recently freed space.

A last item to consider when working with string data is also performance based. Strings usually take up more space than numbers. Thus, when storing numeric values input by the user, convert them to an integer or a real number. Do not save them as strings after the input or output phase of your program is finished. When you need to manipulate these values as numbers, it is more efficient to have converted them only once and not multiple times. For example, suppose an input item is an angle value. Instead of converting the string to a real number angle for manipulation in the program, convert it to an angle value after the input process is finished. But note that it is best to keep everything stored as strings when working with dialog box contents. After the user clicks the OK button, convert the strings to numbers.

The example expressions in Listing 4.1 create strings using a variety of functions. In the first part of the SETQ, the GR symbol is set to the constant string "Greetings "(note the space). Next, the NM symbol is set to the result of the user typing his or her name. The OUT symbol is set to the result of combining the values in GR and NM. Then the operator is asked to supply an integer number. That number is stored in the NUM symbol, converted to a string using ITOA, and stored in SNUM. Next, the OUT symbol is used again to add the number input along with more constant strings. The OUT symbol is then printed.

Listing 4.1   Creating a string.

```
(SETQ GR "Greetings "
      NM (GETSTRING 1 "\nEnter your name: ")
      OUT (STRCAT GR NM)
      NUM (GETINT "\nEnter an integer: ")
      SNUM (ITOA NUM)
      OUT (STRCAT OUT ", you chose " SNUM " today. ")
)
(PRINT OUT)
```

This nonsense example shows that most of the time, you will be using strings as variables and with a SETQ expression. Strings are then used as arguments to other functions to build more complex strings. Because variable names and the amount of space they consume does not need to be defined in Visual LISP, working with and manipulating strings in this language is easy.

Manipulating Strings

Visual LISP provides a nice collection of string manipulation functions. You engage in only a few activities related to the string values themselves: putting strings together, taking strings apart, converting strings, and searching strings for matches with other strings. When building strings for output reports, annotations on drawings, prompting the operator, and any other basic activity, you will probably be using some of the subrs described in this chapter.

This section describes common string manipulation functions: STRCAT, STRLEN, STRCASE, VL-STRING-SUBST, and VL-STRING-TRANSLATE. Simple examples of these functions are shown in Table 4.1. Note that the results of an entry in this table are carried forward to the next row. When SETQ is used to save a value associated with a symbol, that symbol will be used in one or more of the expressions that follow.

Table 4.1 Examples of string manipulations.

Expression	Result
(STRCAT "A" "B" "C" "D" "E" "F" "G" "H")	"ABCDEFGH"
(STRCAT "123" "," "456")	"123,456"
(SETQ A (STRCAT "1" " & " "2"))	"1 & 2"; the A symbol references the string
(SETQ B (STRCAT A " & " "3"))	"1 & 2 & 3"; the B symbol references the string
(STRLEN A)	5
(STRLEN B)	9
(SETQ C "AbCdEfGhIj")	"AbCdEfGhIj"; the C symbol references the string
(STRLEN C)	10
(STRCASE C)	"ABCDEFGHIJ"
(STRCASE C 1)	"abcdefghij"
(SETQ D (STRCAT (STRCASE C) (STRCASE C 1)))	"ABCDEFGHIJabcdefghij"; the D symbol references the string
(STRLEN D)	20
(STRLEN (STRCAT A B C D))	34
(VL-STRING-SUBST "and-uh" "&" B)	"1 and-uh 2 & 3"
(VL-STRING-SUBST "and-uh" "&" B 5)	"1 & 2 and-uh 3"
(SETQ CC "123,456.789")	"123,456.789"; the CC symbol references the string
(VL-STRING-TRANSLATE ".." " ," CC)	"123 456,789"
(VL-STRING-TRANSLATE "AB" "12" C)	"1bCdEfGhIj"
(VL-STRING-TRANSLATE "AB" "12" (STRCASE C))	"12CDEFGHIJ"

Building larger strings

The string concatenation function, STRCAT, combines strings into a larger string. All the arguments to STRCAT must be strings, and the result is a string that combines the various items. Any spaces, commas, or other delimiters you may need to use in the output must be inserted using STRCAT. The STRCAT function can accept from zero to as many arguments as you need to supply.

Converting the case

To convert characters to uppercase or lowercase, you use the STRCASE subr in an expression. STRCASE accepts a single string as an argument followed by an optional flag. If the flag is present and not NIL, the string is converted to lowercase. If the flag is not provided or is NIL, the string is converted to uppercase.

The STRCASE subr changes only the alphabetic characters in a string. Numbers and special characters are unchanged because there is no logical conversion between uppercase and lowercase for these items.

Finding the length of a string

Given zero or more strings as its argument, the STRLEN subr returns the total length of the strings as an integer. The length of the string is the count of the number of characters in the string, including spaces and special characters. The string length is a helpful value when you want to loop through a string and pull out specific information. It can also serve as an indicator as to whether or not input is correct.

Substituting characters in a string

Sometimes you might need to change certain characters in a string. For example, if you are expressing numbers in the various standards around the world, you might need to substitute the decimal character with a comma and visa versa. You might also need to change the spaces and commas separating each order of thousands. For example, the number 45,123.5 in one standard is 45 123,5 in other standard.

To substitute characters in a string, you use the VL-STRING-SUBST subr, which has four arguments. The first and second arguments are the new string and old string, respectively. The third argument is the source string in which to do the substituting. The last argument, which is optional, is an integer indicating where to start making substitutions. One nuance to keep in mind is that the position of the first character in this case is 0, not 1. One way to figure out which number to use with different Visual LISP functions is to remember that all newer functions use 0 as the base, but older functions use 1. You can easily recognize most functions added when Visual LISP made its appearance by their VL prefix.

VL-STRING-SUBST changes only the first occurrence of the pattern string it finds in the source string. If you need to make many changes to the source string, call VL-STRING-SUBST as many times as needed or use the VL-STRING-TRANSLATE subr.

VL-STRING-TRANSLATE replaces characters in a source string. It replaces only characters, not substrings. Given the set to match, the replacement set, and the source string, this function returns a new string. The function matches exact characters, so it is case specific.

Reducing Strings

Many times, you need to take strings apart to form substrings. Visual LISP provides a variety of tools to facilitate this activity, including SUBSTR and the three related functions VL-STRING-TRIM, VL-STRING-RIGHT-TRIM, and VL-STRING-LEFT-TRIM. These functions are introduced in this section. Table 4.2 provides some simple examples.

Table 4.2 Examples of string reductions.

Expression	Result
(SETQ A "123A123B123")	"123A123B123"; the A symbol references the string
(SUBSTR A 1 1)	"1"
(SUBSTR A 2)	"23A123B123"
(SUBSTR A 2 3)	"23A"
(VL-STRING-TRIM "1234567890" A)	"A123B"
(VL-STRING-LEFT-TRIM "1234567890" A)	"A123B123"
(VL-STRING-RIGHT-TRIM "432" A)	"123A123B1"

Returning a portion of a string

The SUBSTR subr returns a portion of a string given a starting location and an optional number of characters to retrieve. SUBSTR is useful because you can strip one character or a small group of characters at a time. SUBSTR has three arguments. The first argument is the string from which you want to extract a portion. The second argument is the starting position in the string, with the first character considered 1. The last argument, which is optional, is the length of the string to be returned.

A common use of SUBSTR is to reduce a string one character at a time to look for delimiters, such as a comma or a space. The basic concept behind analyzing, or parsing, a string is to remove the first character from the string, reduce the string by one character, and then continue until every character in the source string has been analyzed. For example, the series of expressions in Listing 4.2 reduce a string referenced by the ISS symbol by taking one character at a time out of the string, placing it in CH, and doing something with the character just read.

At the end of the chapter are several parsing examples that read a source string and return a list of data extracted from the string. This is a common activity when reading data files created by other programs or devices.

Trimming strings

The VL-STRING-TRIM subr removes characters from the beginning and end of a string. This is useful when processing strings from a file or some other device that pads data with extra spaces or other characters. The arguments to VL-STRING-TRIM are the pattern character set and the string to

Listing 4.2   Reducing a string.

```
(WHILE (> (STRLEN ISS) 0)
   (SETQ CH (SUBSTR ISS 1 1)
         ISS (SUBSTR ISS 2)
   )
   ... ; Do something with CH
)
```

trim. The pattern character set is supplied as a string of one to many characters. The result of the function is the trimmed string.

Two related functions are VL-STRING-RIGHT-TRIM and VL-STRING-LEFT-TRIM. These two functions behave in the same manner and with the same arguments as VL-STRING-TRIM. The only difference is that one trims the right side of the source string and the other trims the left side. As in the VL-STRING-TRIM function, any characters matching the pattern characters are removed.

You cannot use wildcards or groups as pattern characters. If you have a large selection of characters to remove from either end of a string, consider a more specialized string parsing system of your own design.

Searching Strings

String searching is important in many applications. For example, you may have to read the title block of a drawing (where the drawing and project information is typically drawn) and determine whether a part number or other critical data is valid. You can use legacy search utility routines to search strings a character at a time, or you can use Visual LISP search routines, which are much faster because they are compiled routines and not evaluated LISP code. This section describes the VL-STRING-SEARCH, VL-STRING-POSITION, ASCII, CHR, and VL-STRING->LIST subrs. See Table 4.3 for some simple examples.

You will want to do a few tasks when searching strings. The first is to simply determine whether a source string has a matching pattern; this is a string comparison function. For example, you might see whether a string representing a filename has a file extension by detecting a period near the end of the string. Another activity related to searching strings is finding where in a string something is located. Following along with the same example, if you want to remove that file extension, knowing where the period is located makes the task easy.

Visual LISP's string searching utility, VL-STRING-SEARCH, accepts a pattern string, a source string to search, and an optional starting position to begin the search. The result is NIL if no match is found or an integer indicating the position in the source string where the match starts. Because this is a VL function, the positions in the string are zero-based, which means the first character is at position 0.

VL-STRING-SEARCH is used to search for string comparisons of any length. If you are searching for a single character, use the VL-STRING-POSITION subr, which is optimized to search for a single character. The VL-STRING-POSITION subr has four arguments. The first argument is an integer

Table 4.3 Examples of strings searches.

Expression	Result
`(SETQ A "AbCdEfGhIj")Ô`	`"AbCdEfGhIj"`; the A symbol references the string value
`(VL-STRING-SEARCH "CdE" A)`	2; the location is zero-based
`(VL-STRING-SEARCH "cde" A)`	`NIL`; the search is case sensitive
`(SETQ F "C:\\My Documents\\MyFile.Txt")`	`"C:\My Documents\MyFile.Txt"`; the F symbol references the string
`(VL-STRING-POSITION (ASCII ".") F)`	22; the location is zero-based
`(SETQ SLASH  (ASCII "\\"))`	92, the ASCII code for the backslash character
`(VL-STRING-POSITION SLASH F)`	2, the zero-based location of the first backslash in the string as seen from the front of the string
`(VL-STRING-POSITION SLASH F 3)`	15, the zero-based location of the second backslash as seen from the front of the string; the location of the first slash is incremented by 1 to start the search
`(VL-STRING-POSITION SLASH F 0 'T)`	15, the zero-based location of the first backslash as seen from the back of the string
`(SETQ DQUOTE (CHR 34))`	`"\""`, creates a symbol to reference the double quote character.
`(STRCAT "12" DQUOTE " equals a foot.")`	`"12\" equals a foot."`
`(SETQ Slash (CHR 92))`	`"\\"`, creates a symbol to reference the backslash character
`(STRCAT "C:" SLASH "My Documents" Slash "MyFile.TXT")`	`"C:\\My Documents\\MyFile.TXT"`
`(SETQ B "123+100")`	`"123+100"`; the B symbol references the string
`(SETQ BLIST (VL-STRING->LIST B))`	`(49 50 51 43 49 48 48)`; the Blist symbol references the list; the numbers are ASCII character codes for values in the B string
`(SETQ BLIST (SUBST 32 43 BLIST))`	`(49 50 51 32 49 48 48)`; SUBST substitutes 32 for 43
`(SETQ B (VL-LIST->STRING BLIST))`	`"123 100"`; character 32 is a space

containing the ASCII (American Standard Code for Information Interchange) number for the character to be located. The second argument is the string to search. The last two arguments, which are optional, are an integer to indicate where in the string to start the search (zero-based) and a flag to indicate whether the string should be searched from the back. Searching from the back can be handy, for example, when looking for a period that may mark the beginning of an extension in a filename.

Two subrs are used when converting to and from ASCII character codes: ASCII and CHR. (ASCII is a character coding system used by computers. When you create a string, you are actually creating a sequence of ASCII character codes.) The ASCII subr returns an integer representing the ASCII code of the first character in a string provided as an argument to the subr. CHR is the opposite. Given an integer, CHR returns the character as a string containing the one character.

The ASCII subr is often used to make code readable. For example, integer 65 is the ASCII number for A. Instead of inserting the integer 65 in the code as part of a search pattern, it is more readable to have (ASCII "A"). Also, you don't have to memorize the ASCII table for characters such as the period, equal sign, double quote mark, and so forth.

The CHR subr is used more in the construction of strings. This is how you can handle "unprintable" characters or override special characters such as the backslash and double quote. When defining a string, the double quote is typically used to mark the beginning and end of a string. But what if you want a double quote in the string itself? The CHR subr can take number 34, the ASCII equivalent for a double quote, and convert it to a double quote mark or simply use the backslash, as in \".

One last function related to ASCII codes in strings is VL-STRING->LIST. This subr takes a string as its sole argument and returns a list of integers. The list contains one number for each character in the string. ASCII codes as numbers can be handy tools. You can use them to encrypt information using an input string and converting that to numbers. Another application is to write data to a file or external device so that you can monitor the output and make sure no special characters get through and cause a problem at the other end of the transaction. Before writing the string, you convert it to a list of numbers, check to see whether the numbers are within an acceptable range, change any that are not, and then convert the list of numbers back to a string. The VL-LIST->STRING subr performs the reversing process, making such conversions easy to manage.

Comparing Strings

String comparison is when you compare two strings to see whether they are the same or where they differ. Visual LISP provides two powerful functions for finding string matches: WCMATCH and VL-STRING-MISMATCH. WCMATCH is a wildcard match, which means that you specify the search or comparison pattern string using wildcards. Wildcards allow you to specify ambiguous or nonrelevant areas of a string. If you want to know if the value "23" is anywhere in a string, for example, use the wildcard search pattern string "*23*". The asterisks indicate that anything can appear on either side of the digits 23. Table 4.4 lists the wildcard characters you can use in a search pattern.

The WCMATCH subr searches a string to see whether a pattern is matched. It returns a NIL result if the pattern is not matched, and a T (true) result if there is a match. After finding a match, you may use VL-STRING-SEARCH to pull out specific elements. WCMATCH accepts two argument values: the string to search followed by the pattern to match.

In most cases, you use WCMATCH as a test in a conditional expression looking for specific patterns. For example, you may have a program that reads a data file containing variable record data,

Table 4.4 Wildcard characters for WCMATCH.

Pattern	Description
#	Matches any numeric digit, 0 to 9
@	Matches any alphabetic character, A to Z
.	Matches any non-alphanumeric character
*	Matches any string pattern
?	Matches any single character
~	Used as the first character in a pattern to reverse logic, as in NOT
[...]	Matches any characters between the brackets
[~...]	Matches any character not between the brackets
-	Specifies a range (such as A–Z); used inside brackets
,	Separates two patterns
`	Indicates that the next character should be used as is (allows the use of wildcard characters as part of the pattern itself)

such an INI file, which is a common Windows file. An INI file has two types of records: heading records, which have square brackets around them, and data records, which have a name followed by an equal sign followed by some value. The WCMATCH patterns that would recognize these record types are "`[*`]" and "*=*", respectively. Thus, the expression (WCMATCH S "`[*`]") returns T for true if the S string has a header type structure and NIL for false if the S string does not.

Note the use of the single backward quote mark in front of each square bracket. These are required so that the bracket character is used directly. Otherwise, the brackets would be interpreted by the search system as meaning "match any character in between." A search pattern of "[*]" returns true only if the input is an asterisk all by itself. By including the backward single quote, the bracket characters become part of the search pattern. (You may find it difficult at first to create complicated search patterns. If so, spend some time experimenting.)

You can use WCMATCH to check input just read from a data file or some other device (even the keyboard) to assist a parsing system. As such, it is a powerful tool when integrating various applications and devices with AutoCAD.

A related subr is VL-STRING-MISMATCH, which compares two strings and returns the character position offset where they no longer match. You can specify the starting location of the search independently for each of the two strings (as zero-based offsets); these are optional parameters. VL-STRING-MISMATCH is handy when comparing two strings containing directory paths or filenames, product number systems, or drawing information with standard templates.

In many cases where WCMATCH might be used, VL-STRING-MISMATCH will execute faster. For example, suppose you need to compare a part number prefix with a title block or BOM (bill of material) record entry. You might be doing this to navigate to a related drawing or to provide additional information about a reference. If you know the starting locations of the part number in the strings, VL-STRING-MISMATCH tells you whether there is a match faster than WCMATCH.

If the part number string can be referenced using the PN symbol, and the pattern string can be referenced by the PTTN symbol, and each comparison starts at the first character in the string, the following functions are the same. Each returns a NIL result if the pattern string does not match the part number string or true (T) otherwise:

```
(WCMATCH PN (STRCAT PTTN "*"))
(= (SUBSTR PN 1 (STRLEN PTTN)) PTTN)
(= (VL-STRING-MISMATCH PN PTTN) (STRLEN PTTN))
```

Now, which of these three executes faster? And why would anyone care? The second question is easy to answer. No matter how fast you make a function, you will want to make it faster. Either you want to keep improving your work or users will harass you to make something faster.

Back to the first question, which can Visual LISP evaluate the fastest? To understand the answer, you need to examine each expression. In the first expression, you ask Visual LISP to search through a string and see whether anything inside matches the supplied pattern.

In the second expression, you extract a set of characters from the part number string and directly compare those with the pattern string. This results in fewer operations in the computer, because the entire string is not searched for a pattern match. Instead, two strings of equal length are compared directly.

In the third option, the same thing is taking place, but slightly faster. The comparison and substring extraction happen at once in the supporting object code for the function. The result is simply compared (using integer comparison) to the length of the pattern string. As a result, the third option, VL-STRING-MISMATCH, evaluates slightly faster. This can be important when many iterations of the same operation are involved, as is often the case in file handling.

Converting between Strings and Symbols

Visual LISP has two conversion subrs for changing strings into symbols and symbols into strings. The conversion between the two is typically performed when reading symbol names from an external device or file. The read process takes place as a string, and you must then convert the string to a symbol to be used in your program. The reverse process takes place when you want to send a symbol name to an external device or file.

The READ subr converts a string to a symbol name if the string represents a valid symbol name. READ is powerful and can convert strings to other data types, such as numbers. The (READ "TEST") expression returns the TEST symbol name. You take a closer look at the READ subr in a later chapter about converting strings and numbers. The second conversion function is VL-SYMBOL-NAME, which takes a symbol as an argument and returns a string. For example, (VL-SYMBOL-NAME 'Test) returns "TEST" as a string. You must put the single quote in front of the symbol name; otherwise, the function evaluates the symbol and sends the result to the VL-SYMBOL-NAME subr.

Example Functions

This section describes two useful functions for working with string input. A common task in many applications is reading a data file of formatted information, such as X,Y,Z coordinates or a survey instrument download in which each record may be different. Both example functions accept a string and break it into a list of strings. The first example looks for a particular delimiter in the string, such as a comma or a space. The second looks for numbers amongst variable text data and returns a list of just the numbers found.

Note that these example functions are complex for beginners. You might want to revisit them after you learn about other programming concepts such as loops, conditionals, and predicates.

The (PARSE-STRING) function

The (PARSE-STRING) function, shown in Listing 4.3, takes a string and a delimiter character and returns a list containing the string elements bounded by the delimiter. For example, the input string "X,Y,Z" returns the list ("X" "Y" "Z"). If these data items were numbers, you could convert them to something more appropriate to your application. Another example is breaking a sentence into words, as in "The quick brown fox" returning ("The" "quick" "brown" "fox"). One place where you would break input like this into pieces for processing is in a natural-language-based solution.

The(PARSE-STRING) function has two arguments: the input string(INSTR) and the delimiter character (DELIM). The input string must be a string type, but the data supplied by DELIM may be a string or an integer. If it is a string, only the first character is used. If it is an integer, the value is assumed to be an ASCII character code.

(PARSE_IT) has three local variables: RES, INX, and INXP, which all start with a value of NIL. RES will contain the result list of words you create from the input string. INX and INXP are integers that tell you where in the input string the parser is currently looking. INX is the current location and INXP is the previous location, or index.

(PARSE_IT) starts by checking the data type of the argument symbol, DELIM. If DELIM is a string, the ASCII subr converts the first character of the string to an ASCII integer code. If DELIM is not a string, it is checked to see whether it is an integer. If DELIM is neither a string nor an integer, the function uses the value 32, which is the ASCII character code for the space character, " ". This serves as the default delimiter if nothing legitimate is provided. The last check of DELIM is to see whether the integer value is between 1 and 255, inclusive. This is the valid character-code range for the ASCII set. After that expression has completed, we know that DELIM is a valid data type and value.

The INX and INXP symbols are initialized in the same SETQ as DELIM. INXP, the previous location, is set to an initial value of -1. INX is set to the location of the first occurrence of the DELIM character. The values for INX and INXP are zero-based offsets into the input string. It is important to remember which method you are using when writing an application. Are your string index values zero-based or one-based? The answer is up to you, the programmer. In this example, I stored everything using a zero-based index into the string because I was relying on the VL-STRING-POSITION subr to perform the searches for the delimiter characters, and that subr is zero based.

Listing 4.3   Parsing a string to a list.

```
(DEFUN PARSE_It (INSTR DELIM / RES INX INXP)
  (SETQ DELIM
    (IF (= (TYPE DELIM) 'STR)
      (ASCII DELIM)
      (IF (/= (TYPE DELIM) 'INT)
        32
        (IF (> 0 DELIM 256) DELIM 32)))
      INX (VL-STRING-POSITION DELIM INSTR 0)
      INXP -1)
  (WHILE (AND INX
              (< INX (STRLEN INSTR)))
    (SETQ RES
      (CONS (SUBSTR INSTR (+ 2 INXP) (- INX INXP 1))
            RES)
          INXP INX
          INX (VL-STRING-POSITION
                DELIM INSTR (1+ INXP))))
  (SETQ RES (CONS (SUBSTR INSTR (+ 2 INXP)) RES))
  (REVERSE RES))
```

A WHILE loop then begins to go through the entire string. The loop iterates, or repeats, as long as the value in INX is not NIL and as long as the value in INX is less than the length of the INSTR string. WHILE loops and testing expressions are covered in Chapter 7. For now, understand that the next sequence of expressions is repeated as long as both conditions remain true.

In the loop, you are building RES, the return list. CONS, the list construction subr, is used to attach a substring to the RES list. The key component of this expression is the substring extraction. The SUBSTR subr extracts pieces of INSTR. The pieces are defined by the starting character position (one-based) and the number of characters you want. To compute the starting position from the zero-based INX value, you need to add 1. However, the code indicates that you are adding 2 to the value. Why? You are skipping the delimiter. Walk through an example string to see how this works.

Suppose you have the string "123 56 8"; the fourth and seventh positions are spaces, and you are parsing on the space (breaking the string apart at the spaces). At the start of the loop, INX is set to a value of 3 by using VL-STRING-POSITION to find the first space character, which is at an offset of 3 (zero-based).

INXP is set to -1. So adding 2 to INXP provides the starting position of the substring, which is 1 in the first iteration. The length of the substring is computed by subtracting 1 from the difference of INX and INXP. (As you will see in the next chapter, you can combine arithmetic expressions in this manner.) The expression (- INX INXP 1) can be expressed algebraically as (INX - INXP) - 1.

After the substring is extracted, the value of INXP is set to INX. INX is then set to the value from VL-STRING-POSITION for the location of the next delimiter. In the example string, ("123 56 8"), the next space is found at an offset position of 6 (zero-based). To tell VL-STRING-POSITION to search beyond the last space encountered, 1 is added to the value of INXP, the previous location found. If the starting position had not been supplied, the same space would have been located at offset 3.

So in the second iteration of the loop, the INX and INXP symbols have values of 6 and 3, respectively. The substring extraction starts at (INXP + 2), or 5, and proceeds for (INX - INXP - 1), or 2, characters. If this is not clear, write symbol names on a piece of paper and walk though it again to see how it works. After you clear this conceptual hurdle, you will be comfortable manipulating strings using the variety of powerful tools provided in Visual LISP.

When VL-STRING-POSITION can no longer find a matching character, it returns NIL. This terminates the WHILE loop because it repeats only as long as INX has a non-NIL value and is less than the length of the input string.

After the WHILE loop is finished, the last part of the string remains to be pulled out and added to the RES result list. SUBSTR is used again but with only the starting position, (INXP + 2), and no length. When the length is not supplied, the remainder of the string is supplied, which is what you want to get.

The last step of the function is to reverse the RES list. (CONS builds a list by putting new members at the front of the list, so you must reverse the list to return it to its "natural"state.) Because REVERSE is the last expression in the function, the result of REVERSE is returned as the result of the function.

Running PARSE_IT is simple. After loading it, just send it a string, as in the following examples:

```
(PARSE_IT "123 56 8" " ") returns ("123" "56" "8")
(PARSE_IT "10,20,0" ",") returns ("10" "20" "0")
(PARSE_IT "100.0 200.0 300.0" 32) returns ("100.0" "200.0" "300.0")
```

The (STRING_TO_NUMBERS) function

You can use the preceding parsing example in a variety of applications, but it will not work with data that does not contain delimiters. An example of this type of data comes from surveying: "N40:23:50E150.0", which means a bearing at 40 degrees, 23 minutes, 50 seconds from the north in the east direction with a distance of 150. For with this type of data, you need a specialized parsing routine. Listing 4.4 has the answer, the STRING_TO_NUMBERS function. Note that the source code, which is provided on the CD, contains many comments and appears different than the listings presented.

STRING_TO_NUMBERS takes a string and returns a list consisting of just the numbers from the string. For example, a string such as "N40:23:50E150.0" is returned as ("40" "23" "50"

Listing 4.4   Converting a string to numbers.

```
(DEFUN STRING_TO_NUMBERS (INSTR / RES BUF INX CH)
  (SETQ INX 1 BUF "")
  (WHILE (<= INX (STRLEN INSTR))
    (SETQ CH (SUBSTR INSTR INX 1)
          INX (1+ INX))
    (COND
      ((WCMATCH CH "[0-9.]")
        (IF (= CH ".")
          (IF (NOT (WCMATCH BUF "*`.*"))
            (SETQ BUF (STRCAT BUF CH))
            (FLUSH_BUF))
          (SETQ BUF (STRCAT BUF CH))))
      ((= BUF "")
        (IF (= CH "-")
          (SETQ BUF CH)))
      ('T
        (FLUSH_BUF)
        (IF (= CH "-")
          (SETQ BUF CH)))))
  (IF (AND (/= BUF "")
    (NOT (WCMATCH BUF "[+-.]")))
    (FLUSH_BUF))
  (REVERSE RES))
```

"150.0"). This list can be quickly converted to a list of numbers by passing it to the READ subr, as in (mapcar 'read string-list). The values are returned as strings to allow for subsequent string searches back into the source string to find other critical data, such as the letter following the third number, which indicates east (E) or west (W).

The STRING_TO_NUMBERS function represents another way to parse strings. Because you don't know what delimiters you will be using, faster search tools such as VL-STRING-POSITION cannot be used. Instead, this function takes each character from the string one at a time and determines what to do with it.

A conditional expression tests the value of each character in the input string. The first option in the COND expression checks to see whether the CH character matches any of the digits 0 through 9 or the decimal point. Digits are concatenated to the BUF variable as encountered. The second option of the COND expression checks to see whether the BUF variable is an empty string. If the character in the CH variable is a minus sign, it is added to the BUF string. The third option in the COND expression is the default condition (which is always true). In this case, the character in CH is not a digit and BUF contains something. The buffer is flushed and CH is tested for a minus sign as before.

The actions inside this loop continue until the end of the input string is reached, which occurs when INX is greater than the length of the string. At the end of the WHILE loop, the buffer contents are checked to see whether they contain anything worth putting in the RES list. WCMATCH is used again, only this time with a pattern of "[+-.]" to see whether the string in BUF contains just one of these characters. If so, the BUF value is disregarded as if it were empty. If BUF is not empty, the value is flushed to RES in the FLUSH_BUF function. The function is now finished and the result list can be sent back to the calling function. Because CONS was used in the construction of this list, the REVERSE subr prepares the list for direct return from the parsing function.

FLUSH_BUF uses CONS to build the list. Looking at Listing 4.5, FLUSH_BUF is a short routine. But it does a lot thanks to the power of the string handling in Visual LISP. The first thing the routine does is check to see whether the contents of BUF are a single character, such as a plus sign, minus sign, or period. If so, the flush routine empties the contents of BUF by setting it to an empty string and then returns. If not, PROGN signals the beginning of a grouping of expressions.

Listing 4.5   Flushing the buffer.

```
(DEFUN FLUSH_BUF ()
  (IF (NOT (WCMATCH BUF "[+-.]"))
    (PROGN
      (IF (= (SUBSTR BUF 1 1) ".")
        (SETQ BUF (STRCAT "0" BUF)))
      (IF (= (SUBSTR BUF (STRLEN BUF)) ".")
        (SETQ BUF (SUBSTR BUF 1 (1- (STRLEN BUF)))))
      (SETQ RES (CONS BUF RES))))
  (SETQ BUF "")
)
```

The first test in the PROGN grouping is to see whether the first character of BUF equals a period (decimal point). If you intend to convert these strings containing digits to real numbers, the decimal point should not appear as the first character in the string. The FLUSH_BUF function adds a zero character to the front to the string if the first character is a decimal point. The second test checks the end of the string to see whether it ends in a decimal point. (SUBSTR BUF (STRLEN BUF)) returns the last character in the string. Instead of simply appending a zero character, you remove the last character, making the return value an integer if nothing follows the decimal point.

The last character is removed through the expression (SUBSTR BUF 1 (1- (STRLEN BUF))), in which the buffer substring from position one is taken with a character count of 1 less than currently found in the string. (1- (STRLEN BUF)) gets the length of the BUF string and reduces that value by 1. Removing the ending character is one case in which the unary functions (1+ and 1-) are applied. Another is when switching between zero-based and one-based subrs for string manipulation in Visual LISP.

Summary

Strings are an important part of data processing because they often represent the user's input or output. Strings are used in reports, for input data, and for annotations on drawings. This chapter looked at how strings are stored and manipulated. You also explored the subrs related to strings. The primary operations you will perform on strings involve building them from constants or from pieces of strings to form larger strings. Two other common tasks are retrieving parts of strings, or substrings, as well as searching strings for matching characters. The conversion of strings to other data types was briefly mentioned in this chapter; the topic is covered in detail in Chapter 6.

CHAPTER 5

Working with Numbers

Engineering and architectural applications typically involve computations on a grand scale, and the programmer must understand the nature of the numbers used. For this reason, this chapter explores the basic numeric types in Visual LISP and introduces the subrs provided for working with numbers.

Because of the environment in which Visual LISP is typically used, it provides many tools for manipulating numeric data. For more detailed information as well as additional examples involving numeric data types, consult the Visual LISP online help file system.

Integers

The most basic type of number in the computer is the integer. Integers are whole numbers; they have no decimal point and no fractional component. Many computer languages support a variety of integer types, with each a different size (often counted in terms of bytes of memory). Visual LISP, however, provides only one type: a 4-byte (32-bit) integer. This type can hold integers ranging from 2,147,483,647 to –2,147,483,648, which is sufficient for most applications.

Note that the GETINT function, which is used for integer input from the operator, accepts only 16-bit integers. This is an artifact from an older version of AutoLISP.

Integers are commonly used for counting and specifying the byte position in a file. The primary advantage of using integers is that they can be manipulated faster than real numbers.

The primary disadvantage of using integers is that they cannot represent fractions or numbers containing digits to the right of the decimal point. For example, if you divide the integer 1 by the integer 2, the result is 0 — not 1/2. Integers may also not be big enough to hold a result (although it is difficult to think of a computation that requires larger numbers for an intermediate result). When larger numbers or fractional numbers are needed, real numbers are the answer.

Real Numbers

A real number contains a fractional component or a decimal point. Real numbers in Visual LISP can be quite large, with up to 14 digits of precision, which is sufficient for all but the most extreme equations. (In those cases, you may be able to sequence the computation in such a way as to minimize the precision imbalances that may result.) Large real numbers are expressed using exponential notation, such as 6.5e5 for 650,000.

You use real numbers to store not only computer numbers containing decimal points but also angle values. Angle values are stored using the unit of measure known as a radian. A circle contains 2π (two times *pi*) radians. *Pi* (π) is an irrational number, so you never get an exact amount. Thus, when angles are involved, you might see numbers that seem odd. For example, you may be expecting a variable to equal 0 but find that it equals 1e–10 (.0000000001). Data extracted from points may also exhibit this behavior because angles are often involved in that type of computation.

The precision of real numbers won't cause a serious error in your computations as long as you take appropriate measures in your coding. You can follow several approaches.

One approach is to use the EQUAL expression instead of the = expression. EQUAL allows you to define an optional "fuzz factor" for equality testing, in which you specify how many digits of accuracy you want. For example, (EQUAL R1 R2 0.01) tests to see whether R1 and R2 are equal to within 0.01. Applications vary widely in the degree of precision they require in the equality test. For example, a steel beam application that compares equal sizes of steel may have a tolerance of +/– 5 mm. If the units of measurement were in millimeters, the EQUAL fuzz factor would be 5 when comparing lengths of steel beam that are also measured in millimeters.

Another approach when dealing with the precision of real numbers is to multiply the value by the precision desired, truncate the portion of the number to the right of the decimal point, and then divide by the precision multiplier. For example, if you want to use numbers accurate to three digits of precision to the right of the decimal, you would multiply the number by 1,000, remove all digits to the right of the decimal, and then divide by 1,000. In this case, 1,000 is the precision multiplier. Converting the number to an integer and then back to a floating-point number truncates the digits to the right of the decimal point. This type of conversion is the topic of the next section.

Converting between Reals and Integers

Programs can force one type of data to become another type of data through the use of conversion routines. Visual LISP has many conversion routines. The two pertaining to numbers are FIX and FLOAT. (For details on other conversion routines, see Chapter 6.)

FIX converts a real number to an integer by chopping off the numbers after the decimal point and returning the whole number. The value 2.999, for example, is returned from FIX as 2, not 3. The value is not rounded. To round a number, add 0.5 to it before using FIX. Using 2.999 again, adding 0.5 gives you 3.499; apply FIX and the result is 3. If, instead, the source number is 2.499 and you add 0.5, the result is 2.999; apply FIX and it returns 2. This approach is presented as an example function named ROUND in Listing 5.1.

Listing 5.1　Rounding.

```
(DEFUN ROUND (RN)
   (FIX ((IF (MINUSP RN) - +) RN 0.5)))
```

If a number is too large to become an integer (integers can have up to 10 digits or precision, but reals can have up to 14), FIX still removes the fractional component of the number but returns a real number to hold the result.

The FLOAT subr promotes an integer to a real number. An integer manipulated by an integer results in an integer. In Visual LISP, a real number manipulated by any other number always produces a real number result. Therefore, by promoting an integer in a mathematical expression to a real, FLOAT ensures that the result is a real.

Suppose the symbol A has a value of integer 1 and B has a value of integer 2. The expression (/ A B) produces the answer 0. However, the expressions (/ (FLOAT A) B) and (/ A (FLOAT B)) both result in 0.5, a real number. This is because the FLOAT subr promotes A (in the first expression) or B (in the second) to a real number for the division.

Manipulating Numbers as Numbers

Next, you turn your attention to the set of numeric manipulators provided in Visual LISP. From this basic set, you can construct more advanced numeric manipulators. Numeric manipulators work on two types of numbers: numbers as numbers and numbers as bit patterns. This section describes the various subrs available for manipulating numbers as numbers. The second group is described later in the chapter.

When a number is manipulated as a number, rather than as a bit pattern, the number is a value to be used in a computation to produce another number. Table 5.1 shows the various Visual LISP subrs for manipulating numbers as numbers. If you require other subrs, such as arcsine, arc cosine, or tangent, you can simply add them yourself — remember, Visual LISP is a programming language that thrives on expansion through function definitions. An even simpler option is to see whether the function you need is provided on the CD that accompanies this book.

Addition, subtraction, multiplication, and division

The basic math subrs for addition, subtraction, multiplication, and division can accept more than two arguments. Additional arguments are handled like nested functions. For example, the expression (- A B C) is the same as (- (- A B) C), although the nested expression takes slightly longer to evaluate. Likewise, (+ A B C) is the same as (+ (+ A B) C).

The result returned from a math operation is based on the type of data presented. If everything is an integer, the result is an integer. If one or more arguments are real numbers, the result is a real. In Listing 5.2, the value supplied as a parameter in symbol A is converted from degrees to radians. (Note that all trig functions in Visual LISP use radians.) The value supplied in symbol A is divided by 180 (a real number) and then multiplied by Pi (the internal constant). The result of the multiplication is returned as the result of the function.

Logarithm and base *e*

The LOG and EXP subrs are based on the natural logarithm and the mathematical constant *e*, respectively. LOG is the inverse of EXP. If you take the LOG of a number and apply that value to EXP,

Table 5.1 Manipulation subrs for numbers as numbers.

Subr	Operation	Syntax
`1+`	Increment by 1, same as adding 1	`(1+ <number>)`
`1-`	Decrement by 1, same as subtracting 1	`(1- <number>)`
`+`	Addition	`(+ <number> <number> [<number> ...])`
`-`	Subtraction	`(- <number> <number> [<number> ...])`
`*`	Multiplication	`(* <number> <number> [<number> ...])`
`/`	Division	`(/ <number> <number> [<number> ...])`
`LOG`	Natural log of a number	`(LOG <number>)`
`EXP`	*e* raised to the number; the natural antilog of a number	`(EXP <number>)`
`SQR`	Square root	`(SQR <number>)`
`EXPT`	Exponent of a number raised to another number	`(EXPT <number> <number>)`
`REM`	Modulus; the remainder of one number divided by another	`(REM <number> <number>)`
`GCD`	Greatest common denominator	`(GCD <number> <number>)`
`ABS`	Absolute value of a number	`(ABS <number>)`
`SIN`	Sine of an angle in radians	`(SIN <number>)`
`COS`	Cosine of an angle in radians	`(COS <number>)`
`ATAN`	Arctangent; returns angle in radians	`(ATAN <number>)`
`MIN`	Minimum number in a set of numbers	`(MIN <number> <number> ...)`
`MAX`	Maximum number in a set of numbers	`(MAX <number> <number> ...)`
`CVUNIT`	Conversion from one unit of measurement to another	`(CVUNIT <number> <from> <to>)`

the result is the original number. The natural log and anti-log are used in many equations involving forces and in graphing results.

To compute log base 10, divide the log of the number by the log of 10. You can use the example function in Listing 5.3 to compute base 10 logs, which are useful in developing charts and graphs.

Listing 5.2   Converting degrees to radians.

```
(DEFUN D2R (A)
  (*
    Pi
    (/ A 180.0)))
```

Listing 5.3   Computing log base 10.

```
(DEFUN LOG10 (L)
  (/
      (LOG L) (/ LOG 10.0)))
```

Square root and exponent

Raising a number to another number and computing the root of a number are common operations in the type of advanced math performed in engineering. SQR computes the square root, one of the most common roots required in computations. If you need another number root, use the EXPT subr. For example, the expression (EXPT 2 3) returns 8, the result of 2 cubed. The expression (EXPT 8 (/ 1 3.0)) returns 2, the cube root of 8.

To compute the specific root of a number, use the inverse (1 over the number) for the exponent. For example, computing 8 raised to the 1/3 power is the same as computing the cube root of 8.

Using EXPT, you can solve all types of exponents and roots, including the square root (raise a number to the 1/2 power). If you need to use a particular exponent over and over, create a small function for it, such as those in Listing 5.4. When used in your program code, such functions make the equations more readable.

Modulo

The REM subr returns the remainder, or modulo, of a number. REM is helpful when you are converting a number to a fraction, such as inches to feet plus fractions of a foot. To convert inches to feet, divide the inches number by 12 to get the integer number of feet, and then use REM to compute the remainder, which is the number of inches left over.

The FT-IN function in Listing 5.5 returns a list in which the first member of the list is the number of feet and the second member is the number of inches remaining given the total number of inches. If TOTAL_INCHES is supplied as 57, for example, the FT-IN function returns the list (4 9), representing 4 feet, 9 inches.

You can determine whether a number is odd or even by applying REM against the number with a divisor of 2, as follows: (REM <number> 2). If the result of the REM expression is 1, the number is odd. If the result is 0, the number is even.

Listing 5.4   Finding the cube root and square root.

```
(DEFUN CUBEROOT (N)
  (EXPT N (/ 1.0 3)))
;
(DEFUN SQUARE (N)
  (* N N))
  ; Or (EXPT N 2)), which is much slower
;
(DEFUN CUBE (N)
  (EXPT N 3))
;
(DEFUN HYPOT (A B)
  (SQRT
    (+ (* A A) (* B B))))
```

Listing 5.5   Computing feet and inches.

```
(DEFUN FT-IN (TOTAL_INCHES)
  (LIST
    (FIX (/ TOTAL_INCHES 12))
    (REM TOTAL_INCHES 12)))
```

Greatest common denominator

The greatest common denominator is the greatest number by which you can divide two numbers and have a whole number result. For example, the greatest common denominator of 15 and 20 is 5 (5 divides into 15 three times and into 20 four times). The greatest common denominator of 21 and 35 is 7.

The Visual LISP subr for finding the greatest common denominator is GCD. You can use the GCD subr to reduce fractions. Suppose that the result of a computation is 132 over 209. If you apply GCD to 132 and 209, it returns 11. Then divide each value by 11 to reduce the fraction to a value of 12 over 19.

The REDUCEFRACT function in Listing 5.6 demonstrates the use of GCD to reduce two numbers representing the numerator (NUM) and denominator (DEN). For example, the (REDUCEFRACT 10 16) expression returns (5 8), which means you can reduce the fraction 10/16 to 5/8.

GCD works with integers and whole numbers. If you need to work with decimal values, multiply them by 10 raised to the precision you want and then use FIX to reduce the value to an integer. For example, to use a number with a precision of three digits to the right of the decimal, multiply the

Listing 5.6   Reducing fractions.

```
(DEFUN REDUCEFRACT (NUM DEN / DD)
   (SETQ DD (GCD NUM DEN))
   (LIST (/ NUM DD) (/ DEN DD)))
```

number by 10 to the third power (1,000), apply FIX to the number, and then use the result with GCD. Remember to divide the answer by 1,000 before you finish.

Absolute value

The absolute value of a number is always greater than or equal to 0. When ABS is given a negative number, it returns the positive value. When given a positive value, it returns the value unchanged. The primary reason for getting the absolute value of a number is to avoid negative numbers in equations. A classic application of the ABS subr is computing the differences of coordinates. If you want to know the distance along the x-axis between two points, you can subtract one X value from the other X value and then take the absolute value of the result. No matter which X value you select first, the answer is the same.

Sometimes, however, you need to make sure a number is negative. If you subtract the absolute value of a number from 0, you get the negative number every time.

The expression (- <number>) negates the number. A negative number becomes positive, and a positive number becomes negative. The expression (- (ABS <number>)) always returns the negative value of the number. This is the opposite of (ABS <number>), which always returns the positive value of a number.

In Listing 5.7, CHS changes the sign of a number by switching it from negative to positive or vice versa. NEGATE returns the negative of the number, even if the number is already negative.

Listing 5.7   Changing the sign and negating.

```
(DEFUN CHS (NUM)
  (- NUM))
(DEFUN NEGATE (NUM)
  (- (ABS NUM)))
```

Sine, cosine, and arctangent

Visual LISP comes equipped with three elementary trig functions: SIN (sine), COS (cosine), and ATAN (arctangent). These functions work with angles in radians. (As mentioned, a circle has 2π radians.)

Radians are a better unit of measure than degrees for computations involving angles because the size of a circle is directly proportional to the value of *pi*. The circumference of a circle is *pi* times the diameter. The area of a circle is *pi* times the radius squared. Fortunately, Visual LISP provides Pi, a constant for *pi* that you can use in your computations. The Pi symbol is preset in

Visual LISP to the internal system value of *pi* as referenced in the math processor unit of the computer.

Working with radians is simple if you follow two simple rules: Use radians whenever angles are involved, and convert from or to degrees when performing user input and output operations.

You can use the basic functions to create additional functions that perform other computations. For example, the tangent of an angle is equal to the cosine of the angle divided by the sine of the angle, as shown in Listing 5.8. As long as the sine of the angle is not 0, the tangent can be computed. The other function, ASIN, computes the arc sine of a number, which is often useful when working with triangles that have unknown angles or sides. Note that a better version of these functions that includes error checking is on the CD, along with several other functions.

Listing 5.8   Trig functions.

```
(DEFUN TAN (A)
    (/ (COS A) (SIN A)))


(DEFUN ASIN (A)
    (ATAN
      (/ A
        (SQRT
          (- 1
            (* A A)))))))
```

Maximum and minimum

The MAX and MIN subrs return the maximum value or minimum value (respectively) of a group. Note that these functions do not take a list of numbers. Instead, they take a group of numbers presented as individual parameters, such as (MAX 20 25 21 15), which returns 25. The numbers can be symbols but cannot be lists, unless you use the APPLY subr.

To apply MAX and MIN to a list of numbers, you use the APPLY subr, which attaches the subr to the front of the list and then evaluates the result. For example, the expression (APPLY 'MAX '(20 15 10 5)) results in the answer 20. The MAX subr was placed at the front of the list, creating a proper expression that APPLY then passed to the evaluator.

The MAX and MIN functions are handy also in finding the maximum and minimum corners of some geometry, such as a rectangle. For example, the following expression finds the maximum X value in a list of points referenced by the POINT_LIST symbol. A list of points is a data list in which each member is a point list (contains two or three numbers for the X,Y[,Z] ordinate values).

```
(APPLY 'MAX (MAPCAR 'CAR POINT_LIST))
```

APPLY and MAPCAR are list-iteration tools and are covered in Chapter 8. In the preceding example, the MAPCAR expression applies the CAR subr to each member of POINT_LIST. CAR returns the X ordinate value from a point list, and MAPCAR saves the results of each CAR for each member in

POINT_LIST. The resulting list is then supplied to APPLY, which applies the MAX subr to the front of the list to find the maximum number in the group. If this seems confusing, don't worry. The example uses several features you have not learned yet.

Unit conversion

The CVUNIT function allows you to quickly convert numbers in one unit of measure to another, such as millimeters to inches. The function has many conversion formulas, which are stored in a text file that you can manipulate to add new conversions and units of measure. (See ACAD.UNT in the Support directory of AutoCAD for a list of all the unit conversions supported by CVUNIT.)

CVUNIT has three arguments. The first is either a number or a list of numbers. The second and third arguments are the names of the units of measurement to convert from and to, respectively. The measurement names you use in an expression are common names or abbreviations, such as M, Metres, Meter, or Meters for meters and in, inches, or inch for inches.

When converting multiple numbers, it is much faster to use the unit conversion factor. To get the unit conversion factor, apply the CVUNIT function to the value 1.0. For example, given a set of numbers to convert from meters to inches, get the result of (CVUNIT 1.0 "METER" "IN"), which is 39.3701, and then multiply that number by all the values in metes to get the values in inches.

Manipulating Numbers as Bit Patterns

Now that you've read about the different ways to manipulate numbers as numbers, it's time to look at the other group of numeric manipulators: those used with numbers as bit patterns. A bit it represented using a 0 or a 1. Bits are base 2 (0 and 1), whereas most counting systems are base 10 (0 through 9).

The combination of bits makes a number. For example, the bits 00, 01, 10, and 11 represent the numbers 0, 1, 2, and 3, respectively. Table 5.2 shows the primary base-2 placement equivalencies. These numbers show the value in decimal for the primary bit locations in an eight-bit number. Each time you shift the bit one to the left, the decimal value is increased by 2 to the next power, as in $2^0 = 1$, $2^1=2$, $2^2=4$, $2^3=16$, and so on.

Table 5.2 Decimal to binary conversion.

Decimal	Binary
1	0000 0001
2	0000 0010
4	0000 0100
8	0000 1000
16	0001 0000
32	0010 0000
64	0100 0000
128	1000 0000

When working with binary bit patterns, each place is often referenced in terms of its decimal equivalent because we use integers to store combined binary values. Thus, if you need to set the one bit and the four bit, you add 1 and 4 to get 5. The value 5 has two bits set to on.

Programmers often use integers to store a group of flags or bits indicating a yes or no status. When the bit is on, the flag indicates a true, or yes, status. AutoCAD has several bit-encoded numbers in entity data lists. For example, each layer table entry has a bit-encoded integer. It is set to 1 if the layer is frozen, 2 if the layer is to be frozen by default in new viewports, 4 if the layer is locked, 16 if an XREF object is involved, and so on. The layer table object can have more than one bit setting at a time. For example, the layer can be both frozen and locked (bits one and four).

Table 5.3 lists the Visual LISP subrs available for the bitwise manipulation of numbers. Integer data types should be used as arguments and expected as results. Although bit-encoded values rarely exceed sixteen bits (2^{16} = 65,536), plenty of room is available if necessary (up to 32 bits worth).

Table 5.3 Manipulation subrs for numbers as bit patterns.

Subr	Operation	Syntax
LOGAND	Logical AND	(LOGAND <number> <number>)
LOGIOR	Logical inclusive OR	(LOGIOR <number> <number>)
LSH	Logical bitwise shift	(LSH <number> <# of bits>)
BOOLE	General-purpose Boolean logic test	(BOOLE <operator> <number> <number>)
~	One's complement, a bitwise "not" operation	(~ <number>)

When grouped, 8 bits form a byte. One or more bytes (depending on the computer and the application language) form a word. In Visual LISP, each word is 4 bytes (32 bits) long.

Two operations are typically employed on a single word: one's complement and bit shifting. In one's complement, each bit is flipped: 1 becomes 0 and 0 becomes 1. In a shift operation, each bit is moved to the left or the right. As new bits are added, they are set to 0. As bits move beyond the end of the word, they are lost. (Another operation called rotating the bits moves bits off one end and onto the other end. Visual LISP supports only logical shifting, not rotating.)

Shift operations are rarely used to set flags. Instead, shift operations are typically used in building encryption or password verification systems. Bit shifting is also a fast way to multiply or divide by 2. Each shift to the left is the same as multiplying by 2, and each shift to the right is the same as dividing by 2, as shown in Table 5.4.

You can perform logical operations in which the two words, or bit patterns, are combined to produce to a result. The two most common operations performed on words are AND and OR (also called an inclusive OR). AND is true if all conditions are true; OR is true if either condition or both conditions are true. The LOGAND and LOGIOR subrs perform these two operations.

Table 5.4 Bit shifting.

Operation	Binary	Decimal
Original bit pattern	0010	2
Shift left 1	0100	4
Shift left 2	1000	8
New bit pattern	0101	5
Shift left 1	1010	10
Shift right 1	0010	2

LOGAND compares two integers on a bit-by-bit basis and returns an integer that is the result of a logical AND operation. Only bits that are the same in both patterns are returned. For example, if you AND the bit patterns 0011 and 0010, the result is 0010.

LOGIOR compares two integers on a bit-by-bit basis and returns an integer that is the result of a logical inclusive OR operation. An inclusive OR means that the resulting bit is true (on, or 1) if either or both test bits are true. For example, if you OR the bit patterns 0011 and 0010, the result is 0111.

LOGAND is frequently used to isolate an individual bit in a bit-encoded integer. For example, the expression (LOGAND <bit-coded-integer> 12) results in 0 if neither bits four nor eight are set (4 plus 8 equals 12). If bit four is set, the result is 4. If bit eight is set, 8. If both are set, the result is 12.

LOGIOR is used to update a bit-encoded integer. You can force the setting of a particular bit (or group of bits) while leaving the others unchanged. For example, the expression (LOGIOR <bit-coded-integer> 12) forces bits four and eight to be set in the result. The other bits in the original bit-encoded integer remain untouched in the result.

You will see more of the LOGIOR and LOGAND subrs as you explore entity data lists (beginning in Chapter 12), where it is common to encounter bit-encoded integers. The logical OR and AND operations just described are part of what is commonly referred to as Boolean logic. You can create the other operations typically found in Boolean logic by using the BOOLE subr.

Custom Boolean Logic

The BOOLE subr allows you to build a custom Boolean logic test using a binary-coded operation description. The operation description tells the BOOLE subr what to do with bits encountered in the two integers that follow the operation description in the parameter list. Using BOOLE you can construct any logical operation based on comparing two bits. The custom logical test can be applied to two integers in your programs. Although logical OR and AND testing is provided in Visual LISP, you might need other types of Boolean operations. The BOOLE function allows you to define any type of logical operation for use in your applications.

In the operation description, you provide a mapping of the results you want by describing what to do if the bits are certain values, as shown in Table 5.5. If you wanted the test to return true when both bits are 1, you need the first entry. The bits in each integer are compared based on the operation bit mask.

A bit mask is a collection of bits used for testing. For example, if you need to test the first and third bits to see whether they are on, you would use a bit mask of 0101 (value of 5). In the BOOLE function, the bit positions in the mask indicate which tests will result in true. A bit mask of 2 + 4 = 6 (binary 1010) results in tests that are true when the bits compared in two integers are opposites or complements of each other.

Table 5.5 BOOLE operation bits.

Bit mask	Integer 1	Integer 2
1	1	1
2	1	0
4	0	1
8	0	0

Adding the proper bits from column one in Table 5.5 allows BOOLE to form the standard Boolean logic operators AND, OR, and XOR (logical exclusive OR). Bit mask 1 by itself is a logical AND, bit masks 1 and 4 combine to form the XOR. The result is true if either bit but not both bits are true. Bit masks 1, 2, and 4 together make IOR (inclusive OR). You can create other bit tests, such as testing to see whether the bit in integer 1 is set regardless of integer 2. That test would combine bit masks 1 and 2 only.

When using bit masks and integer flags as AutoCAD does, you may find it useful to use the BOOLE function to extract information from the bit-encoded flag. In most cases, the LOGIOR and LOGAND functions suffice, but XOR and NOR are sometimes handy when working with a series of bit patterns or when encrypting data to be stored in a hidden place in a drawing. (NOR is defined by using bit mask 8.)

Listing 5.9 shows the BOOLE subr in action. In this function, a string is supplied as the ST parameter and is encrypted using the integer value in KEY. The encrypted string is returned as the result of the function. You can use encrypted strings in extended data to protect it from prying eyes. (Extended data is string data attached to AutoCAD entities; you learn more about extended data in Chapter 14.) The encryption function uses some of the string utilities covered in Chapter 4 as well as a WHILE loop, which has not yet been discussed in detail.

The logic of the function is easy to follow. The function starts by setting the RES symbol to an empty string. RES will be the resulting encrypted string. A WHILE loop then starts and repeats as long as the ST symbol points to a string that contains more than zero characters.

In the WHILE loop, the first character in ST is extracted and stored in CH. SUBSTR then shortens ST, starting at the second character to the end of the string. Note that all this is still inside the same SETQ expression. As long as you supply a symbol and an expression that evaluates, you can put as many items in a single SETQ as necessary.

Still in the same SETQ, the ASCII subr converts the value saved with the CH symbol (the first character in the ST string at the start of the loop) to an integer. ASCII takes a character string and returns the integer code for that character. Next, the BOOLE subr is used to XOR the ASCII character

Listing 5.9   Encrypting using BOOLE.

```
(DEFUN ENCRYPTSTRING (ST KEY / CH RES)
  (SETQ RES "")
  (WHILE (> (STRLEN ST) 0)
    (SETQ CH (SUBSTR ST 1 1)
          ST (SUBSTR ST 2)
          CH (ASCII CH)
          CH (BOOLE 6 CH KEY)
          CH (CHR CH)
          RES (STRCAT RES CH)
    ))
  RES)
```

code of the current character and the value supplied as KEY in the parameter list. Then CHR converts the now-encrypted integer in CH back to a string with a single character. That character is then appended to the RES string and the loop is finished.

Each character in the ST parameter string is converted using the same KEY number. To decrypt the string, apply the same function again with the same key. Thus, to get at your data, you must know the key number as well the location of the key; a casual hacker will not find it. You can increase the complexity of the encryption by increasing or decreasing KEY after each iteration so that each character is XOR'd with a different value. With some experimenting, you can find clever ways to lock your data so that only your application can make sense of it.

Summary

Working with numbers is an important part of programming, and selecting the right type of number for the application at hand is just as important. Integers are good for loop counters, for keeping track of places in strings and such, and for counting. Real numbers, which contain fractional or decimal components, can have up to 14 digits of precision, making them suitable for most engineering and scientific calculations.

The Visual LISP language is rich in operators for manipulating numbers. Moreover, programmers can use these operators as the foundation for creating additional operators.

This chapter also introduced the use of integers for storing binary flags as bit-encoded numbers. (Bit-encoded numbers are encountered in entity data lists, which are covered in a later chapter.) The Boolean logic system was described as a way to test bit settings in a bit-encoded value.

CHAPTER 6

Converting Numbers and Strings

In programming, the primary data elements you work with are numbers and strings (sequences of characters). In AutoCAD, you work with dimensions, which are strings containing numbers representing parameter data, and applications often must report the results of computations in string format to users, files, and drawings.

This chapter explores the Visual LISP subrs for converting between strings and numbers. Integer and real numbers are covered as well as two uses of real numbers, scalars and angles. In addition, radians and how you use them in Visual LISP are also described in this chapter.

Integers and Strings

Two simple subrs convert data between integer format and string format. The ATOI (ASCII TO Integer) subr takes a string containing digits and returns the value they represent as an integer. For example, (ATOI "100") returns the integer 100.

If ATOI is presented with a string that contains both characters and numbers, it converts as many numbers as it can until it encounters a non-numeric character. For example, the expression (ATOI "12AB34") returns the integer value 12.

When presented with something it cannot translate to an integer, ATOI returns a value of 0. For example, (ATOI "AB12") returns 0 because the first characters are non-numeric and cannot be converted. Therefore, it is important to remove any formatting characters or other non-numeric characters from the string before trying to convert it to an integer.

The opposite of ATOI is ITOA (Integer TO ASCII). ITOA converts an integer value to a string of digits. For example, (ITOA 100) returns the string "100". If the value is negative, a negative sign is inserted in front of the string. For example, (ITOA -23) returns "-23".

If you need to pad leading or trailing zeros, do so after converting the numbers to strings. Listing 6.1 shows a function that you can use for the formatted conversion of a positive integer to a string. The expression (INTSTRING 17 4) returns "0017".

Converting Strings to Real Numbers

Listing 6.1   Converting an integer to a string with padded digits.

```
(DEFUN INTSTRING (NUM DIGS)
  (SETQ NUM (ITOA NUM))
  (WHILE (< (STRLEN NUM) DIGS)
    (SETQ NUM (STRCAT "0" NUM)))
  NUM)
```

Two subrs are available for converting strings to numbers representing scalar values. A *scalar* is a distance or value other than a point, vector, or angle.

The ATOF (ASCII TO Float) subr converts a string to a real, or floating-point, number. Note that ASCII and string are often used interchangeably. Technically, when dealing with normal strings, you should use the term ASCII string. Other types of strings based on code pages and different strategies of data storage are outside the scope of Visual LISP.

The ATOF subr is similar to the ATOI subr. ATOF can translate most strings starting with a numeric character to a numeric data type that can be used in expressions calling for numbers. Given a string such as "0.12ab", ATOF returns the real number 0.12. ATOF does not require a leading zero, so the string ".12ab" is translated to the same value.

ATOF accepts exponential notation. Given the string "0.12e2" (which is 0.12 times 10^2), ATOF returns the real number 12.0. Listing 6.2 contains a utility that you can use with both ATOI and ATOF to convert numbers. The utility removes characters from the front of a string until it encounters a numeric character. The expression (NUMBERONLY "ab12de") returns "12de", which passes to ATOF or ATOI and returns 12.

Listing 6.2   Removing non-numeric characters from the front of a string.

```
(DEFUN NUMBERONLY (ST)
  (WHILE (AND (> (STRLEN ST) 0)
    (WCMATCH ST "[~0-9.-]*"))
      (SETQ ST (SUBSTR ST 2)))
  ST)
```

Sometimes strings representing numbers are in a special format, such as feet and inches. The ATOF subr will not work well with these strings because it stops at the first non-numeric character in the translation. In those instances, use the DISTOF subr instead.

DISTOF (DIStance TO Float) was provided to convert strings in standard AutoCAD formats to floating-point numbers. DISTOF uses the current number-generation system variables in AutoCAD to determine how to translate the string provided. For example, if you type (DISTOF "17'-10\"") at the command prompt and the LUNITS system variable is set to 3 (engineering) or

4 (architectural), the result is 214.0, the correct conversion of 17 feet, 10 inches to total inches ((17 * 12)+10). When LUNITS is not set to 3 or 4, you get NIL as an answer

You can control the units for conversion with DISTOF in two ways. One, you can use the SETVAR subr to establish the unit setting. The expression (SETVAR "LUNITS" 3) sets the units to engineering style. Two, you can override the LUNITS setting in the DISTOF expression by supplying the units mode after the string to be converted.

If you want to try every LUNITS setting in a program to see whether you get a conversion, use a utility like CONVERTDISTANCE in Listing 6.3. This utility loops through all five unit settings, using the units override to change the current setting to try a conversion. When the utility gets a non-NIL result, it is saved using the local RES symbol for return at the end of the function.

Listing 6.3   Converting distance by testing all unit types.

```
(DEFUN CONVERTDISTANCE (S / LU RES TMP)
  (SETQ LU 1)
  (REPEAT 5 ;Five types to test
    (SETQ TMP (DISTOF S LU)
          LU (1+ LU))
    (IF TMP (SETQ RES TMP)))
  RES)
```

Almost every application must convert strings to numbers. For example, all user input and output related to dialog boxes is performed using strings. Thus, it is important to be able to convert strings to numbers you can use in the program. But it is equally important to be able to convert numbers to strings.

Converting Real Numbers to Strings

To use a number in a dialog box, as a component in a dimension, or as an annotation in a drawing, you must first convert the number to a string. When dealing with file output, it may be necessary to convert numbers to specific string formats as well. Visual LISP contains a powerful subr named RTOS that converts real numbers to strings. This conversion utility is for scalar values. You look at how to convert angles in the next section.

Experienced AutoCAD operators already know the UNITS command and how to use it to create dimensions or to get more detailed information about objects in the CAD system. The RTOS subr has the same capabilities as the UNITS command but does not require you to set any system variables. If given just a number to convert, RTOS does use the system variables to see which format options to use. But when using alternative units of measure or precision, it is not necessary to adjust the LUNITS and LUPREC system variables. Instead, the values are supplied as optional parameters to RTOS.

The LUNITS settings are shown in Table 6.1. RTOS accepts one of these values as the second parameter. The precision is supplied as a third parameter. RTOS takes the number and applies the conversion rules inside AutoCAD.

Table 6.1 LUNITS **settings.**

Setting	Description
1	Scientific notation
2	Decimal
3	Engineering (feet and decimal inches)
4	Architectural (feet and fractional inches)
5	Fractions

When you use a LUNITS setting of 3 or 4, the input real number is assumed to be in inches. The number of feet is computed by dividing twelve into the input value. The remainder is the number of inches. Any fractions of an inch are displayed based on the setting of LUPREC.

When LUNITS is set to 3, the fractional part of an inch is returned in decimal notation. With a unit setting of 4, a fraction is used. For example, the value 33.125 is returned as "2'-9.125\"" when you use a setting of 3 and a precision setting of 3. The same input value results in "2'-9 1/8\"" with a setting of 4 and a precision of 3. The precision setting affects the output. Using the same example of 33.125 but with a precision of 2 results in the strings "2'-9.13\"" and "2'-9 1/4\"" for modes 3 and 4, respectively.

A LUNITS setting of 5 results in fractions using the number directly. Given 33.125 and a setting of 5 and a precision of 3, the result is "33 1/8". There are no extra double and single quotation characters denoting feet and inches.

The UNITMODE system variable can change the output of the RTOS subr for modes 3, 4, and 5. By default, UNITMODE is set to 0 and results in the values you've seen thus far. When UNITMODE is set to 1, the output changes slightly. All the spaces are squeezed out and the string looks like one you type at the command prompt. For example, "2'-9 1/8\"" becomes "2'9-1/8\"" with the hyphen moved and all spaces removed.

These conversion utilities should provide the basics for all you need to work with scalar real numbers. In most cases, you will be working with distances for dimensions, and any of the modes will work well. When working with measurements that do not represent distances, modes 1, 2, and 5 work best because they do not convert to feet and inches. One recommendation is to never trust the system settings; always supply values to the RTOS conversion subr so that you know exactly what is expected. If you want to provide your users with the capability to set these values, consider saving them to a global symbol for reference throughout your application. That way, you can isolate and check them at appropriate times and override the values when needed. Next, you turn your attention to the conversion of angles.

Working with Angles

Visual LISP uses angle values expressed in radians, which is not the method of measuring angles that most people are accustomed to. After all, most people know how to turn 45 degrees to the right, but wouldn't know what to do if told to turn *pi* over four radians to the right. Before you learn about converting and working with radians, you need a solid understanding of radians in general.

The conventional angular measurement is in degrees. A circle has 360 degrees. The number 360 was selected because it was the nearest "good number" to 365, the number of days in a year, when the seasons come full circle. There is no mathematical reason why degrees should be used because they actually increase the amount of work needed to solve a problem involving angles and circles. For example, to compute the arc length given the angle and radius, you multiple the radius by the angle, and multiply that result by the factor *pi* over 180. The *pi* over 180 factor is a conversion factor. It converts the angle value in degrees to radians. You can reduce this equation by simply storing the angle measurement in radians to begin with so that a conversion is no longer required.

In the radians units of measurement for angles, a circle has 2π (2 times *pi*) radians. That means half a circle is *pi*, a quarter circle is *pi* over 4, and so forth. The number *pi* is a special number because it relates the radius of a circle with the circumference or arc length. But *pi* is an irrational number, which means it has no final value; the decimal numbers keep going on and on. As such, radians are often expressed as fractions of *pi*. In Visual LISP, the value of *pi* is provided as a constant, so you do not need to establish a value for it before using it in a calculation.

Most languages use radians as the internal storage unit for angles. If your program must convert radians and degrees, the process is simple. The functions in Listing 6.4, R2D and D2R, are utility functions for converting radians to degrees (R2D) and degrees to radians (D2R). To convert from degrees to radians, you divide 180 into the product of *pi* and the degrees value. To go to degrees from radians, multiple 180 by the radians value divided by *pi*.

Listing 6.4   Converting degrees and radians.

```
(DEFUN R2D (R)
  (* (/ R PI) 180.0))
(DEFUN D2R (D)
  (/ (* D PI) 180.0))
```

Fortunately, Visual LISP provides two powerful subrs for converting angular values to and from strings. ANGTOS takes an angle in radians and returns a converted and formatted string. ANGTOF takes a string containing an angle value and converts it to an angle value in radians.

In both the ANGTOF and ANGTOS subrs, you can specify the angular units. If these values are not supplied, AUNITS, the default system variable value, is used. The angular units for these two subrs are the same as the AUNITS system variable and are shown in Table 6.2. Experienced AutoCAD operators should be familiar with these values and the types of angle strings that result from their use.

Table 6.2 AUNITS **settings.**

Setting	Description
0	Degrees
1	Degrees/minutes/seconds
2	Grads
3	Radians
4	Surveyor's units

When using ANGTOF and ANGTOS, the unit setting is optional. If not supplied, the default AUNITS value is used as Visual LISP attempts to determine the value of the supplied string. If the current AUNITS setting is 0, for decimal degrees, and you supply ANGTOF with a number, the number is assumed to be in decimal degrees unless otherwise specified. If ANGTOF performs the conversion, it returns the angle value in radians, a real number . Should ANGTOF fail in the conversion, it returns NIL.

In most cases, the AUNITS setting of 0 will suffice. The problem with using a setting of 1 is that the degrees are labeled with the character d and not the degree symbol. When using conventional AutoCAD text, the degree symbol (ASCII code 176) might appear as the result of a dimension. If you were to output the string to a text object, the %%d special format control might be used. As such, a common practice is to substitute the degree symbol or the special control characters with d before or after a conversion using ANGTOS or ANGTOF. The VL-STRING-SUBST subr can be quite useful for the task.

When working the conversion subrs, keep in mind also that the ANGBASE system variable setting changes the output result if it is not 0. Your programs should take this into account when converting angular measurements.

The last aspect to be aware of when working with angular units is the sign of the angle. Normally, angles are measured as positive in the counterclockwise direction. If you supply a negative angle value for conversion to ANGTOS, the result is positive as wrapped around the circle. For example, the conversion of *pi*/4 results in 45 degrees. Negative *pi*/4 yields 315 degrees. This is the correct answer, but may not be what you were planning to display. You can use the function in Listing 6.5 if you want the sign of the angle to survive the translation. Note that this signed angle utility should not be used with survey units because the result would be confusing in that context.

Listing 6.5   Converting a signed angle to a string.

```
(DEFUN SANGTOS (AA AU P / RES)
  (SETQ RES (ANGTOS (ABS AA) AU P))
  (IF (MINUSP AA)
    (SETQ RES (STRCAT "-" RES))
  RES))
```

Converting a String to a List of Numbers

You can use the READ subr (introduced in Chapter 4) to convert strings to numbers as well as symbols. And if the string is properly formatted, READ can convert it to a list of numbers in one expression. Properly formatted means that spaces are between each number and there are no non-numeric entries. The string "12 45 56.12" is a proper string. The string "12 ABC 56.12" is not because "ABC" is non-numeric. Given a properly formatted string, concatenate an open parenthesis at the front and a close parenthesis at the end and pass that string to READ. The result is a list of numbers, as in (READ "(12 45 56.12)"), which returns the list (12 45 56.12).

This mechanism is frequently used when reading data from a file containing space-delimited numbers. (Space delimited means there is a space or tab between each number in each line of the file.) The expression (READ (STRCAT "(" LN ")")) appends a parenthesis to each end of the string in LN and then passes that value to the READ subr. The result, assuming LN holds a string of numbers, is a list of numbers. The next example utility demonstrates how you can use READ to convert numbers coming from a data file.

Example: Importing and Using Point Data

A frequent task that Visual LISP is called on to perform is to import data from a file and draw something based on that data. An example is a survey notes set or graph points calculated by a program running outside AutoCAD. The file to be processed by the example application is an ASCII text file, with each line containing the X, Y, and Z ordinate values for a point in space. The program draws a point object at the coordinates supplied. And just to make things interesting, the coordinates in the data file can be either space delimited or comma delimited.

The utility, called (C:POINTSIMPORT), is shown in Listing 6.6. This example is just a seed for you to grow into something useful for your own applications. Some aspects of the utility have not been covered yet. For example, the example demonstrates modifying code, that is, program code that changes.

(C:POINTSIMPORT) is a command function, which means you can run it from the command line of AutoCAD by typing the name of the function without parentheses. The first action in the function is to request an input filename using GETFILED, a common utility dialog box subr. For now, note that GETFILED either returns a string containing a filename selected by the operator or returns NIL, indicating that the operator selected cancel in file dialog box. Thus, immediately after the GETFILED expression is a conditional test to see whether the FH symbol evaluates to a non-NIL value.

If FH is non-NIL, it contains a filename and that file is opened in read mode. The file handle returned as a result of the OPEN expression is saved in FH. You no longer need the filename; you need only the file handle to read the file. Visual LISP symbols can be reassigned in this manner. Just set the symbol to a new value (using SETQ), and the data type is reassigned automatically.

The next step in the function is to retrieve the first line of data from the input file using READ-LINE. This subr returns a string that is a line of text read from the file, where each line ends with the newline character (or characters). (The newline character is created in a text editor when you press the Enter key for a carriage return and line feed.)

Listing 6.6   Importing point data from a file.

```
(DEFUN C:POINTSIMPORT ( / FH LN LN2PT PT)
  (SETQ FH (GETFILED "X,Y,Z Data file" "" "" 0))
  (If FH
    (PROGN
      (SETQ FH (OPEN FH "r")
            LN (READ-LINE FH)) ;get first line
      (PROMPT (STRCAT "\n" LN))
      (COND
        ((WCMATCH LN "*,*") ;comma delimited
          (DEFUN LN2Pt (L)
            (SETQ L (VL-STRING-TRANSLATE "," " " L)
                  L (STRCAT "(" L ")"))
            (READ L)))
        ((WCMATCH LN "* *") ;space delimited
          (DEFUN LN2Pt (L)
            (READ (STRCAT "(" L ")"))))
        ('T
          (PROMPT "\nDid not recognize format.")))
      (IF LN2Pt
        (WHILE LN
          (SETQ PT (LN2Pt LN)
                LN (READ-LINE FH))
          (COMMAND "_POINT" PT)))
      (CLOSE FH))))
```

The input to this program from the file is a line of text, such as "1,1,1" or "2 2 2". The next task is to figure out what kind of data you are working with in this run of the program and prepare accordingly. The preparations involve defining a function to handle the input format. To see how this happens, find the COND expression in the program code. The first test in COND is to see whether the input line of text in LN matches the pattern for comma-delimited input, which is "*,*". If the text line matches, the next step in the program is to define a function named LN2PT. In Visual LISP, defining a function on-the-fly, in the middle of evaluating another function, is perfectly legal.

When the program encounters the DEFUN expression, the evaluator simply creates a symbol (if one does not already exist) with the name immediately following the DEFUN subr and assigns the associated expressions to the symbol for later reference. This is perhaps the most elementary way to create code that adapts to the environment it is working in: Define a common symbol name to handle each unique circumstance that you expect. The example function handles two types of translations of strings to points, but the adaptive translation function concept could support more exotic formats as well.

Look closer at the definition of the LN2PT function in the middle of the code. For the comma-delimited input string, the VL-STRING-TRANSLATE subr is called to convert the commas to spaces. An open and a close parenthesis is concatenated to the front and end, respectively, of the changed string, which is passed to the READ subr for conversion to a list of numbers.

The alternate definition of LN2PT is found in the other conditional option for a space-delimited format. If WCMATCH returns true for a pattern match of "* *", the input file must be space delimited. The comma-delimited check took place first. If the space-delimited test had been performed first, the result might be questionable because the string "1, 2" (note the space between the comma and the 2) returns true for a pattern of "* *". In a COND expression, the sequence of testing is important.

LN2PT is defined only if the format in the first line of text was recognized. If the line was not recognized, a prompt is issued and the LN2PT symbol is not assigned. Because LN2PT is a local symbol, it is bound to NIL and thus you can test for a non-NIL assignment to see whether or not to proceed.

Assuming LN2PT was defined to a function, the program enters a WHILE loop that iterates as long as the LN symbol has a binding that is non-NIL. In the WHILE loop, the LN2PT function is called with the value in LN. The resulting point, PT, is sent to the drawing as a POINT entity object using the COMMAND subr. At this point, you might want your application to do something else, such as draw connecting lines or create a polyline. That is where you can transform the program into something that you find useful. You can add support for more format types in addition to the space-delimited and comma-delimited types, or you can expand the recognition and processing logic in the LN2PT function.

Summary

This chapter wraps up a few loose ends regarding strings. Specifically, you explored how to convert between numbers and strings, with an emphasis on real numbers. Real numbers can be used to represent scalars and angles. A scalar is anything that is not an angle and can represent distances, mass, scales, and much more. Angles in Visual LISP are manipulated using radians as a unit of measure, and this chapter explained radians in more detail as well as presented two utility subrs for converting between angles and strings.

Strings are essential in programming applications. They are the primary communication between your program and the outside world, conveying information as well as posing queries and getting answers. As you create applications for AutoCAD, you will make frequent use of string and number conversions, and the subrs introduced in this chapter will become common tools.

CHAPTER 7

Using Conditionals and Loops

Almost all of the example functions and utilities you've looked at so far have included conditionals and loops, critical components in programming computers. A conditional is a test, the result of which causes your program to take a particular path. A loop is a repeating group of program code that works with lists of data or that collapses on an answer through an iterative process such as those commonly used in engineering computations involving linear algebra.

In this chapter, you explore the concepts behind conditionals and then look at the many options available for testing data in Visual LISP. The two basic conditional structures, IF and COND, are formally introduced, and you learn how to choose the right one for your programs. The chapter then describes a related structure, the loop.

Conditionals

The difference between a script and a program is logic. A script plays back a series of commands in order. It will not deviate from that sequence except to stop working when something is wrong. You may have developed scripts in AutoCAD for menu macros or command streams (a sequence of commands). You can save a command stream in a text file with an SCR extension. These SCR files are called script files and can be played back using the SCRIPT command. Although scripts can be useful for combining AutoCAD commands that you use frequently in sequence, that is all they can do. If you must apply some sort of logic to when the commands are used, you need to look at a programming language that supports conditionals.

A conditional is simply a test with associated code that executes if the test is true or false. For example, suppose you have a utility that annotates graphics in a drawing. A typical conditional test in is whether the annotation should be placed above, below, to the left, or to the right. You might ask the operator to select the location of the annotation, but you still need to do some calculations, which vary based on the selection. Now suppose that the operator wants the annotation to the left of the graphic, and your routine is uses the AutoCAD TEXT command. By default, the TEXT command expects the point input at the bottom-left corner for placing text. You can select options from the command line for alternative locations, but they introduce a change in the command sequence.

To handle changes in the command sequence based on circumstances or to expand the commands available to provide even more options, the programming language you use must support logical branching in the code, or conditionals. The most simple form of logical branching is the IF conditional. In the IF conditional, a test is performed. If the test is true, there is a place for an expression to be evaluated. After the expression is evaluated, the program continues forward. If the test is false, that expression is skipped and program execution continues past that point. The IF conditional is the most basic type of logic that can be used in a computer programming language and serves as the foundation for other conditionals.

The IF conditional is typically read as "if then." The IF part is the test that is either true or false. The THEN part is the expression evaluated when the IF part is true. This conditional can be expanded to IF-THEN-ELSE, where the ELSE part is an expression that is evaluated when the IF part is false. The expanded version provides two independent paths for the program to take. When the IF path is taken, the ELSE path is skipped. When the ELSE path is selected, the THEN path is skipped.

The logic of an IF-THEN-ELSE structure is like driving down a road and coming to a fork, with a sign indicating that the two roads eventually end up at the same place, but each offers different scenery.

Sometimes just having two choices is not enough. You can nest IF-THEN structures to form IF-THEN-ELSE IF... type logic chains that keep testing deeper and deeper in the ELSE path. Figure 7.1 shows this sort of logic in a flowchart. (In a flowchart, a diamond is a test, or IF conditional. Blocks represent an expression or a group of expressions.) Reading down the flowchart, when the first test is false, the second test is performed. If the second test is false, the third test is performed, and so on. Note that all paths lead back to the same path.

Although this is an acceptable way to develop

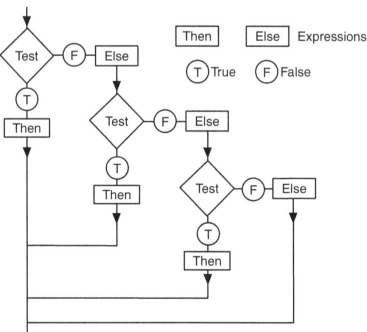

Figure 7.1   If-Then-Else flowchart.

applications containing advanced logic, many languages, including Visual LISP, offer a better alternative. The alternative structure contains multiple tests that cascade in the same way as a series of IF-THEN-ELSE structures, but it is much easier to read and manipulate. The name typically associated with the alternative structure can vary based on the programming language. Visual LISP calls such a structure COND, Pascal uses CASE, and C++ uses SWITCH. The effect is the same: A series of tests take place in sequence.

Returning to the example, suppose that the operator can choice to position the annotation to the left or right of the graphic or above or below the graphic. The TEXT command has four different responses to provide at the text location prompt based on the operator's selection. The program needs a test to see what location option was selected and an expression (or two) to handle each possibility. The following shows what that might look like if you use a series of IF statements.

```
IF (put text to left?) THEN
    Text left point
  ELSE IF (put text to right?) THEN
       Text right point
     ELSE IF (put text above?) THEN
          Text above point
        ELSE
          Text below point
```

Compare this with the next example, which uses a COND expression. The COND version is much easier to read — and is therefore much easier to maintain or improve.

```
COND
    (put text to left?)  Text left point
    (put text to right?) Text right point
    (put text above?) Text above point
    OTHERWISE   Text below point
```

Although the primary difference between the IF and COND structures is readability, you need to consider a few other differences as well. You look at those in more detail shortly. First, however, you look at the heart of the conditional, the test expression.

Test Expressions

A test expression produces either a NIL or non-NIL result. A NIL result is equivalent to false, and a non-NIL result is true. Because all Visual LISP expressions return a result, they are all valid test expressions. Many of the examples in this book take advantage of this aspect of Visual LISP.

Note, however, that some Visual LISP expressions are valid but are not suitable because they always return a particular value, such as NIL, every time they run.

Many Visual LISP subrs are intended for use as a predicate, which is a true-or-false test. For example, the three types of equality testing subrs do nothing but check equality between items in slightly different ways. They all return a NIL or T result just like WCMATCH, which you've seen in several examples.

To make things a little easier to digest, the discussion of predicate expressions is divided into three groups: numeric values, data types, and string values.

Testing numeric values

Table 7.1 shows the numeric value testing subrs in Visual LISP. Note that although you use these subrs primarily for testing numeric values, you can sometimes apply them to strings too.

Table 7.1 Numeric value testing.

Subr	Description
=	Equality test. Compares numbers as well as strings. Must match exactly. This subr may not be suitable for values computed as a result of trig functions or angles. For those cases, see EQUAL.
/=	Not equal test. Compares numbers as well as strings.
>	Greater than test. Compares numbers to see whether the first one is greater than the second.
>=	Greater than or equal test. Compares numbers to see whether the first one is greater than or equal to the second.
<	Less than test. Compares numbers to see whether the first one is less than the second.
<=	Less than or equal test. Compares numbers to see whether the first one is less than or equal to the second.
EQUAL	Equality test for numbers, strings, and lists. You can apply a fuzz factor to all numeric comparisons. The fuzz factor accounts for slight differences due to floating-point errors resulting from trig functions.
MINUSP	Checks whether a number is less than zero.
ZEROP	Checks whether a number is equal to zero.

With the exception of EQUAL, MINUSP, and ZEROP, you can supply more than a pair of numbers for testing. For example, if you want to test whether A, B, C equal the same amount, the expression is (= A B C). Another example is testing whether X is between 0 and 1 by using (< 0.0 X 1.0). When the evaluator is presented with this sort of expression, it breaks the arguments into pairs. The (< 0.0 X 1.0) expression is the same as (AND (< 0.0 X) (< X 1.0)), but the first expression takes up less space and evaluates a little more quickly.

Speed of evaluation is why MINUSP and ZEROP appear in the list. You could test for negative or zero values using an equality or relationship test, as in (< X 0.0), which tests whether the value in X is less than 0. Although (MINUSP X) and (< X 0.0) are the same from a logical standpoint in programming, they differ in execution speed. The relationship test involves the evaluation of two symbols. The evaluator must get the values of both x and the 0.0 constant. Then it subtracts one from the other and sees whether the answer is negative or positive. The last test of plus or minus is performed by checking the sign bit of the number in the computer. Determining whether a bit is set at the most fundamental level of the computer is a fast test, and MINUSP exploits this fact. It simply loads the number value into the registers of the computer and checks the sign bit. With no subtractions and only one value to manipulate, MINUSP is much faster as a result. The same situation exists with the ZEROP subr.

You might ask, "How much faster?" The answer is, not enough to worry about with today's computers. But not too many years ago, when machines ran slower by an order or more of magnitude, the difference was enough to merit making these options available to programmers.

You can use the EQUAL test with numbers as well as with lists of numbers. As such, EQUAL is the preferred subr for testing the equality of points. EQUAL can also use a fuzz factor, which specifies the limits of precision to test for equality. For example, suppose that your program has produced a calculated result of 10.0000000001, which most reasonable people consider to be equal to 10. If you set two symbols to these values and presented them to the equality subr (=), however, it returns a false, or NIL, value.

To correct this, specify the fuzz factor when defining the EQUAL expression. The fuzz factor follows the two items being tested. For example, to test for equality between two symbols P1 and P2 to a precision of four decimal places, the expression is (EQUAL P1 P2 0.0001). The 0.0001 value is the fuzz factor.

A fuzz-factor-based equality check works by subtracting the two values and comparing the absolute value of the result to the fuzz factor value. If the value is greater than the fuzz factor, the two values are considered not equal. If the value is less than or equal to the fuzz factor, they are equal.

To illustrate, set P1 to 10.001 and P2 to 10.0 using a SETQ expression, as in (SETQ P1 10.001 P2 10.0). Next, compare the two values using EQUAL:

```
(= P1 P2) ; NIL
(EQUAL P1 P2) ; NIL
(EQUAL P1 P2 0.01) ; T
(EQUAL P1 P2 0.001) ;T
(EQUAL P1 P2 0.0001) ; NIL
```

You can use the fuzz factor to determine whether numbers are nearly equal for more than just trig computation errors. For example, you can determine whether a beam is within a number of millimeters of another size or determine how many factors of some unit a measurement deviates. Listing 7.1 shows a simple example that returns a color code based on tolerance bands.

You pass two values to the function: the value as read from some instrument and the nominal value as determined by the function or the design. If these values vary by less than 1 percent, "GREEN" is returned. If they vary by more than 1 percent but less than or equal to 2 percent, "YELLOW" is returned. If the difference is greater than 2 and less than or equal to 5 percent, "ORANGE" is returned. Anything greater results in "RED".

Listing 7.1   Returning the amount of deviation as a color code.

```
(DEFUN DEVIATIONCOLOR (ACTUAL NOMINAL)
  (COND
    ((EQUAL ACTUAL NOMINAL (/ NOMINAL 100.0)) "GREEN")
    ((EQUAL ACTUAL NOMINAL (/ NOMINAL 50.0)) "YELLOW")
    ((EQUAL ACTUAL NOMINAL (/ NOMINAL 20.0)) "ORANGE")
    ('T "RED")
  )
)
```

In Listing 7.1, the deviation percent is determined as a factor of the NOMINAL distance provided. To find 1 percent of the nominal, divide it by 100. To find 2 percent, divide by 50 (half of 100).

Testing data types

Because of LISP's dynamic nature in working with symbols, you may not always know what type of data a particular symbol is housing. For example, Visual LISP enables you to specify keywords before requesting input for a number or a point. This means that the response of the input system may be a number, a point, NIL, or a string. How do you know what type of data was provided? Visual LISP has several tools for testing data types, and they are listed in Table 7.2. The operation of most of these tests is obvious, but there are a few subtle points to understand. Because NIL is both a list and an atom, it has its own special test (NULL). You find out why NIL is considered a list in the next chapter, when you explore how lists are constructed. For now, it is important to know that NIL produces a true response from (ATOM), (LISTP), and (NULL). A binding of NIL to a symbol results in a false response from (BOUNDP). When setting up a test sequence for data types, it is critical that you consider these things because the possible data types you are seeking dictate the order of the tests. If you need to rule out NIL, use the (NULL) test first to remove it from consideration.

Another way of check data types in symbols is to use the TYPE subr as part of a test expression. TYPE returns a symbol for the type of data supplied: 'STR for string, 'INT for integer, 'REAL for double-precision floating point, 'LIST for a data list (or NIL), and 'PICKSET for a selection set. You can then make an equality check to see whether TYPE matches one of the known symbols for types. For example, the (= (TYPE X) 'STR) expression tests the X symbol to see whether it is a string type.

You have already seen the EQUAL and (=) subrs, so why a third form of equality checking, the EQ subr? This third option has only specialized uses, so it is used the least. The EQ subr tests to see whether the objects being compared are the same thing, not just an equivalence. That is, EQ tests to see whether the objects that the symbols reference are at the same location in system memory. A typical use for EQ is to see whether a list or function has been modified.

Table 7.2 Data type tests.

Subr	Description
NUMBERP	Checks whether the data type is an integer or real. Returns 'T for numeric data types or NIL otherwise.
LISTP	Checks whether the data presented is a list. Returns true if data is NIL.
ATOM	Checks whether the data presented is an atomic data type. Note that NIL will also return a true response from this subr.
BOUNDP	Checks whether the symbol presented is bound to anything other than NIL. The symbol is provided in quoted form (not evaluated) to be tested.
EQ	Checks whether two expressions evaluate to the same object.
NULL	Checks whether the symbol presented is NIL.

Testing string values

Although we have already talked about string handling, the string testing subrs are listed in Table 7.3 for your convenience. Refer to Chapter 4 for information on string handling and string comparisons.

Table 7.3 String comparisons.

Subr	Description
=	Case-sensitive comparison of strings
WCMATCH	Wildcard search of string
VL-STRING-POSITION	Finds matching character position
VL-STRING-SEARCH	Finds matching string position

When checking for a particular string value in a test, you can use the STRCASE subr to convert strings to uppercase or lowercase, thereby resulting in a case-insensitive comparison. If string A has a value of "AbC" and string B has a value of "abc", the (= A B) expression returns NIL. The strings are not equal in a case-sensitive comparison. The (= (STRCASE A) (STRCASE B)) expression returns T because both strings are converted to uppercase before the comparison.

In most cases, you will be testing an input value against you own internal constants. It is a good idea to get in to the habit of converting all strings to either uppercase or lowercase for comparison and just stay with whichever standard you prefer. That way, your code is consistent for future updates. My preference is to convert all comparison strings to uppercase simply because it involves less typing (you don't need the Convert to lowercase flag).

Combining tests

Many times during programming, you will need to combine tests. You may want to know whether a particular layer is current and whether a particular dimension style is both available and current so that you can make changes before drawing something. Although you can create a series of expressions testing each option, readability and modularity suffer, making corrections or changes later more difficult.

A better way to combine tests is to use the logical AND and OR subrs. The AND combination returns a true result only if all tests combined return a true result. OR returns true if any or all combined tests return a true result.

To combine tests in Visual LISP, just wrap the combination expression around the tests to be combined. For example, if you want to test whether the A symbol has a binding, is a string, and equals "ABC", you would use the (AND (boundp 'A) (= (type A) 'STR) (= (strcase A) "ABC")) expression. When combined in this way, the evaluator starts with the first test on the left and continues until it encounters a NIL result or the end of the grouping expression.

The fact that an AND combination stops if a NIL result is encountered is of particular importance in Visual LISP programming. In the example expression, the conversion of A to uppercase fails and causes an error if the A symbol is bound to something other than a string. Thus, the test to see whether A has a binding and whether the type of data is a string takes place first. This feature allows you to do combinations of tests to validate data.

OR comes in handy when looking for error situations or for values outside a legal range. It returns true if any one of the tests are true, which means you can test opposite extremes. For example, the following expression checks to see whether the A symbol is a number, is negative, or exceeds 100:

```
(OR (NOT (NUMBERP A)) (MINUSP A) (> (FIX A) 100))
```

In other words, you are testing the A symbol to see whether it is a number between 0 and 100. The OR test returns true if any one of these tests is true. The first test in the expression checks to see whether A is a number and reverses the response using NOT. Thus, it will be true if the value in A is not a number. The second test checks to see whether the value in A is less than 0. The first test established that A was a number. Had it failed and A not been a number, NUMBERP would have returned NIL and the NOT would have made it T, causing the OR expression to halt and return a T result itself.

Differences between IF and COND

The testing expressions are applied most frequently in IF and COND expressions. These are the two basic conditional branching control subrs in Visual LISP. The principle difference between the two is that IF is used when you have one thing to test. That one test may be a combination test (using AND or OR), but the primary concern is that there is just one test with two possible outcomes (true or false) and with two possible program branches — the THEN expression and the ELSE expression. The ELSE expression is optional. Sometimes you want to use only the THEN expression, such as when checking to see whether a layer has already been created. If the layer has not been created, create the layer; otherwise, just carry on.

COND involves multiple tests, although it could be just a single test if that is what you want. In fact, when building applications, it is not uncommon to start with a COND that has one branch. The intent is to build the options at a later time, and COND allows for easy expansion of an existing logic set. Suppose you have a program that allows the operator to select zoom settings. You might start with some basics and then add more at a later time as users begin to request updates and improvements.

Whereas IF has the ELSE clause, COND often considers the last option as "otherwise" if the test will always evaluate as true. This is typically accomplished by using T itself as a predicate in the last option of a COND. If all else has failed, the T is true and that code is evaluated.

The syntax of the IF and COND expressions follows. Values inside brackets ([and]) are optional. In the IF expression, the ELSE clause is optional. So too are the predicate 2 and otherwise in COND.

```
(IF <predicate>
   <THEN expression>
   [<ELSE expression>]
)

;

(IF <predicate>
   (PROGN
      <THEN expressions>
   )
   [(PROGN
      <ELSE expressions>
   )]
)

;

(COND (<predicate 1>
        <expressions>
      )
      [(<predicate 2>
        <expressions>
      )]
      [('T
        <OTHERWISE expressions>
      )]
)
```

Note that you can have multiple expressions in the COND cases, indicated by the plural <expressions> under <predicate 1>. Any number of expressions (including zero expressions) can appear before the balancing parentheses. Each parameter in a COND expression is a list containing a predicate as the first member followed by expressions to evaluate if the predicate is true.

The IF expression, on the other hand, allows for only one expression in the THEN position and one in the ELSE position. These groupings have no balancing parenthesis — just the one for the IF expression itself. To get around this restriction, you use the PROGN subr, which defines an anonymous function without parameters. This subr allows you to group expressions. The PROGN subr is used most frequently in relation to the IF expression, as shown in the second IF syntax. When using PROGN in an IF expression, any number of expressions may fit in the THEN or ELSE branches.

Conditional branches are useful tools in programming because they allow your code to make decisions and act based on the data available. Some say this gives the computer intelligence. As a programmer, it all comes down to conditional branching and the capability to repeat, or loop. Loops are the next topic because they, like conditionals, relate to program sequence control.

Loops

Looping, or the capability of a computer to tirelessly repeat a task over and over, is its greatest aspect. Through this mechanism, you can solve advanced mathematical problems and manipulate data on request. There are three basic structural types of loops. The differences between each type have to do with when you leave the loop or make the decision to leave the loop.

Generally, you decide whether or not to leave a loop at some point in the code each time the loop iterates, or repeats. That decision process may be something as simple as reaching a counter value (as in "do this 100 times") or something more complex (as in "do this until blue pigs fly").

The three types of looping structures are based on the location of the exit test. The test can occur at the front of the loop, at the end of the loop, or in the middle of the loop. After you determine which structure you want to us, you apply the Visual LISP looping control tools, REPEAT and WHILE. Of these two, only the WHILE loop can be adapted to all three types of loop structures. The REPEAT loop is a direct count iteration that loops for a predetermined number of times. You look at the REPEAT loop first, and then you look at the WHILE loop and how you can adapt it to basic looping structures.

The REPEAT loop is the simplest looping structure in Visual LISP:

```
(REPEAT <number> <expressions>)
```

The number is an integer determined before the REPEAT loop starts. You cannot change the number after the loop is underway. REPEAT loops are useful when you know in advance how many times you want the code to execute. And example REPEAT loop is building a log-log chart to fill a particular area in a drawing. Another example is inserting some detail at set intervals along a line (the REPEAT counter would be based on the length of the line divided by the interval size). REPEAT is simple and intended for the simplest of loops. After a REPEAT loop starts, it ends only if it has an error or finishes the count.

The WHILE loop is more versatile. The syntax follows:

```
(WHILE <predicate> <expressions>)
```

The expressions are evaluated over and over, as long as the predicate returns a non-NIL value. As such, the termination of the loop is controlled by the contents of the loop. Whereas the REPEAT loop iterates for a set number of times, the WHILE loop iterates as long as conditions call for it to continue. So, unless you want the program to continue forever, you must provide something in the expressions that allows the WHILE loop's predicate test to fail.

A classic example is a WHILE loop based on user input. In the WHILE loop, the operator tells the program what it wants to do next. If one of those options is to exit the program and that option is selected, the program can take whatever actions are needed to exit the loop and the program.

It is easy to see how the WHILE structure can test before the loop. The predicate is located at the front of the loop and no expression evaluates whether it is not true. So how do you implement the other two logical loop structures, the ones that test at the end of the loop or at the middle of the loop? You use flag variables, as demonstrated next.

The basic WHILE loop syntax is simple. The expressions are evaluated as long as the predicate test is true. If the test fails on the first try, the loop expressions are never evaluated. Note that in this syntax, the test occurs at the beginning of the loop.

If you need to reverse that logic and evaluate the loop expressions at least one time, use one of the basic structures shown in the following. In this WHILE loop syntax, the test is at the end of the loop:

```
(SETQ DOIT 'T)
(WHILE DOIT
   <expressions>
   (IF (NOT <continuation test>) (SETQ DOIT NIL))
)


(WHILE
  (PROGN
    <expressions>
    <continuation test>
  )
)
```

In the first version, the DOIT symbol is set to true. The loop iterates as long as the DOIT symbol is not NIL. Following the DOIT test are the expressions, and then a test is conducted to see whether the exit condition has been met. Note that a NOT is used. The predicate is checking to see whether the loop should continue in most cases where this structure is used. NOT reverses the answer and then sets the DOIT symbol if the loop is not to continue. Another way to accomplish this would be to simply save the result of the predicate test to the DOIT symbol directly.

The second part of the code places the entire WHILE loop iteration inside a PROGN for the predicate of the loop. The last expression evaluated is the result of the PROGN expression, which allows this structure to evaluate the loop contents at least once before leaving the loop.

The next two WHILE loop syntaxes show how you can structure WHILE loops to test in the middle of the loop, although the need for this is rare in well-designed programs. You may want to have the program evaluate half the WHILE loop code at least once, and then check for the exit condition. When that is the case, use whichever format you find more readable:

```
(SETQ DOIT 'T)
(WHILE DOIT
    <expressions part 1>
    (IF (not <continuation test>)
        (SETQ DOIT NIL)
        (PROGN
            <expressions part 2>
        )
    )
)
```

Following is the second version of a WHILE loop that tests in the middle of the loop:

```
(WHILE (PROGN
        <expressions part 1>
        <continuation test>
    )
    <expressions part 2>
)
```

The predicates in a WHILE loop are the same as those in COND and IF expressions, and the same rules apply. If something evaluates to NIL, it is false. Any other value is true.

Beginning programmers often find it difficult to understand how to structure the testing for the iterations in a WHILE loop. Sometimes just writing the problem down, using the word while, can clarify how you should structure the program.

Example: Importing Text from a File

What follows is a complex example that contains many Visual LISP features that have not been covered yet. I advise you to proceed with caution and come back to the example later too.

Although the program is complex, the concept behind it is simple. We want a function that reads lines of text from a file looking for a line that begins with an asterisk. The program outputs any it finds to the drawing, until the end of the file is reached. To figure out how to program the application, I will rephrase the concept using the term `while`:

> While text is read from the file, if the text line starts with an asterisk, output it to the drawing.

Now that I have described the program, the next step is to refine the description and syntax. In trying to anticipate the needs of the operator using a command as just described in one sentence, I've greatly expanded the description. When writing programs, you need to expand each step as you refine your description into pseudocode:

> Open a text file selected by the operator for input. Ask for a text starting point in the drawing. While text can be read from the file, process it. Processing the text involves testing to see whether the string just read from the file starts with an asterisk. If it does, the text will be placed in the drawing. Before outputting the text to the drawing, remove the prefix asterisk. Next, output the text string at the text point location. Move the text point location down by one and half times the text height and repeat the `WHILE` loop. When finished, close the file.

After reviewing the previous description, I decided to improve the design. Sometimes an operator may want to bring text into a drawing at multiple locations. Logic for such an operation can be added by including the following in the program description:

> When two asterisks are encountered, have the operator select a new text point location in the drawing. Then remove the first asterisk to output the text at that location, and proceed as before.

Listing 7.2 contains a text file import utility based on this design. The `IMPORTTEXT` command function reads a text file selected by the user and imports only lines tagged with an asterisk as the first character.

The command function starts by requesting a file name from the operator using `GETFILED`, the standard file dialog box utility. If `GETFILED` returns a file name, `FH` will have a non-NIL value so the predicate for the `IF` expression will be considered true. `PROGN` groups all the expressions associated with the `THEN` expression of the `IF`. Because you want to do more than one thing as a result of getting a good file name, `PROGN` is required.

`PROGN` first opens the file in read mode and requests that the operator supply a text point. The point 0,0,0 is presented as a default value. Following the `GETPOINT` input is another `IF` expression in which you check whether the `TP` symbol has a null binding, indicating that a point was not input using `GETPOINT`. If that is the case, the `TP` symbol is set to a list containing 0 for the X, Y, and Z values.

With the file open and the starting text point known, the next task is to start reading the file. The first step is to check the line just read for an asterisk. If an asterisk exists, you use the text line for output. The `WHILE` loop contains a `SETQ` in the predicate. The `SETQ` contains a `READ-LINE` subr that returns a text line from a file or `NIL` if the end-of-file is encountered. It is perfect for a predicate test in this application. Because `READ-LINE` returns `NIL` at the end-of-file, the `WHILE` loop

Listing 7.2   Importing text.

```
(DEFUN C:IMPORTTEXT ( / FH LN TP TMP)
  (SETQ FH (GETFILED "Text file to import" "" "" 0))
  (IF FH
    (PROGN
      (SETQ FH (OPEN FH "r")
            TP (GETPOINT "\nText point (0,0,0): "))
      (IF (NULL TP)
        (SETQ TP (LIST 0.0 0.0 0.0)))
      (WHILE (SETQ LN (READ-LINE FH))
        (IF (= (SUBSTR LN 1 1) "*")
          (PROGN
            (IF (= (SUBSTR LN 1 2) "**")
              (SETQ TMP (GETPOINT TP "\nNew text point: ")
                    TP (IF TMP TMP TP)
                    LN (SUBSTR LN 2))
              (SETQ TP (POLAR TP (* 1.5 PI)
                              (* 1.5 (GETVAT "TEXTSIZE"))))
              )
            (SETQ LN (SUBSTR LN 2))
            (COMMAND "_TEXT" TP "" "" LN))))
      (SETQ FH (CLOSE FH))))
  (PRINC)
)
```

terminates when the file is completely read. The WHILE loop continues to repeat as long as READ-LINE can return a string and put it in LN.

With a string in LN, the first character is tested to see whether it equals an asterisk. If so, another PROGN is started because you need to do a few things in this case as well. First, you check to see whether there are two asterisks, which signifies the desire for a new text insertion point. If that case is met, the program asks for the new insertion point with the current value of TP as the default. If the operator enters a new point, it is stored in TMP; otherwise, TMP is NIL. The next part of SETQ tests TMP to see whether it is non-NIL. If so, TMP is placed in TP. Otherwise, TP is placed back in TP. The text line is then reduced by another character to remove one of the two asterisks from the front. The second asterisk is removed after the IF is finished. At that time, the text in LN is output to TP.

Note that this version assumes that you do not have a style with a constant text height set. If this function fails when testing, check the current text style and set the default text size to 0.

Summary

In this chapter, you explored conditionals and loops, the two most important branching tools for programming applications. Both make use of predicates, the expressions that return either a NIL or non-NIL answer. Predicate tests are provided in Visual LISP for strings, numbers, and data type comparisons. Some of the tests are specific and fast. Others are more versatile.

The EQUAL predicate test allows you to test numbers and lists of numbers for equality with a fuzz factor. The fuzz factor is a tolerance for the comparison so that floating-point shifts and trig function results can be tested properly. The normal equal test (=) is useful for testing strings as well as numbers, but the match must be exact: Strings must match in both case and character and the numbers must match exactly, to the insignificant digit.

Visual LISP provides two types of conditional branching subrs: IF and COND. IF allows for one test, and COND allows for a group of tests in a cascade-like structure. The IF expression sometimes requires PROGN to expand the number of expressions that can be evaluated in either the THEN or ELSE parts. COND does not require PROGN because the entire predicate and expressions are defined in a list (they have surrounding parentheses). This structure permits any number of expressions.

Loops in Visual LISP are direct iterations based either on a predetermined number using REPEAT or on the more versatile WHILE structure. WHILE can be manipulated so that the exit, or breakout, test takes place at the front, end, or middle of the loop.

CHAPTER 8

Working with Lists

LISP is an acronym for List Processing (not Lost In Stupid Parentheses, although sometimes one does wonder). A list is an ordered collection of data; the organization of the list is up to the programmer. Some lists are expected to have a standard structure, such as lists of points or lists of entity object data that AutoCAD should process.

Lists can be made up of any data type, including other lists. And lists can contain any mixture of data. For example you could have a list that contains a layer name with a count of entity objects, color code, last Z elevation used, and so forth. You could then create a list containing multiple copies of the previous list described for each layer in a drawing. It is up to your application to keep track of what you are working on.

In this chapter, you look at how to build and access data in lists. Then you look at some specific list types in AutoCAD programming, such as point lists and association lists. Lists representing point data are important in AutoCAD, and you will explore several subrs for manipulating points. You then dig deeper into lists by learning about the concepts of list storage that LISP employs. By the end of the chapter, you should know how to create a list of your own design and manipulate it using several techniques.

Creating a List

Lists are created either all at once or in pieces. Most applications build on existing lists that are started using the LIST or QUOTE method. When you use these subrs to create a starting list, it generally contains only the basics. You then use other subrs to add data to or retrieve data from the list.

A list can be extensive or simple. An example of an extensive list is parameter data (that can be accessed by name) for all the types of windows in a particular construction job. A simpler list might be one that is built as the application runs. For example, an application that tracks lumber used would start by building a list based on the first piece of lumber selected for use. As more lumber is used, the list grows.

The LIST and QUOTE subrs differ in one major respect. When you use QUOTE to build a list, the elements in the list are not evaluated. Thus, if a symbol is used, the symbol becomes part of the data list, not the data referenced by the symbol. LIST, however, allows the evaluator to evaluate symbols as they are used to construct the list.

You can think of the difference between LIST and QUOTE this way. If you know all the data in advance when coding the application, you can use QUOTE. If you need to use data generated during the application run, you must use LIST. For example, if you knew the values for the X, Y, and Z ordinate values for a point at programming time, you could use QUOTE or LIST to create the point list. If you have just calculated these ordinates, however, you would use LIST. Table 8.1 shows the basic actions for creating symbols using the LIST and QUOTE methods.

Table 8.1 Examples of creating lists.

Expression	Result
(SETQ A 1 B 10 C 100 D "ABC")	Set up some symbols
(SETQ L '(A B C D))	(A B C D), a list of symbols
(SETQ L (list A B C D))	(1 10 100 "ABC"), a list of data evaluated from the symbols
(SETQ L '(1 2 3))	(1 2 3); constants were used with no symbols
(SETQ L (LIST A B C 'D))	(1 10 100 D); note the quote in front of the D symbol, which causes the symbol name to be returned rather than evaluated

Adding to a List

To add data to lists, you use the APPEND and CONS subrs. In the simplest terms, APPEND adds data to the end of a list, and CONS adds data to the front of a list. APPEND also allows you to work with multiple lists as you merge them into a single list. CONS allows you to add only one item at a time to a list.

CONS is significantly faster than APPEND and is thus preferred for building lists on the fly. In LISP, you often build lists in reverse order and then reverse them as needed. Many example functions from this book use CONS to construct a list inside a loop and then reverse the list at the completion of the loop. As you will see later, this operation is not difficult for LISP due to its approach to list storage.

The APPEND subr takes two or more lists and runs them together to return a longer list. You cannot use atomic data types such as strings and numbers. You can use only lists as arguments to APPEND. One way to think of APPEND is that it snips the parentheses between the lists supplied as arguments, as shown in Figure 8.1.

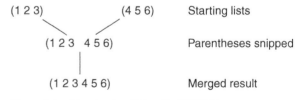

Figure 8.1   Merging two lists with APPEND.

A common mistake made by Visual LISP programmers is to use APPEND with two point lists, as shown in the figure. The result is a list with six elements, which may not be the desired result. If you want to merge two point lists to form a resulting list of two points, you must nest the lists.

Suppose that you stored the first list, (1 2 3), using the PT1 symbol, and stored the second list, (4 5 6), using the PT2 symbol. The following expression

```
(APPEND PT1 PT2)
```

results in

```
(1 2 3 4 5 6)
```

This expression

```
(APPEND (LIST PT1) (LIST PT2))
```

creates a nested list

```
((1 2 3) (4 5 6))
```

So too will the (LIST PT1 PT2) expression.

To add members after you build an initial list containing lists, you must wrap the new member in a LIST expression as it is added to the nested list. If you stored the nested list just described using the PTS symbol and the new point was named PT3, the following expression adds the new sublist to the end of the PTS list:

```
(APPEND PTS (LIST PT3))
```

Table 8.2 demonstrates the APPEND subr in action with a few different lists. Note the use of the LIST subr to wrap extra parentheses around some of the data to allow for proper nesting while merging.

Table 8.2 Examples of CONS and APPEND.

Expression	Result

(SETQ
  A (LIST 1 2 3)
  B (LIST 4 5 6)
  C (LIST 7 8 9))
	Sets up the A, B, and C data lists

(SETQ AA (APPEND A B C))	(1 2 3 4 5 6 7 8 9); created from the individual lists
(SETQ AA (APPEND (LIST A) (LIST B)))	((1 2 3) (4 5 6))
(SETQ AA (CONS C AA))	Adds C to AA from the previous step to form ((7 8 9)(1 2 3)(4 5 6))
(APPEND AA C)	((7 8 9)(1 2 3)(4 5 6) 7 8 9)
(SETQ AA (LIST A))	((1 2 3))
(SETQ AA (CONS B AA))	Adds B to AA to form ((4 5 6)(1 2 3))
(SETQ AA (CONS C AA))	Adds C to AA to form ((7 8 9)(4 5 6)(1 2 3))
(REVERSE AA)	((1 2 3)(4 5 6)(7 8 9)); note that the internal lists did not get reversed

The CONS subr is used to construct a list from the back forward. You might wonder why at first, but consider that a list built in this way is behaving like a stack. A stack is a logical data organization in which the first thing in, or pushed, is the last thing out, or popped. (Put another way, the last thing in is the first thing out.) Because CONS puts things at the front of a list, you can think of it as pushing data onto the front of the list. When you access the list, the first thing you see is the last thing that was added.

Lists can be made to behave like a stack by getting the CAR and CDR composite primitives involved. CAR retrieves the front of a list, and CDR removes the front of the list. CAR and CDR used in combination are the same as popping off the stack, and CONS is the same as pushing onto the stack. You look at these two subrs in more detail later in this chapter.

Instead of a stack structure in your application, you may want to just build a list quickly and with the minimal coding. In that case, use CONS, as shown in Table 8.2. When you have finished building the list, simply use the REVERSE subr to change the order of items in the list. For example, in Table 8.2, the REVERSE subr is shown with the AA nested list. When REVERSE was used, only the outermost list was reversed, not the inner lists. This situation comes up only when working with nested lists as shown. A single level list is reversed, as you would expect. For example, (REVERSE (LIST 1 2 3)) returns the (3 2 1) list.

Storing and Accessing Lists in LISP

In this section, you look at how lists are stored and accessed in the LISP environment. The heart of a list in LISP is the cons cell, so-named probably because the CONS subr is used to create cells. The cons cell is comprised of two components labeled A and D. (These labels have to do with the original computer LISP was developed on and refer to two parts of an internal register.) I just consider them to mean "A list element" and "Dee rest of dee list."

The cons cell is shown in Figure 8.2. In this figure, a symbol (or another cons cell) points to the cons cell. The cons cell contains two pointers. The first, called A, is a pointer to the list data element. Keep in mind that the data element being pointed at may be an atom, such as a string or a number, or another list, in which case it would point to another cons cell. The second element of a cons cell, D, points to a cons cell

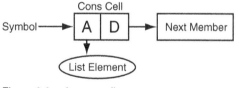

Figure 8.2   A cons cell.

for the next member of the list. A list ends when the D component does not point to another cons cell. You come back to that later. For now, just consider that all normal lists end with a D pointer to NIL.

Figure 8.3 contains a typical list structure diagram. The list of integers, (1 2 3), is shown graphically. A symbol points to the first cons cell. The A pointer of that cell points to the value

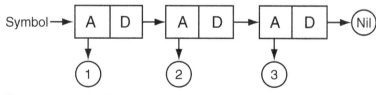

Figure 8.3   A typical list structure.

1, and the D pointer points to the second cons cell in the list. In the second cons cell, A points to the value 2 and D points to the third cons cell. You can keep following the D track until you reach the last cons cell, at which point D points to NIL, signifying the end of the list.

At first glance, using cons cells to store lists of data may seem odd. However, two things about this design make it powerful. First, pointers are just pointers. You can quickly traverse a list to a specific location. Second, pointers can point to anything you want. The location they point to contains the information about the type of data stored there (such as an integer, a real number, or a string). Cons cells can also point to other cons cells, allowing list structures to take on all sorts of forms, such as the ((1 2) 3 4) list in Figure 8.4.

Figure 8.4 contains a nested list named AA in which the first member is a list. The AA symbol points to the

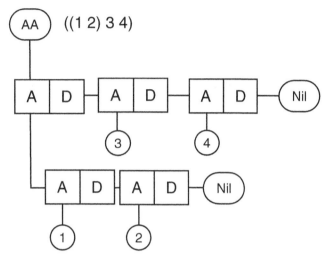

Figure 8.4   A nested list structure.

opening cons cell. From that cons cell, the A pointer points to another cons cell that represents the first member of the nested list. The D pointer continues down the list, as in the previous figures. At the end of each list, D points to NIL.

By layering cons cells, you can build any type of list structure. The form that a list can take has no technical limits, though it might have practical limits based on your own requirements.

Accessing data using specialized subrs

Storing data in a list is only a small part of list manipulation. The real power of LISP is revealed when accessing data from a list. Many subrs are dedicated to specialized tasks in list manipulation. For example, the LENGTH subr returns the integer count of the number of element in a list, and the LAST subr retrieves the last member of a list. (These subr names are easy to remember, but LISP has a long history and many of the subrs used to manipulate lists are not as easy to decipher, such as CAR and CDR.)

To demonstrate some important aspects of the list handling subrs, I'll use the AA list in Figure 8.4, which is ((1 2) 3 4). You might want to follow along in AutoCAD. Start by setting the AA symbol to the list:

```
(SETQ AA '((1 2) 3 4))
```

Next, using the LENGTH subr, you can see that the (LENGTH AA) expression returns 3. This subr counts only the uppermost level cons cells in a list. It does not count any of the lower-level ones. The first element was considered to be one entry in the list despite the fact that it is a list itself containing two elements. If you think of this subr as counting cons cells and not data elements, the concept makes sense.

The LAST subr returns the last element in the list, so (LAST AA) returns 4, the last data element. The last data element was found by locating the last cons cell, which has a D pointer that does not point to another cons cell. (The last D points to NIL.)

NTH retrieves any member in a list. You provide the offset into the list as one of the arguments to the subr. The system simply counts that many cons cells, and then returns the contents pointed to by the A pointer. NTH starts with an offset of 0 and retrieves data from the uppermost level of a list. (NTH 0 AA) returns (1 2) list, the first element in the AA list. (NTH 1 AA) returns 3, the contents of the second element in the AA list.

MEMBER searches a list for a matching value. Given an item to match, MEMBER returns a pointer to the cons cell for the matching element, which can also be thought of as the remainder of the list. (MEMBER 3 AA) returns the (3 4) sublist. When there is no match, as in (MEMBER 10 AA), NIL is returned.

Another basic subr used in list manipulations is SUBST, which substitutes new values for members in a list. Arguments to the subr include the list, the old value to be replaced, and the new value. All instances of the old value in a list are replaced with the new value. The (SUBST 6 3 AA) expression returns the ((1 2) 6 4) list. The item being substituted must be at the upper level of the list. (SUBST 6 2 AA) results in an unchanged list because the value 2 is not visible at the upper level of the list structure.

These subrs provide the tools needed to manipulate lists in a variety of manners. But they don't aid in accessing nested data lists and in getting even more specific information from a list. Suppose you want the second member of the list that is the first element of AA. The (NTH 1 (NTH 0 AA)) expression produces the result, but it is difficult to read. LISP has a more direct approach available for accessing pieces of lists.

Accessing data using composite primitives

For direct access to a list, you use the CAR and CDR composite primitives, which come from the original LISP language. They are called composite primitives because they can be combined. CAR stands for Contents of the A Register, which is the value associated with the first A in a list. For example, (CAR AA) returns (1 2) because that is the first element in the list. CDR stands for Contents of the D Register. For example, (CDR AA) returns (3 4) or the "Dee rest of the dee list" after removing the first element. Composite primitives are useful when manipulating lists but the only problem is that reading them in program code is odd.

You can combine primitives to provide access to nested lists. To get to the first value in the first list of AA requires the CAR of the CAR of AA, or (CAR (CAR AA)). You can combine the primitives to make the (CAAR AA) composite primitive. The action takes place starting from the R and working backwards to the C. Each A is the same as CAR, and each D the same as CDR. Thus, the CADR composite primitive performs the CDR primitive first and then the CAR. (CADR AA) is the same as writing (CAR (CDR AA)). The combined form hot only requires less typing but also runs faster.

To retrieve the second value from the nested list, use (CAR (CDR (CAR AA))), or (CADAR AA). Starting at the AA symbol in Figure 8.4, follow the pointer to the first cons cell in the list. From there, follow the A pointer to the first cons cell in the nested list. Now take the D pointer to the second cons cell and then follow the A pointer to the data element itself (which is 2).

To retrieve the second item from the list, the composite primitive is (CADR AA). Again, reading the composite primitive backwards starting just before the R, the symbol points to the initial cons cell. Follow the D route to the second cons cell. From there, follow the A route to the data itself (which is 3).

The only restriction with composite primitives is that you must know the list's format in advance. For most applications, this is not an issue because the data list is generally defined first to carry the required items.

Another aspect of composite primitives is that they have been defined for up to four As and Ds. If you need to go deeper into a list, use the NTH subr or just nest the composite primitives. Table 8.3 shows a variety of composite primitives operating on the ((1 2) (3 4) (5 6)) nested list.

Table 8.3 Examples of composite primitives.

Expression	Result
(SETQ AA '((1 2) (3 4) (5 6)))	Sets AA to ((1 2) (3 4) (5 6))
(CAR AA)	(1 2)
(CAAR AA)	1
(CADAR AA)	2
(CADR AA)	(3 4)
(CAADR AA)	3
(CADADR AA)	4
(CDR AA)	((3 4) (5 6))
(CDDR AA)	((5 6))
(CADDR AA)	(5 6)
(CAADDR AA)	5
(CAR (CDADDR AA))	6

Because points are stored as lists containing three numbers, you can use the CAR, CADR, and CADDR composite primitives to get the X, Y, and Z ordinate values, respectively, from a point or vector. For example, the function in Listing 8.1 uses these three composite primitives to extract a point's ordinates one at a time. Each value is then converted to a string using RTOS to create a point with commas between each number. You may want to adjust the RTOS and ANGTOS conversion parameters to suite your application needs. This function does not perform error testing, but the version on the CD does. Please refer to that version when using this utility in your own work.

Special List Types

LISP has a few special list structures that are used frequently in Visual LISP programming when manipulating AutoCAD entity objects using something called an entity list. You explore entity lists

Listing 8.1   Converting a point list to a string.

```
(DEFUN PT_STR (PT)
  (STRCAT
    (RTOS (CAR PT) 2 3)
    ", "
    (RTOS (CADR PT) 2 3)
    ", "
    (RTOS (CADDR PT) 2 3)
  )
)
```

in later chapters (starting in Chapter 12). In this section, you learn the basics of two special list structures, the dotted pair and the association list.

Dotted pair list structure

As mentioned, a list is terminated when the D component of a cons cell does not point to another cons cell. A normal list ends with the D component pointing to NIL. If the D component instead points to an atom, as in Figure 8.5, the list is called a dotted pair.

You can create a dotted pair in two ways. One, you can use the CONS subr with an atom instead of a list. For example, the (CONS 1 2) expression creates the dotted pair (1 . 2). Two, you can simply use a quote and type the dot (period) where it is needed. For example, the (SETQ B '(1 . 2)) expression creates the (1 . 2) dotted pair and saves it using the B symbol as a reference.

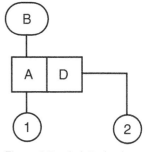

Figure 8.5   A dotted pair.

A dotted pair is rarely used in other LISP implementations and offers only one main advantage: It uses less memory for a list with only two elements because an entire cons cell is eliminated. This was important when memory for LISP applications was limited. The initial releases of AutoLISP, the predecessor to Visual LISP, ran in just 64 kilobytes of memory. From today's perspective, it is hard to fathom a program running in such a small amount of memory. But because of the long legacy of Visual LISP, the dotted pair is used quite a bit in AutoCAD-related programming.

Association list structure

You use an association list to associate data with a key. A *key* is something that you can search for or locate by name. In this section, you look at the simple structure behind an association list and see how it can be used to solve many different requirements for data retrieval.

The structure of an association list has only two basic rules. The first is that each member of the main list must be a list. Atoms cannot appear in the uppermost list. The sublists in an association list do not have to be the same size or structure, but they must be lists.

The second rule is that the first data element in each list must be a key. The key can be any type of data, but all keys should be of the same data type. Keeping the keys unique enables you to access all members of the association list without further manipulation. If you instead have two entries with the same key, you must follow a multiple-step process to get at the data for the second entry.

You use the ASSOC subr to access an association list. When ASSOC finds a matching key entry in the association list, it returns the sublist. If no match is found, it returns NIL. Table 8.4 contains an example association list and a series of accesses.

Table 8.4 Examples of association lists.

Expression	Result
(SETQ AA '(("A1" 1.0 2.0) ("B3" 2.5 3.5) ("C2" 7.1 8.3)))	The AA symbol references the (("A1" 1.0 2.0)("B3" 2.5 3.5)("C2" 7.1 8.3)) nested list
(ASSOC "A1" AA)	("A1" 1.0 2.0)
(SETQ B (ASSOC "B3" AA))	The B symbol references the ("B3" 2.5 3.5) list
(CADR B)	2.5; CADR returns the second element in a sublist
(CADR (ASSOC "A1" AA))	1.0
(CADR (ASSOC "C2" AA))	7.1
(ASSOC "D5" AA)	Nil; there is no entry for "D5"
(LENGTH AA)	3, the number of sublists in the AA list
(SETQ AA (CONS '("D5" 5.5 6.6) AA))	The AA symbol references the (("D5" 5.5 6.6)("A1" 1.0 2.0)("B3" 2.5 3.5)("C2" 7.1 8.3)) nested list
(LENGTH AA)	4
(CADDR (ASSOC "D5" AA))	6.6; CADDR returns the third element in a sublist

In the listings in this book, you can see many other examples of association lists and dotted pairs. They are useful not only for housing your own data but also when accessing entity-related data. In fact, most Visual LISP programmers use association lists and dotted pairs when they work with entity data lists. The reason is that entity data lists are association lists with integer keys. And most of the data lists in the entity association list are dotted pairs. You explore entity data lists in later chapters (starting with Chapter 12) as you study the tools for accessing AutoCAD drawing data.

Looping through Lists

Visual LISP provides two powerful subrs for looping through data lists, FOREACH and MAPCAR. The primary difference between the two is what they return as a result of a loop. FOREACH returns the result of the last iteration of the loop. MAPCAR returns a list containing the result for each iteration of the loop. You may wonder why such a difference exists and when you would select one rather than the other. The answer has to do with the purpose of the loop.

If the loop goes through a list and outputs data, the results of each iteration are not important, so you would use FOREACH. Most loops you will create based on lists are like this. You will want to do something with the data to achieve a result in the loop, and you will not be looking for a list result.

Other times, you want to manipulate each member of a list in the same way and keep the resulting list, so you would use MAPCAR. For example, if you have a list of points and want to offset them ten drawing units, a MAPCAR loop accomplishes this feat in the fewest possible lines of programming. (I like to think of MAPCAR as meaning Multiple Applications of CAR. In other words, it does the same thing as CAR but multiple times through an entire loop.)

The FOREACH expression uses a local symbol name to house the elements of the list during the loop iterations. Each time the loop starts, the next member in the loop is referenced by the local symbol. For example, using the AA list in Table 8.4, the following expression prints the association keys found at the beginning of each sublist ins AA:

```
(FOREACH A AA (PRINT (CAR A)))
```

The (CAR A) part of the expression extracts the first element of the list in the A symbol. This symbol houses each individual list member from AA.

MAPCAR is sometimes difficult to work due to its syntax. The basic syntax seems simple enough:

```
(MAPCAR '<expression> <list> [<list> ...])
```

For example, the (MAPCAR 'CAR AA) expression returns a list of the first elements in the AA list from the previous examples. For basic manipulations such as those in Table 8.5, you can use a single expression. The number of lists provided as arguments must meet the basic requirements of the expression. The plus (+) expression can work with two or more numbers, so you can supply two or more lists as seen in the examples. Adding and subtracting vectors or points stored as a list (like the ones in the examples) is greatly simplified with the MAPCAR expression. It just looks strange when reading the code until you get used to it.

But what if you need more than a single expression? How do you expand MAPCAR for that purpose? The solution is to define a function that solves the problem for you. Suppose you want to add the numbers in the AA and BB lists, and then divide the sum by 2. No single expression can accomplish this, so you have to define a function for that purpose. If you define a function named MIDDLE, for example, with two arguments that are both numbers, the (MAPCAR 'MIDDLE AA BB) expression returns the answer you are after.

To expand a MAPCAR expression, you can also define an anonymous function instead of a new function. An anonymous function has no name but sports the same features as a function (bound symbols, local symbols, and multiple expressions). You create an anonymous function with the LAMBDA subr. LAMBDA is similar to a combination of PROGN and DEFUN. It is like PROGN in that it

Table 8.5 Examples of MAPCAR.

Expression	Result
(SETQ AA '(2 3 4) BB '(5 4 3) CC '(7 8 9))	Sets up three symbols that each reference a list with three integer data elements
(MAPCAR '+ AA BB)	(7 7 7), the summing of the individual values in AA and BB
(MAPCAR '- CC BB)	(2 4 6), the difference of each element in the CC and BB lists
(MAPCAR '+ AA BB CC)	(14 15 16), the summed list
(MAPCAR 'MIN AA BB CC)	(2 3 7), the minimums from each list

provides an opportunity for more expressions when only one is allowed. It is like DEFUN in that it has a parameter list of symbols that go on the stack during the evaluation. Novice programmer might be intrigued with they come across LAMBDA in your code because it is not always clear what LAMBDA is doing.

When working with points, vectors, and matrices, MAPCAR can be a powerful tool because it allows you to perform operations to all members equally with minimal coding. Later in the chapter, you look at point list operations as well as more examples of point manipulations. Some of those examples use the LAMBDA expression. When you see LAMBDA in the code, just think of it as its own function definition. It is a function without a name, and is used in only one place in the code.

Sorting Lists

One of the first problems you will most likely encounter when working with data lists is the need to sort the data in a particular order, perhaps for a report or for part of a drawing table. For that type of task, you use the VL-SORT subr, which accepts a list and a comparison operator to be applied to the list. Like in the MAPCAR expression, the comparison operator can be a single subr or a function. But unlike the MAPCAR expression, the comparison expression must accept two arguments and act like a predicate in that it returns a true (non-NIL) or false (NIL) answer. This expression is applied to all the members of the list to produce a sorted list as a result. Duplicate values are removed from the resulting list.

Following is a simple example:

```
(VL-SORT '(4 1 2 0 5) '<)
```

This expression returns the (0 1 2 4 5) list. The less-than operator (<) compares each element in the list to produce a sequence in ascending order. If you used the greater-than operator (>), the result would be a list of numbers in descending order.

When lists are more complicated, the comparison operator is more complex as well. This is another case where you can define a function or use the LAMBDA expression to expand the routine. The logic of your sorting system is up to you because you define the method of testing.

Listing 8.2 shows a set of functions that use VL-SORT to create a set of more descriptive sort functions to assist in your programming efforts. These functions sort a list of points by X or Y ordinate values. A third function is provided as an example of sorting based on the distance from a known point.

Listing 8.2   Sorting lists.

```
(DEFUN SORT_BY_X (PTS)
  (VL-SORT
    PTS
    '(LAMBDA (P1 P2)
       (< (CAR P1) (CADR P2)))))


(DEFUN SORT_BY_Y (PTS)
  (VL-SORT
    PTS
    '(LAMBDA (P1 P2)
       (< (CADR P1) (CADR P2)))))


(defun Sort_By_Distance (PTS PT)
  (VL-Sort
    PTS
    '(lambda(P1 P2)
       (< (distance P1 PT)
          (distance P2 PT)))))
```

Point Lists

The previous examples demonstrated the sorting of point lists. Point lists are just lists of numbers with two or three values, such as (1 2 3) or (5.3 1.2 0.0). The three values represent the X, Y, and Z ordinate values for the point. You can also think of the values as representing a vector to be calculated. As seen earlier in this chapter, the (MAPCAR '- P1 P2) expression returns the vector difference between two points lists.

Table 8.6 lists the subrs that you will use most often with point lists. Some of these subrs are dedicated to the manipulation of point lists; others are borrowed from the general-purpose LISP library of tools. Points are something you will use frequently when programming Visual LISP applications in AutoCAD. As such, you will find that you use the subrs in this table frequently.

Table 8.6 Point list manipulation subrsp.

Subr	Description
ANGLE	Computes the angle off the X-axis between two points
CAR	Retrieves the X ordinate value
CADR	Retrieves the Y ordinate value
CADDR	Retrieves the Z ordinate value
DISTANCE	Computes the distance between two points
INTERS	Computes the intersection of two vectors defined by four points
OSNAP	Returns a point matching the object snap option with a given point
POLAR	Given a base point, distance, and angle, computes a new point
TRANS	Converts a point from one coordinate system to another

The ANGLE and POLAR subrs involve angles. Remember that all applications must use radians internally as the unit of measure for angles. Thus, the ANGLE subr returns an angle in radians for two points relative to the X-axis. And POLAR expects the angle value supplied to be in radians.

When manipulating points, the ANGLE, DISTANCE, POLAR, and composite primitives are used the most often. A typical application problem is to accept input from the user in the form of points and then calculate new point locations based on those input values.

The function in Listing 8.3 is useful when working with user-supplied or variable input. This function tests a value to see whether it is a point list. The function can serve as a predicate that checks to see whether a data list represents a valid point list. The function combines several predicates for testing data types as well as some list tools.

Listing 8.3   Testing whether data is a point list.

```
(DEFUN IS_POINT? (PT)
  (AND
    (LISTP PT)
    (NOT (NULL PT))
    (APPLY 'AND
      (MAPCAR 'NUMBERP PT))
    (OR (= (LENGTH PT) 2)
        (= (LENGTH PT) 3)
    )
  )
)
```

To be considered a point, the data must meet all the criteria, so you use an AND expression because it returns true if all predicates inside it are true. To be a point list, the item must be a list and not an empty list. The LISTP and NULL predicates perform these tests. The next criterion is that all data items in the list must be numbers. To solve this problem, the list manipulators are called into action. You apply the AND subr to the lists that results from testing each element in the list with the NUMBERP predicate. If any element is not a number, the NUMBERP returns NIL, which causes the AND to return NIL. The last criterion for being a point list is that there be only two or three numbers. A two-number list is a two-dimensional point list, and a three-number list is three-dimensional.

If all these conditions are met, the IS_POINT? function returns a true result. Otherwise, NIL is sent back as the response.

The MAPCAR expression is useful when manipulating lists, particularly point lists. If you need to do something involving the ordinates of a group of points, MAPCAR can probably help.

Table 8.7 demonstrates the MAPCAR subr in action with point lists. For these examples, assume that any symbol starting with P is a (P1, P2) point list, V is a vector list (the same a point list but with a different meaning to the application), and PTS is a list of points.

Table 8.7 Examples of point list manipulations.

Expression	Description
(MAPCAR '- P2 P1)	Vectors from P1 to P2
(MAPCAR '+ P1 V1)	Adds the V1 vector to the P1 point
(/ (APPLY '+ (MAPCAR 'CAR PTS)) (LENGTH PTS))	Calculates the average X value of points in the PTS list
(/ (APPLY '+ (MAPCAR 'CADR PTS)) (LENGTH PTS))	Calculates the average Y value of points in the PTS list
(SQRT (APPLY '+ (MAPCAR '(LAMBDA (V) (* V V)) V1)))	Calculates the square root of the sum of the squares

Point computations are important in AutoCAD applications development. One subr that you may find helpful is the OSNAP subr. OSNAP applies an object snap to a point to refine the point value based on graphics in the drawing. You can use OSNAP to home in on an end point, a center point, or another snap point of an object given a point on the object. OSNAP provides assistance for command processing in that it provides the point AutoCAD would select under operator control. Commands such as BREAK and others require exact points related to the graphics on the screen, and that is where OSNAP is usually applied.

Example: Getting Information from a Point List

Listing 8.4 contains a sample function for obtaining information from point lists. It demonstrates the primary point list manipulators as it takes two points supplied by the operator and creates a report on the screen about the two points. The data shown contains the points selected after conversion by PT_STR, which was introduced earlier in this chapter, along with the vector displacement between the two points. The distance and angle between the points is then displayed.

Listing 8.4   Getting information about points.

```
(DEFUN C:PINFO ( / P1 P2)
  (SETQ P1 (GETPOINT P1 "\NLOCATE FIRST POINT: "))
  (IF P1 (PROGN
      (SETQ P2 (GETPOINT P1 "  SECOND POINT: "))
    (IF P2 (PROGN
        (TEXTSCR) ;SWITCH TO TEXT SCREEN VIEW
        (PROMPT
          (STRCAT
            "\nCOORDINATES:\n\tP1 = " (PT_STR P1)
            "\tP2 = " (PT_STR P2)
            "\nVECTOR:\t" (PT_STR (MAPCAR '- P2 P1))
            "\nDISTANCE: " (RTOS (DISTANCE P1 P2) 2 3)
            "\tANGLE: " (ANGTOS (ANGLE P1 P2))
          ))))))
  (PRINC)
)
```

Coordinate Transformations

Sometimes you need to transform a point list from one coordinate system to another. The primary coordinate systems in AutoCAD are the World Coordinate System (WCS), the User Coordinate System (UCS), and the Entity Coordinate System (ESC).

You might encounter other coordinate systems transformations, such as converting points from a block definition to a location in the drawing. Blocks are defined as relative to a base point and are transformed when inserted into the drawing. Block insert transformations include an offset point, a scale factor set, and a rotation angle.

To perform coordinate transformations, you have two choices. The simplest is to use the TRANS subr in Visual LISP. TRANS accepts a point list, a source coordinate system definition, and a target coordinate system definition. It returns a new point list. The coordinate system definitions could be a code number (for some standard systems), an entity name, or a three-dimensional extrusion vector. Following are several code numbers:

0	for WCS
1	for UCS
2	for the model space display coordinate system
3	for the current paper space display coordinate system

The display coordinate systems are a combination of what you see on the screen and the vantage point you are using to look at the model.

When converting entity related points, you should understand that although an entity is created on a given UCS, it is not stored in that manner in AutoCAD. Instead, each entity uses what is called the Entity Coordinate System (ECS). When an entity is created with a UCS that is not the WCS, a coordinate system is created for that instance of the entity called the ECS. This comes into play when you access an entity from the AutoCAD drawing database. If the entity has an extrusion vector that is not the WCS (0,0,1), you must pass the data points through TRANS. Use the entity name and the WCS code 0 to transform the data points to the World Coordinate System.

Sometimes TRANS cannot convert the data for you, such as when you are determining points relative to an inserted block. A block is defined with all data points relative to the base point of the block. Thus, if you have a block containing a line from 1,1 to 2,1 and that block is inserted at position 10,20, the line coordinates are 11,21 to 12,21. To get the new coordinates, you must add the insertion point values to the line's end point values. That is simple. But what if the block was rotated and scaled at insertion? Now you must perform three different transformations: apply the scaling factors, apply the rotation, and do the translation (shift to a new insert point).

Listing 8.5 contains a function that performs the block coordinate system to World Coordinate System transformations just described. You can use this utility to locate points relative to an insertion given the data from the block definition. You supply two parameters to the function: the point to be transformed and a reference to the insertion entity object. The reference to the insertion entity can be an entity name or an entity data list. We have not covered the details regarding entity names and data lists yet, so let's take a quick look at that part of the program before getting into the list manipulations.

The BLK_2_WCS function uses the value supplied in BLK as the reference to the block insertion. BLK is either an entity data list or an entity name, and the first step in the program is to test the type of data supplied to BLK. If BLK is a list, the routine assumes that it is an entity data list and works with it as provided. If the type of data in BLK is an entity name (ENAME), the ENTGET subr retrieves the entity data list. The result of the first SETQ assignment is that BLK now points to an entity list.

Using the entity data list in BLK, the insertion angle (A) and insertion point (P) are extracted. Entity lists are association lists, and the key is the integer code number for the item as defined in the AutoCAD DXF file specification. With experience and by using the online help files, you can determine that the code numbers 50 and 10 return the insert angle and point, respectively, for a block insert instance. To get the value from the entity list, ASSOC is used with the code number (sometimes called a group code). The result returned from ASSOC is applied to the CDR subr to

Listing 8.5   Converting block coordinates to world coordinates.

```
(DEFUN BLK_2_WCS (PT BLK / A P)
  (SETQ BLK (COND
            ((LISTP BLK) BLK)
            ((= (TYPE BLK) 'ENAME) (ENTGET BLK))
            )
        A (CDR (ASSOC 50 BLK))
        P (CDR (ASSOC 10 BLK))
        PT (LIST
             (* (CAR PT) (CDR (ASSOC 41 BLK)))
             (* (CADR PT) (CDR (ASSOC 42 BLK)))
             (* (CADDR PT) (CDR (ASSOC 43 BLK)))
             1.0
             )
        TM
          (LIST
            (LIST (COS A) (- 0.0 (SIN A)) 0.0 (CAR P))
            (LIST (SIN A) (COS A) 0.0 (CADR P))
            (LIST 0.0 0.0 0.0 (CADDR P))
            )
        PT (MAPCAR
             '(LAMBDA (TC)
                (APPLY '+
                  (MAPCAR '* TC PT))) TM)
    )
  (LIST (CAR PT) (CADR PT) (CADDR PT))
)
```

retrieve the value. CDR is used because the entity data in the entity data list is stored as dotted pairs, and CDR returns the value pointed at by the D component of the cons cell.

The PT point is now ready to be scaled based on the scale factors in the block insert. Group codes 41 through 43 provide the keys to the association list for the X, Y, and Z scale factors. These values are extracted using the CDR and ASSOC subrs in concert. The values are then applied directly to the data point values in PT. The X component of PT (CAR) is multiplied by the X scaling factor (code 41), the Y component (CADR) by the Y scaling factor (code 42), and the Z component

(CADDR) by the Z scaling factor (code 43). The result of multiplying all these values is stored back in PT as a list.

Things get trickier in the next part. You are going to construct a transformation matrix that translates the coordinates and rotates all at once. The transformation matrix is a 4 x 4 matrix that combines the translation equations (add the insertion point to the data point) with the rotation equations (apply block rotation to the data point). (I don't go into the details of building the composite transformation matrix.)

You multiply the data point (plus the extra 1.0 added to the end) to achieve the transformation of coordinates. The real key is how the matrix is defined as a list. The TM matrix is defined as a nested list of four elements, and each element contains four numbers. The sixteen numbers are arranged in the list to represent the rows of the conversion matrix. The point, defined as a 4 x 1 matrix, is multiplied to the 4 x 4 matrix. The result is a 4 x 1 matrix in which the first three values are the transformed point.

To perform the matrix multiplication, MAPCAR multiplies each row by the data point. TC is a local symbol containing each row from the matrix as extracted by the outermost MAPCAR. Given the row, APPLY sums the result of multiplying each value in the inner MAPCAR. That result is sent back from the outer MAPCAR as a list of four numbers. The first three are extracted to build the returning list of the function.

If you can see how MAPCAR and APPLY work in concert with nested lists to solve matrix problems, you have mastered a complex part of LISP programming. If you don't see this, don't worry because list manipulation becomes more comfortable with practice.

Summary

This chapter covered a lot of ground. Lists are the primary tools for manipulating data in LISP. The LISP system allows you to define lists of any structure using a system of cons cells that connect everything in the computer's memory. By understanding the cons cell system, you can begin to see how most of LISP's list manipulators work. From that understanding, you can see what steps are needed to solve a problem involving a list of data.

The methods for creating a list are simple. You can use the LIST subr to define a new list or use a QUOTE expression with a set of constants. You can increase a list by using CONS to build a new cons cell at the front of the list or by using APPEND to merge lists. Quite a few list manipulation subrs are available to then access and modify the contents of data lists. Refer to the online help to learn more about the list manipulation subrs.

You also learned about several types of lists, including dotted pairs, association lists, and point lists. The first two types of lists are used extensively in the manipulation of entity data lists. Dotted pairs came to Visual LISP from AutoLISP as a tool to provide data in the minimum amount of memory. The association list simply presents a nice way to organize data that will vary, as you would expect given the variety of entity objects you might encountered when developing applications for AutoCAD users.

To best exploit the powers of Visual LISP, you should feel comfortable with point lists and basic list structures. You do not need to be an expert with MAPCAR and other subrs, but you should know that they exist. As you improve your skills in Visual LISP programming, you will find that the list is a convenient and powerful concept that you can exploit in a variety of creative ways.

CHAPTER 9

Basic User Output

What good is a computer if it cannot display the results of computations in a meaningful manner? Without the capability to display output, both as text and as graphics, Visual LISP would be useless to us. This chapter describes the essentials of Visual LISP output. I describe the components of the interface from a programmer's point of view and also introduce the primary subrs for generating output.

Building AutoCAD Commands

The main reason for programming in Visual LISP is to expand the capabilities of AutoCAD. And that is best accomplished by creating your own commands for AutoCAD. If you are the sole user of your programming effort, you are free to experiment with alternative input formats and command structures. But if you are writing code for others to use, the situation is less flexible. When writing code for other AutoCAD users, you need to make your interfaces appear like AutoCAD as much as possible. This is important for both input (the topic of the next chapter) and output.

Another thing to consider is the users relationship with the software. For example, if your program performs a large number of computations and requires extensive time to accomplish that task, you should output a message at regular intervals to let the operator know that the program is still running. Many Windows applications use a progress bar to indicate the status of the application. Unfortunately, Visual LISP cannot comply in that regard with ease (in some cases, you need more code to display a progress bar than to perform the computations). You must use other alternatives, most of which involve using the command line or text area of output. You could highlight entities as they are processed to indicate the status of an operation, but if the entities are not in the display window, the operator sees nothing and may wonder whether the application has stopped running.

The next time you write a program that takes a while to complete its computations, write it so that nothing is reported to the screen. How many seconds of runtime before you begin to wonder whether it is working okay? Keep in mind that you wrote the program and know what it is doing at this step. Another operator will mostly likely be without a clue as to how it works and what the routine is doing at any given time. In experiments conducted in the early 1980s regarding the ergonomics of CAD/CAM interfaces, I found that in most interactive computer graphics environments, the operator needed to see a response in less than a second to feel that the computer was working. And in repetitive tasks involving longer computation times, a message or update needed to be placed on the display every second or two to satisfy the operator that the computer was still working on the problem.

You should keep a few other considerations in mind when writing commands for operators. Your new commands should not get in the way of normal operations. It is not a good idea to redefine existing AutoCAD commands on a whim. AutoCAD operators with lots of experience may be counting on obscure features of some of these commands; if you've rewritten them, you should provide the same flexibility.

Extra prompts and messages disrupt operators and sometimes make them concentrate on the wrong things. This is especially true when a problem comes up in the field and you are troubleshooting over the phone. For some reason, AutoCAD operators never seem to see the area of the screen you are most interested in seeing. The lesson here is that if something is critical to the operation, it should stand out: Use a dialog box or highlight the output with asterisks at the beginning of the line.

Here's a tip: Supply an extra utility that enables some symbols referenced in the software. When these symbols are true, or on, it indicates that the operator wants more information displayed. The information then provides indications as to how well the software is doing or where it may be failing. This approach allows you to supply a streamlined input/output system for normal operations and the capability to switch the software to debug mode if needed.

The Command Line and the Graphics Screen

In your Visual LISP programs, most output will be to the command line and the graphics screen. The command line is part of the text screen, as it is known by AutoCAD operators. Prompts and messages are typically placed on the command line. Graphics screen output is normally the result of adding new entity objects or modifying existing ones, although you could post messages in a drawing if that was the best way to convey a message to the operator.

The GRAPHSCR and TEXTSCR subrs switch the display of the graphics screen and the text screen or command line. In Windows, that means the focus is set to the window desired, which is brought to the foreground if it is not already there. The effect is the same as pressing the F2 key, but now the toggling is accomplished under programmer control.

Sometimes, you want to display data to the user in a text format, but you won't have enough room if the command-line area of the graphics window has been reduced to one line. An example is the LIST command in AutoCAD: When you select an object, the details of that object are displayed on the screen and those details often require multiple lines of text, especially if multiple entity objects have been selected. A program that computes a lot of numbers may need display the results of each computation and key variables as it progresses through the computations. This is a classic example of when you might direct the work-in-progress report to the text screen for display.

Command-Line Output

In this section, you turn your attention to the subrs for producing output. Keep in mind that the output mechanism is a like a line printer. When you print something to the text screen and then send a new line, the line previously written is scrolled up one position and cannot be changed without some clever programming. If you need to produce graphics output, that is what AutoCAD is best at doing. But for basic text reports, the following subrs work great. These subrs output to the AutoCAD command line as well as to a text file opened in w (write) or a (append) mode.

PRIN1 is the basic print operation. Given a symbol, it prints the value of the symbol. Given a quoted symbol, it prints the symbol name. If the value to be printed is a string, any control characters are printed as ordinary characters in slash format. Control characters are special symbols in a string that you can use to format the output. When you use PRIN1, control characters are printed as if they were regular characters of no significance.

PRINT is like PRIN1, except a new line is printed first, then the evaluated symbol output is sent to the command line or the file, and then a space is printed following the output. Control characters are printed in slash format. Both PRIN1 and PRINT are useful when debugging a complex application because data can be displayed on the text screen or written to a log file without worrying about format control.

PRINC is another version of PRIN1 in which control characters in strings are expanded. This means newline and tab characters are executed as part of the string. Otherwise, the output of PRINC is identical to that of the other PRIN subrs.

Listing 9.1 shows results from the command-line using the PRIN subrs. Each of the subrs returns a value that is the string printed, which is why it appears to print the string twice. The \t inserts a tab.

Listing 9.1   Using PRIN at the command line.

```
COMMAND: (SETQ S "\tMoon")
"\tMoon"
COMMAND: (PRIN1 s)
"\tMoon""\tMoon"
COMMAND: (PRINC s)
Moon"\tMoon"
COMMAND: (PRINT s)

"\tMoon" "\tMoon"
```

The PRINC subr is the only one suitable for outputting text that contains formatting information in the form of control characters. Note that even the double quotes do not appear in the example dialog in Listing 9.1.

Another interesting use of the PRINC and PRIN1 subrs is to force a function to not output its results to the command line when returning. You might have noticed PRINC or PRIN1 at the end of most command functions (that is, functions whose name begins with C:). Command functions — unlike the rest of the functions you write and use in Visual LISP — are not expected to return values. Instead, command functions are expected to do something and then return to the Command prompt without any further output. It is annoying to see NIL or some other message appear at the end of a command, especially if you don't know what it means. In some cases, the very presence of such text on the command line prompts a call to technical support.

When you use PRINC or PRIN1 at the end of a function that is returning to the command line in AutoCAD, the function is said to have a silent exit. If PRINC or PRIN1 is not the last expression in the function, the result of the last expression evaluated is returned to the command line. You might want this when debugging, but users do not appreciate seeing this type of message.

String output

Two additional subrs provided for the output of string data with format expansion are PROMPT and WRITE-LINE. You can use both to output string data to the command line; any control characters in the string are expanded. That means \t (tab) is replaced with empty spaces to the next tab mark, and \n (new line) advances to a new line, scrolling the text screen up one.

The difference between PROMPT and WRITE-LINE is that PROMPT always returns NIL and WRITE-LINE returns a copy of the string written. In addition, you can direct WRITE-LINE output to a file opened in write or append mode.

The ALERT subr also outputs strings, but not to the command line. Instead, ALERT outputs text to a pop-up dialog box that appears in the middle of the AutoCAD screen; nothing more can happen until the operator clicks the OK button. ALERT accepts only a string for output. If you want to output data values, you must convert them to strings and then concatenate them to a single output string.

The string for an ALERT box can contain control characters, so you can format the output data to the same degree as you can for command-line output. For example, you can use tabs and new lines to format the message into something more readable.

Note that if you need more extensive interaction with the operator using a dialog box, you have to create the dialog box yourself using the information presented in a later chapter (Chapter 11). Dialog boxes are easy to create after you understand how they work and what the tools can do for you.

The ALERT dialog is a quick way to display a message. Messages to the command line may be missed, but a dialog box that requires the operator to click OK to continue cannot be skipped. However, use the ALERT subr only for the most important messages. Routine messages used for debugging or to simply to let the operator know the status of the program should be directed to the command line or a text file.

Non-string output

When you want to display numeric information to the text screen or as part of an alert box, you should usually convert the numeric values to a string. You then concatenate the strings to build the output message. The ANGTOS, ITOA, and RTOS subrs provide ample control for converting numbers.

But what about other data types such as entity names and mixed lists? The PRINC, PRINT, and PRIN1 subrs print non-string data to the command line or to a data file. However, if you need to display non-string data as a string in an alert, use the VL-PRINC-TO-STRING subr. This subr and the VL-PRIN1-TO-STRING companion subr use the PRINC or PRIN1 conversion-to-string rules. Instead of outputting directly to the command line or to a file, they return the string as a value for use in a function.

AutoCAD Command Output

By combining logic and AutoCAD commands, you can create powerful tools for operators as well as a productive environment for many applications. The complete suite of AutoCAD commands is available to Visual LISP programs through a pipeline. (A pipeline is a communications channel through which data or commands can flow. A program can establish a pipeline to another program so that the first program can control the second.) The pipeline is one way, so if something goes wrong at the command side, the calling program will not know immediately. (In fact, the calling program must take extra steps to see whether there was a problem with the command stream sent though the pipeline.)

To send output to the AutoCAD drawing system through the pipeline, you use the COMMAND subr. COMMAND allows the program to send one part of a command at a time to the AutoCAD command line. It is as if you were typing the commands, except now the process is under computer control. COMMAND accepts any number of arguments. If supplied with no arguments, it is the same as sending a Cancel to the command prompt. Using an empty string is the same as pressing the Enter key. Each argument to COMMAND is sent one at a time to the AutoCAD command processor. Any symbols used in the COMMAND argument set are evaluated before they are sent to AutoCAD for processing.

For example, the following expression generates a line from the point in P1 to the point in P2. The LINE command expects a continuous stream of points and is terminated when you press the Enter key. Consequently, this expression must issue an Enter key to terminate the LINE command:

```
(COMMAND "_LINE" P1 P2 "")
```

Perhaps the biggest problem with COMMAND is that it is a one-way communication. Errors are not immediately reported back to the calling program. This means the program can get out of synch with the AutoCAD command processor, resulting in data sent in response to the wrong prompts. In most cases, the result is a series of invalid inputs.

Command errors

A few mechanisms for determining whether operations were successful are available, but the best tool is prevention. By checking ahead, you can save a lot a processing time. For example, if you are going to put something on a particular layer, you should first check to see whether the layer exists. Another check might be to see whether another command is running that could interfere with the operation of this command. Try to anticipate problems. In my experience, however, no matter how hard you try to imagine what an operators might do, they always seems to find something you didn't think about.

In most cases, you can catch an error before it occurs by checking the AutoCAD system variable settings or the tables. The tables are where a drawing's layer names, style details, and more reside. We learn more about system variables shortly and the tables in a later section about accessing the drawing database.

Another tool for catching COMMAND stream errors is the VL-CMDF subr. VL-CMDF is similar to COMMAND except its arguments are pre-evaluated by the AutoCAD command processor to see whether they are okay. If they are, AutoCAD executes the command stream and VL-CMDF returns a true value. If any of the arguments are invalid as far as the command processor is concerned, VL-CMDF returns NIL. VL-CMDF is forgiving when it comes to arguments and makes an effort to use what you supply.

An important difference between VL-CMDF and COMMAND occurs when user input takes place, that is, if you use a GETxxx type subr in the command stream. With VL-CMDF, the input operation is performed before the command starts. COMMAND performs the input operation while the command is running. Why is this important? Consider the task of dragging a block for insertion. VL-CMDF asks for an input point before the graphics figure is dragged along with the cursor on the screen. COMMAND presents a copy of the block by the cursor (provided the block has a near-zero base point) that is dragged to the insertion point. If you want your command stream to look and feel like AutoCAD, use COMMAND.

Finish what you started

When you use the COMMAND stream subr, be sure to finish what you started! Although you do not need to complete the command sequence in a single expression, you should complete the command in your function. A command left hanging after a Visual LISP routine has finished is usually a sign that something went wrong.

For the most part, terminate any command sequences underway within your program. This requires a thorough understanding of the actual command sequences, some of which change based on settings in the system. An example is the TEXT command stream. If the current style has a text height of 0.0, the TEXT command requests the text height during the command. If the current style has a non-zero text height, that prompt is skipped. Your routine could easily stumble on this nuance of the TEXT command.

To learn the command sequences, run AutoCAD and try them out. Many commands have dialog boxes for the input of variable parameters, and these will not work well for Visual LISP programming. If a given command seems to have a dialog box interface only when the command is typed at the command line, type the command with a hyphen as the starting character. For example, when you type the LAYER command at the command prompt, a dialog box appears, regardless of the system variable settings. If you type -LAYER instead, there is no dialog box and the prompts for the command options appear on the command line.

When you use the Visual LISP COMMAND pipeline to send commands to the AutoCAD system, the assumption is that you want the non-dialog box command interface. (COMMAND "LAYER") starts the layer command at the command line, not in a dialog box. By placing a hyphen in front of the command name, you force the non-dialog box interface — and can then learn the command sequences that Visual LISP works with to achieve the desired results.

If you want the dialog box to appear for a command started by Visual LISP's COMMAND pipeline, the INITDIA subr should be evaluated before the COMMAND subr. When INITDIA is evaluated, the next commands that have dialog box interfaces use the dialog boxes and not the command-line sequence. You can use INITDIA to force the display of the PLOT or LAYER dialog box.

For example, if you want the LAYER dialog box to pop up in your application, use the following expression:

```
(INITDIA) (COMMAND "_LAYER")
```

The LAYER dialog box appears and allows you to manipulate the layer table as desired. When you click the OK or CANCEL button in the dialog box, control returns to your program with the changes (if any) made to the layer table.

Note the underline character at the front of the string in the COMMAND expression. Three possible characters can appear before a command name: an underline, a period, or a hyphen.

The hyphen signifies that the command should be used without dialog boxes; this is needed sometimes with commands started by Visual LISP, such as the VBA RUN and LOAD commands. To turn off the dialog box, add a hyphen (or use the VL-VBALOAD and VL-VBARUN subrs).

The period is used when the command has been undefined. Commands can be undefined and replaced with new commands of your own design. If you want to make sure you are running the original AutoCAD-supplied version of the command, put a period in front of the command name. Calling a command that has been redefined in Visual LISP can sometimes result in an error at run time.

An underline makes sure you are using a single language for the commands. AutoCAD is supplied in multiple languages. If your Visual LISP programs might be running in an environment using some language other than English, you can put an underline at the front of the command name to force AutoCAD to recognize the English command name. Unlike the period and the hyphen, the underline character may be used also inside commands to force the responses to the commands to be accepted in only English. (Although this restriction requires additional effort for developers not working in the English language because they must know the English command equivalencies, one language had to be selected. And because AutoCAD was written in English and most developers spoke English when the decision was made to incorporate this feature into the LISP environment, that is the language of choice.)

System Variables for Output

Several system variables in AutoCAD can change the way things are output and displayed to the operator. For example, you may want to turn off the AutoCAD command echo so that the operator does not see commands issued from Visual LISP programs. This makes the entire sequence run faster and simplifies the text displayed to the operator in the command area. (More than one operator has canceled a Visual LISP macro because a stream of unreadable messages appeared at the command prompt.)

You can access an AutoCAD system variable using the GETVAR subr with the name of the system variable. Different system variable data types could be returned, but your program will be expecting them. If you request the name of the current layer, expect a string. If you request the current text size, expect a real number.

Visual LISP can establish the settings of system variables using SETVAR. Supply the variable name and the new value to the SETVAR subr to make the change. If the system variable is read-only, however, you cannot change the setting with SETVAR. In many cases, they cannot be updated because they relate to the system configuration or hardware. In other cases, you may have to run a series of AutoCAD commands to update them.

To see which variables are read-only, type the AutoCAD SETVAR command and view the far right side for the read only string. Any system variables marked as such cannot be updated through the SETVAR mechanism.

The most important system variables for Visual LISP programmers are listed in Table 9.1 along with a short description. More information about these system variables and many others can be found in the online help for AutoCAD.

Table 9.1 Commonly used system variables.

System Variable	Description
ACADVER	Returns a string telling you what version of AutoCAD is running
ANGBASE	The base angle orientation changes some commands in AutoCAD; angle calculations in Visual LISP have to be adjusted by this value
AUNITS, AUPREC	The angle unit style and precision setting
CDATE	The system date and time in almost display-ready format
CLAYER	The name of the current layer
CMDACTIVE	Indicates whether or not a command is active
CMDECHO	Echoes commands to the command line when run inside Visual LISP
CMDNAMES	The command names currently active
CTAB	The currently set model or layout space tab
DATE	The system date and time in computation-ready format
DWGNAME	The drawing name
DWGPREFIX	The folder where the drawing is located
EXPERT	Changes in expert mode change the sequences of prompts, especially the "Are you sure?" type prompts
UNITS, LUPREC	The units and precision for non-angle numbers
OSMODE	A bit-encoded integer with the object snap modes currently set
_PKSER	The package serial number for AutoCAD
TDCREATE	The time and date, in Julian day format, when the drawing was created

Table 9.1 Commonly used system variables. (Continued)

System Variable	Description
TDINDWG	The time in days that the drawing has been worked on
TEXTSTYLE	The name of the current text style to retrieve text-generation information
UCSNAME	The name of the current UCS

Listing 9.2 contains two utility functions that I use frequently. They get the current setting of a group of system variables, which you might use when starting an application in which you will change some of the settings. The GETSYSVARS function is given a list of system variable names to retrieve and returns an association list with the variable name followed by the current value of that variable.

Listing 9.2   Setting and saving system variables.

```
(DEFUN GETSYSVARS (SLIST)
  (MAPCAR '(LAMBDA (S)
     (IF (LISTP S) (SETQ S (CAR S)))
     (LIST S (GETVAR S)))
  SLIST))


(DEFUN SETSYSVARS (SLIST)
  (FOREACH S SLIST
    (SETVAR (CAR S) (CADR S))))
```

The SETSYSVARS function accepts a list of the same format created by GETSYSVARS and sets the variables back to their original settings. This function is evaluated on the way out of the application to restore the system variables to the values they had when the operator started the application. (This function can help avoid technical support calls.)

The only restriction in using these functions is that the system variables supplied must be read/write. If they are read only, the SETSYSVARS function will fail because there is no way to test whether a variable is read only in advance.

Example: Reporting Dates and Times

The final example in this chapter reports the time spent drawing as well as additional details such as the drawing name, the directory, the last time saved, and when the drawing was created. This simple function, shown in Listing 9.3, demonstrates the use of PROMPT with format control characters embedded in the string, specifically the \n (newline) and \t (tab) characters. When the function is run at the command prompt, a formatted report is presented to the operator. This function also demonstrates system variable access of the time system used to keep track of time and dates in AutoCAD.

Listing 9.3   Reporting the drawing date and time.

```
(DEFUN C:DATES ()
  (PROMPT
    (STRCAT
      "\n\tDrawing: " (GETVAR "DWGNAME")
      "\n\tDirectory: " (GETVAR "DWGPREFIX")
      "\n\tCreated: " (J2D (GETVAR "TDCREATE"))
      "  " (JTIME (GETVAR "TDCREATE"))
      "\n\tLast saved: " (J2D (GETVAR "TDUPDATE"))
      "  " (JTIME (GETVAR "TDUPDATE"))
      "\n\tHours in dwg: " (JTIME (GETVAR "TDINDWG"))
    )
  )
  (princ)
)
```

STRCAT constructs a string that is passed to the PROMPT subr. Most of the work in this function takes place in the STRCAT expression, where the string is built. That work involves translating the date and time information in AutoCAD to something that makes sense to people. AutoCAD records dates and times using a time system called Julian days. This system offers a significant advantage in computations involving dates and times. Unlike the calendar system, the Julian days system has no month names, no variable number of days in a month, no leap years, and no other disturbances in the count. Julian days are simply a count of the number of days that have elapsed since a set date.

Julian date-based systems did not suffer any Y2K problems and do not have trouble with computing elapsed time at the end of the day — or any other time period. You simply subtract the values to achieve a difference in days. The fractional part of the number represents the hours and minutes as a fraction of a day.

The JTIME function in Listing 9.4 accepts a Julian date and returns the time of day based on the fractional component. The number of hours is that value times 24. Take away the remaining fraction and multiple by 60 to get the number of minutes. Multiply that fraction by 60 again and you have the number of seconds. As you can see, the Julian days system offers a significant advantage in computing elapsed times.

Listing 9.4   Converting time formats.

```
(DEFUN JTIME (JDT / HH MM SS) ; JDT is Julian Date/Time
    (SETQ JDT (- JDT (FIX JDT))
          HH (* JDT 24.0)
          MM (* (- HH (FIX HH)) 60.0)
          SS (* (- MM (FIX MM)) 60.0))
    (STRCAT (ITOA (FIX HH)) ":"
            (IF (< (FIX MM) 10) "0" "") (ITOA (FIX MM)) ":"
            (IF (< (FIX SS) 10) "0" "") (ITOA (FIX SS)))))
```

The DATES function also makes use of the J2D function. J2D is supplied on the CD and is a useful utility for converting Julian days to Calendar days. Given a Julian date, the function returns the month, day, and year as a string suitable for printing. Like JTIME, J2D can be adjusted to fit specific needs.

Summary

Most applications must report the results of computations and the status of the current situation. When reporting textual information, output can be generated to the command line or the text screen. For graphics, you can use the COMMAND subr to control AutoCAD within Visual LISP.

The combination of commands and logic control can produce powerful command enhancements in AutoCAD. The result is improved productivity because the system responds to you instead of you responding to its demands.

AutoCAD's commands are designed to interact with the user, not with a computer program. Visual LISP must sometimes use special characters to invoke the proper command sequence and take extra steps to enable dialog boxes and other features in the system. All commands with dialog boxes accept a hyphen at the start to disable the dialog box so that you can learn the command-entry sequence, which is the sequence used by the Visual LISP COMMAND subr.

An important aspect of command processing in AutoCAD is the status of certain system variables. This chapter introduced the important system variables in AutoCAD as related to Visual LISP programming. You learned about utilities for preserving the values of the system variables that change during an application as well as a tool to reset them when the program finishes.

Output is just one part of the picture. All programs in this book and on the CD make use of output in one way or another, unless they are simple utilities. The next part of the picture, input, is even more important.

CHAPTER 10

Basic User Input

Most programming languages have a way to accept string input and convert it to a particular data type. But Visual LISP, because it runs in a CAD/CAM environment, must do more than just accept basic input in the form of numbers or strings. Visual LISP's input system must be able to accept points, entity selections, selection sets, window selections, angles, and distances, as well as numbers and strings.

Operator input in the Visual LISP environment can be accepted in three ways: in a dialog box, from the graphics screen, and from the command line. The next chapter introduces dialog boxes and their components. In this chapter, you look at command-line and graphic screen input. Virtually all applications written in Visual LISP use at least one of the subrs described in this chapter.

Building AutoCAD Commands

Like output, the input to a command function should parallel the AutoCAD system as much as possible — even if you have a better method in mind. (If you are writing code only for yourself, however, improve the interface to suit your fancy.) When writing code for a large community of AutoCAD users, it is best to keep the essence of the command like AutoCAD. That means supplying a default value whenever possible and including options in the same form when prompting the user. The normal approach is to provide a prompting question, and then present the options (if any) between the [and] characters, with the default option following between the < and > characters. The entire prompt should end with a colon and a space. Commands built in this manner will appear familiar to AutoCAD operators.

Another item to consider when building AutoCAD commands is the action of transparent commands such as transparent zoom and pan. This is not an issue when using the elementary input subr library because those routines know how to respond properly. When using more advanced input systems, however, you can run in trouble. One key to success is planning. And when planning, try to keep the input as simple as possible. You can still provide an expert mode with minimal error handling but more dynamic input options, but don't make it the default for beginners.

Visual LISP Input

From the Visual LISP programmer's perspective, input is received from three places: the command line, the graphics screen, and dialog boxes. Command-line input consists of keyboard entries or menu selections that duplicate keyboard-entry sequences. Graphics screen input consists of points returned when the pointing device is clicked in the graphics window. Although the graphics screen is a two-dimensional device, points are returned as three-dimensional coordinates. Dialog box input is always string based and can utilize a variety of input mechanisms, such as text boxes, buttons, lists, radio buttons, and sliders. Dialog boxes, which are more complex than the other two types of input, are covered in Chapter 11.

You should think carefully about the best input system for your application. The choice you make will help determine whether or not users deem your program to be user friendly. Programs that are not user-friendly are inflexible and often have too many input requirements. User-friendly software is flexible, giving the user choices when asking for input. For example, in a routine that draws circles, the routine should not accept only the radius or only the diameter of the circle to draw. Instead, the routine should allow the operator to enter either one. In addition, the operator should be able to enter those values at the keyboard, on the graphics screen by showing a distance, or by selecting an existing circle.

Does making user-friendly software require more lines of code? It usually does, especially when dialog boxes are involved. However, Visual LISP provides a powerful subr library that makes the job of working with command-line and graphics input a lot easier. And the savings in support and the gains in productivity due to user acceptance will make the extra coding effort worthwhile. Remember, users are your customers. Your software should work with them, not against them.

Command-Line Input

You start your exploration of the input subrs in Visual LISP with command-line input, which generally consists of a prompt to the text screen or the command line asking the user for a bit of information. In most cases, if the user chooses not to enter anything, the result from the input subr is NIL. I say most cases because the string input subr returns an empty string instead of NIL when the user presses the Enter key instead of typing a string. The command-line input subrs are shown in Table 10.1. The syntax for these subrs is essentially the same. All have a prompt string, except the string input subr, which can accept an optional, non-NIL, non-string parameter to signify that spaces are allowed in the input string.

Table 10.1 Subrs for command-line input.

Subr	Description
GETINT	Gets an integer value from the command line
GETKWORD	Gets a keyword string from the command line
GETREAL	Gets a double-precision real number from the command line
GETSTRING	Gets a string value from the command line

In most cases, GET expressions are used inside a SETQ, where the value obtained is saved for reference later. The reason to save the value and not just assume a good value was supplied is that you must check all user input for validity. Users will test the limits of your software, so anticipate that by always testing to see whether input is acceptable.

Following are some sample GET expressions. These are the most basic GET expressions. The only one to note is the GETSTRING subr. If the first parameter is not a string and is not NIL, the input string can contain spaces. If the first parameter is a string or is NIL, the input string cannot contain spaces and pressing the spacebar has the same result as pressing the Enter key.

```
(SETQ IVAL (GETINT "\nEnter an integer: "))

(SETQ RVAL (GETREAL "\nEnter a real number: "))

(SETQ SVAL (GETSTRING "\nEnter a string: "))

(SETQ SVAL (GETSTRING T "\nEnter a long string: "))
```

Another way to get good input is to use the Visual LISP INITGET tool to initialize the input system. INITGET allows you to define keywords as well as input conditions. The GETKWORD subr requires that you use INITGET to define the keywords you will accept, but it is optional for all the other GET subrs in Visual LISP. INITGET does a lot of error checking for you.

The error-checking flags for INITGET are shown in Table 10.2. These flags are passed as bit-coded integers. To activate any one of the tests, add the bit number to the integer code supplied to INITGET. In this way, you can combine tests. For example, you can combine the non-zero and non-negative tests to allow only numbers greater than 0. (Note that you would still have to test the upper limit in your program.)

Table 10.2 Principle flag settings for INITGET.

Setting	Description
1	No null or empty entries allowed
2	No zero entry allowed
4	No negative entry allowed
8	LIMCHECK system variable is applied against the next point input
32	Use dashed lines for a rubber-band line or box during graphics input
64	Force a two-dimensional distance input even if three-dimensional points are input for GETDIST

An example of using INITGET with keywords is shown in the YESNO function in Listing 10.1. YESNO is a simple user input function that asks a yes-or-no type question. If the answer is Yes, the function returns T; otherwise, the function returns NIL. The default answer is a parameter to the function and can be a string or a flag. If it is a string, it is used directly. Otherwise, the default value, DEF, is replaced with a Yes or No string.

Listing 10.1 Inputting yes or no.

```
(DEFUN YESNO (PR DEF / TMP)
  (INITGET 0 "Yes No")
  (IF (/= (TYPE DEF) 'STR)
    (IF (BOUNDP 'DEF)
      (SETQ DEF "Yes")
      (SETQ DEF "No")))
  (SETQ TMP
    (GETKWORD
        (STRCAT PR " <" DEF ">: ")))
  (IF (NULL TMP) (SETQ TMP DEF))
  (= TMP "Yes")
)
```

The DEF default string is displayed as part of the prompt for the GETKWORD subr. The rest of the prompt consists of two constant character strings, " <" and ">: ", along with the PR prompt parameter. The value returned from GETKWORD is saved in the TMP symbol.

After the GETKWORD is completed, TMP is tested to see whether it has a value. If not, the default value is put in TMP. The value of TMP is then tested to see whether it equals Yes or No. If it equals Yes, the functions returns the value 'T. If it equals No, the NIL value is returned.

Some of the bits in the INITGET settings are for point input. The 1, 2, and 4 bit codes are used most frequently for number input. To activate these settings, add the codes together. For example, a code of 7 means you will not accept 0 input, negative input, and a null entry. All you need to do is test for any upper limit that might apply. If no upper limit is applicable, your program doesn't need to do anything except use INITGET.

Listing 10.2 uses INITGET and tests whether the input is in a particular range. This is the type of utility you can use in applications to save programming time. Using a library of input routines that solve standard input functions can help give your applications a professional polish.

The GETRANGE function issues a prompt (PR) and then waits for integer input. A WHILE loop iterates as long as the TMP value is bound to NIL. In the WHILE loop, an INITGET subr prepares the input to not accept null inputs. Then GETINT is called with the PR prompt string and the value input by the operator is placed in TMP.

TMP is tested to see whether the value is greater than or equal to MN and less than or equal to MX. If not, TMP is set to NIL so that the WHILE loop will repeat again. Otherwise, TMP retains the value, the loop exits, and TMP is evaluated to send its value back as a result for the GETRANGE function.

Another example of the GET subrs in action is shown in Listing 10.3, where you create a new GETREAL version. This version of the input function uses a default value displayed with a prompt. GETREAL1 has two arguments: a prompt string and a default value passed as PR and DEF, respectively.

Listing 10.2 Inputting integers with a range check.

```
(DEFUN GETRANGE (PR MN MX / TMP)
  (WHILE (NULL TMP)
    (INITGET 1)
    (SETQ TMP (GETINT PR))
    (IF (NOT (<= MN TMP MX))
      (SETQ TMP NIL))
  )
  TMP
)
```

Listing 10.3 Inputting real numbers with a default value.

```
(DEFUN GETREAL1 (PR DEF / TMP)
  (SETQ TMP
    (GETREAL
      (STRCAT
        PR
        " <"
        (RTOS DEF)
        ">: ")))
  (IF (NULL TMP)
    (SETQ TMP DEF))
  TMP)
```

Inside the GETREAL1 function, a GETREAL expression establishes a value for TMP. The prompt for GETREAL contains a STRCAT expression, which concatenates the PR prompt string with the DEF default value, after converting it to a string with RTOS. That's a lot going on in a single SETQ expression. Sometimes it helps to read the code from the innermost parentheses, as in the following. Take the real number DEF and convert it to a string. Concatenate that string with the constant strings " <" and ">: " and the PR parameter string to form a prompt string for the GETREAL expression. Then save the result of GETREAL in TMP.

After the GETREAL expression and SETQ have finished, the value of TMP is tested to see whether it is null. A null value indicates that the operator simply pressed Enter, meaning he or she accepted the default value. Null value detection will result in TMP being set to the value in DEF. The last action of the function is to return the result of evaluating TMP, which is either a number as entered in GETREAL or the DEF value on return.

Graphics Input

Because Visual LISP runs inside AutoCAD, it must have some way to permit the programmer to obtain data from the graphics screen. A program can get several items of information from graphics input, such as point locations, angles, distances, entities, and selection sets. Whereas command-line input requires keyboard or menu activity, graphics input involves the pointing device and clicking.

Note that all graphics input subrs support command-line input in some fashion. This means you can enter a distance or angle in response to a prompt instead of always showing the value graphically. In addition to command-line input options, the GET functions also support the activities of the INITGET subr in preparing the input system. INITGET settings can be used to force the operator to enter a point without leaving the associated GET function.

The primary graphics input subrs for Visual LISP are shown in Table 10.3. Because of their variety, you have more programming options when using these subrs. Graphics input is accomplished using the pointing device or keyboard. In some cases, you can either locate points or type a scalar value. As the programmer, you have control over which options you make available in your functions. You can elect to give the operator all the options or you can limit them. For example, when requesting a distance value, you can allow the operator to show two points (the distance is calculated between them), or have the operator show a single point with the other supplied by your program, or force the operator to type a value at the keyboard.

Table 10.3 Subrs for graphics input.

Subr	Description
GETCORNER	Point input for the opposite side of a box
GETDIST	Enter value or show point(s) for the distance
GETANGLE	Enter angle value or show point(s) for the angle
GETORIENT	Enter or show the angle value relative to BASEANG
GETPOINT	Point input
ENTSEL	Select a single entity object
NENTSEL	Nested entity selection with point and translation matrix
SSGET	Select one or more entity objects and save them as a selection set or PICKSET object

The GETDIST, GETANGLE, GETORIENT, and GETPOINT subrs accept an optional base point as the anchor for a rubber-band line drawn to the current cursor location. The rubber-band line exists only while the input routine is actively in control of the system. After a point is selected, the rubber-band line disappears. The rubber-band line can be either a solid line (the default) or a dashed line. A dashed line is used when INITGET has been evaluated with a bit code of 32 just before the GET subr.

Angles and distances can be entered at the keyboard or graphically. When entered graphically, two points must be supplied. If a base point is used for rubber-band line generation, that point is considered the first of the two required points. Angular input occurs in the current units and is converted to radians automatically.

Points input with GETPOINT and GETCORNER can be defined at the keyboard by typing the coordinates. AutoCAD-operator-level object snap modes work as well. In addition, relative point locations can be defined using the keyboard, just like entering any other point in AutoCAD. In other words, GETPOINT and GETCORNER operate like the majority of AutoCAD commands when asking for point input.

The GETCORNER subr displays a rectangle from the required base point to the current cursor location. It provides the opposite corner of the input for a window-type selection. The orientation of the rectangle produced by the GETCORNER subr is always square to the edges of the graphics display, no matter what the current UCS. The point returned from GETCORNER is in the current UCS, just like GETPOINT.

Listing 10.4 contains an example function for the GETPOINT and GETCORNER subrs. GETWINDOW accepts a prompt string as a single parameter and ask for two points from the operator. If two points are provided, they are returned in a nested list; otherwise, the result is NIL.

Listing 10.4 Inputting window points.

```
(DEFUN GetWindow (Pr / P1 P2)
  (SETQ P1 (GETPOINT Pr))
  (IF P1
    (PROGN
      (SETQ P2 (GETCORNER P1 " other corner: "))
      (IF P2
        (LIST P1 P2)))))
```

Operators can select entities in Visual LISP by either selecting objects one at a time or constructing a selection set. For most commands, operators are accustomed to creating selection sets and are comfortable with the Select Objects: prompt and its options. Entity selection takes place with a pick box when you use any entity input routine, including selection set input.

The entity selection routines return entity-name data elements, and the SSGET subr creates a pick set. These data objects, which are covered more in later chapters (starting with Chapter 12), provide tools by which you can specify a specific entity or set in response to an AutoCAD command prompt. An example of the entity selection is provided in the next section.

Example: Moving and Rotating an Entity

You have covered enough information about Visual LISP to begin writing useful functions, such as the one presented in Listing 10.5. The C:MOVROT command function combines the AutoCAD MOVE and ROTATE commands in a single command that works with one entity at a time. This routine is meant to serve as a springboard for additional command combinations. It is typical of a large library of AutoCAD command macros that you may want to create for your own purposes.

The function has four bound or local variables: RT for the rotation, P1 and P2 for the points, and EN for the entity that will be moved and rotated. As the program starts, a prompt is issued to the operator announcing the beginning of the command. This prompt gives the operator immediate feedback to his or her command entry, providing the sense that "all is well." The rotation, RT, is set to 0 as an initial default value, and the program is ready to begin accepting entity selections for the move and rotation operations.

A WHILE loop begins and repeats as long as the operator selects an object. ENTSEL returns NIL if nothing is selected or if the Enter key is pressed. A NIL return from ENTSEL terminates the WHILE loop. A non-NIL return from ENTSEL indicates that an entity has been selected, and the code proceeds inside the WHILE loop with the entity name information in the EN symbol.

The first action inside the WHILE loop is to ask the operator for the base point. GETPOINT returns a point list if a point is clicked or NIL if the Enter key is pressed with no input. The operator is free to select any point on the screen. Provided such a selection is made, P1 now contains a non-NIL value and the program continues deeper into the nest with another GETPOINT using P1 as a base point. The second GETPOINT return is saved in P2.

The move command can be run only if you have two points, so the next test is to check whether P2 has a non-NIL value. If so, the AutoCAD move command sequence is sent to the command line.

The sequence for the MOVE command is identical to typing it on the command line. First the _MOVE command starts. The underline character at the beginning of the name is for international operations. The MOVE command requires at least one entity. EN is supplied as the only entity to be moved, and a pair of double quotes follows. That pair is the same as pressing the Enter key, thereby moving the command to the next input.

The base point, P1, and the to-point, P2, are supplied last to the COMMAND to finish the AutoCAD move operation. If the P2 value is NIL, the COMMAND sequence is skipped and P2 is set to the value in P1. This happens because you will be using the P2 value in the rotation operation. GETANGLE prompts the user for a rotation angle to apply. The result of GETANGLE is stored using the P1 symbol reference.

Note that a STRCAT inside the GETANGLE prompt concatenates the prompt and the last rotation value used in RT as the default. That way, the operator can use the same angle over and over by just pressing the Enter key. Thus, if GETANGLE returns a value that is non-NIL, the operator has entered or shown a new angle of rotation, and that value is stored in P1. P1 is tested for a non-NIL value; if it is non-NIL, the RT symbol is updated to the new value.

Next, the COMMAND subr is used again to call the rotate command into action with the entity name provided at the start of the WHILE loop. Note that the angle value in RT must be converted to the current units. Supplying RT directly to the COMMAND subr ends up sending a value in radians when a value in degrees may be expected. It is rare to have AutoCAD units set to radians for angular measurement. ANGTOS is used to convert a value in radians to degrees.

The MOVROT routine loops each time the operator selects another entity to process. At the end of the loop, PRIN1 forces a silent exit to the command processor.

Listing 10.5 Moving and rotating.

```
(defun C:MOVROT (
                /    ;; Local Variables
                RT   ;; Rotation (radians)
                P1   ;; Base point
                P2   ;; To point
                EN   ;; Entity to manipulate
                )
  (prompt "\nMove & Rotate")
  (setq RT 0.0)
  (while (setq EN (entsel "\nChoose an object: "))
    (setq P1 (getpoint "\nBase point: "))
    (if P1
      (progn
        (setq P2 (getpoint P1 " to point: "))
        (if P2
          (command "_MOVE"
                    EN
                    ""
                    P1
                    P2)
          (setq P2 P1)) ;else save P1 in P2
        (setq P1 (getangle P2
                            (strcat "\nROTATION <"
                                    (angtos RT)
                                    ">: ")))
        (if P1 (setq RT P1))
        (command "_ROTATE"
                  EN
                  ""
                  P2
                  (angtos RT 0 8))
    ))
```

Listing 10.5 Moving and rotating.

```
    )

    (prin1)

    )
```

This example function can be thought of as a template for other AutoCAD command combinations that work with single entities. Entity objects are covered in much more detail in a later chapter (starting in Chapter 12), where you see how they can provide even more powerful editing utility options.

Summary

Input — the way an operator interacts with your software — is one of the most important aspects of programming. Visual LISP provides a variety of input vehicles, including entering data at the command line, pointing at things on the graphics screen, and interacting with a dialog box. The first two are covered in this chapter. The more complex dialog boxes are the topic of the next chapter.

User input through the command line or graphics screen is the most common form of accepting data from the operator. Visual LISP provides a host of subrs that you can use for that purpose. All GET subrs, except GETSTRING, return a NIL value if the operator provides an empty entry. In addition, you can send a prompt string to the command line when the GET subr is running.

It is the responsibility of the program to test the input supplied by the user to make sure it is proper for the application. That testing can be partially accomplished using the INITGET subr to prepare the input system. INITGET provides a facility to force non-NIL input, non-zero input, non-negative input, as well as other types of input. In many cases, INITGET can reduce the amount of testing your program must do with input data.

The point-input systems allow for the entry of points using either the graphics screen or the keyboard. In most instances, they can behave just like the AutoCAD commands, accepting entities, object snaps, windows, and so on. Using the basic GET subr library, you can create input systems that look and feel like regular AutoCAD commands.

When using the input tools provided in Visual LISP, it is best to make your prompts look as much like an AutoCAD-generated prompt as possible. That means your input options should include default values whenever possible as well as keyword options presented between brackets.

The quality of your application's input and output plays a big part in how a user feels about your software, so you should take the time to think carefully about these aspects of an application.

CHAPTER 11

Introducing Dialog Boxes

A dialog box is a rectangular area of the screen where data is displayed and selections are made using a pointing device and the keyboard. Operators can select elements in the order they want, but they can select only the items you decide to enable and display. In this way, dialog boxes provide the programmer with an excellent tool for controlling input alternatives.

In this chapter, you find out how to create a dialog box in Visual LISP, a process that is different in other programming languages such as Visual Basic and Visual C++. Other languages have easy-to-use graphical editors. In Visual LISP, you design dialog boxes in a Dialog Control Language file using a text language, and then display the file to see how the dialog box looks.

Dialog box programming is more complex than basic command-line input or graphics input, and in this chapter I introduce only the basics. For details, see the online help in Visual LISP.

How Dialog Boxes Work

In this section, you begin by looking at how dialog boxes work and what is needed from a programming point of view to make one work. The major components that make up a dialog box are shown in Figure 11.1. Here, you look at how the components work from a programmer's perspective.

First, a dialog box is designed and programmed before the application runs. Although some dialog

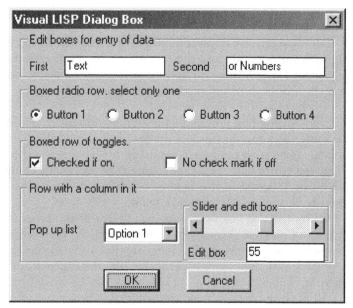

Figure 11.1 The components of a dialog box.

boxes may alter their appearance when the program is running, the majority of the layout must be completed before you can test and run the application. In some environments, such as Visual Basic, you design a dialog box (called a form in that language) by using a graphics design tool to select and place objects. In Visual LISP, the dialog box layout is defined using DCL (Dialog Control Language); the placement of an object relative to other objects is determined by its order in the source file.

Second, a dialog box is rectangular and made up of rectangular areas. The rectangular areas are called tiles in Visual LISP. Think of ceramic tile, where each tile is a different size. As you lay out the tiles, they are oriented parallel to a baseline so that they will fit in the rectangular region. If you move the tiles, the size of the rectangle changes. Visual LISP tiling works the same way, but with a lot more flexibility. You can resize most of the tiles in Visual LISP so that they fit together nicely.

Third, tiles are like objects. If you understand object-oriented programming, you know what that simple statement means! If you don't, that's okay. It means tiles contain properties, or attributes, and have associated methods, or functions. Visual LISP uses the terms attributes for data elements associated with the tile (such as its name) and callback functions for the functions defined to react to a change in the tile. Tiles are not real objects in the truest sense of object-oriented programming, but they exhibit some object-like features.

Fourth, all data communication with tiles and dialog boxes is accomplished using strings. When you want to send data, you send a string. When you attach a callback function, you supply a string. And when the callback function is invoked through the dialog box, it sends strings. Data conversion and data checking are handled during each communication with the dialog box. This gives the programmer control over each aspect of the input process in an isolated environment. There are some numeric communications with tiles but mostly regarding their various modes, or states, and not data.

Fifth, the process involved in displaying the dialog box, preparing the tiles with data, interacting with the operator, and then returning the results are the same for all dialog boxes, as is the sequence of steps. After you have created your first dialog box, the next will be similar. The differences will be in the details such as what specific types of tiles are used and how the callback functions behave with the data provided.

Sixth, dialog box programming supports modular concepts by isolating the input and some of the output to a specific function set designed around the dialog box itself. Modular program development and testing can be accomplished by defining a single function entry for your input request. Then you return data values for testing. The processing component of the application you are creating can be tested in this manner while the dialog boxes are developed at another time or by another person on a development team.

Seventh, dialog box programming is event-driven programming, which requires that you set up a series of possible events with consequences. As the events occur, the consequences play out. In dialog box programming, the events are tiles and the consequences are callback functions. When a user does something with a particular tile, the callback function is invoked and does something about it.

All of these concepts meld to form dialog box programming. In the next section, you see how these concepts work together in an example application.

Creating a Dialog Box

Suppose that you want to build a program that accepts input from the operator using a dialog box. The first step is to create the Dialog Control Language (DCL) file, which defines the initial layout of the dialog box. (You can always return to the DCL and make changes.)

The next step is to define a function that serves as the primary dialog box driver. This function loads the DCL file and then displays the particular dialog box you want to see. You can store more than one dialog box definition in a DCL file. After the dialog box is displayed, the program can place default data into the dialog box tiles, set up the callback functions, and establish the initial modes for the tiles. The mode control establishes whether or not a tile is enabled

After the preparations are finished, the dialog box is started and your primary dialog box driver program waits for the dialog box to be finished. At this point, control is turned over to the operator to choose and manipulate the elements of the dialog box. As tiles are manipulated, the callback functions run. Callback functions are permitted to change the modes and values in other dialog box tiles, so a callback function can produce significant changes in the user's interface, including displaying another dialog box on top of the initial dialog box.

Dialog boxes are terminated when a callback function requests an exit or the operator clicks a button such as OKor Cancel. At this point, the dialog box driver program takes control again. An integer code is passed back to the driver program indicating the exit option that the operator selected. If the OK button was clicked, the driver program prepares the data for returning to the master program that started the driver. The simplest way to return data is as a direct result of the driver function. If the Cancel button is clicked, the driver program typically returns NIL and none of the variables change. The dialog box DCL can be unloaded before the exit of the driver function to free memory for other dialog boxes. However, if you will be using the same dialog box DCL contents again in the application, just leave it open and close it when you are completely finished.

This is just one possible sequence for program flow with a dialog box. Another is to set up retirement buttons so that the operator can go to the graphics screen and make a selection or input a point. This type of operation is still considered retiring the dialog box because you are getting it off the screen to display the graphics window. Typical programming of this type of dialog box interaction places all the main dialog box driver logic, with the exception of the DCL load and unload subrs, into a loop that iterates until one of the exit conditions is met.

The DCL file is an ASCII text file that you create with the Visual LISP editor and save with the DCL extension (by choosing the Save As option and then selecting DCL for the Save as Type option). When you save the file (even an empty file), the editor recognizes that you are writing a dialog box source file.

The syntax of a DCL file is different than Visual LISP syntax because you are defining a screen layout rather than a program. Every object in the DCL file has the same syntax:

```
[NAME ]: ITEM [ : ITEM …] { ATTRIBUTE = VALUE; … }
```

NAME is something you can use to reference the tile or dialog box in your application. Normally, you use NAME only when defining the dialog box object itself. ITEM is the name of a previously defined tile type. It can be a reserve name or something of your own design. You typically have one ITEM, but you can have more than one if needed. The attributes for the DCL object are between the braces.

Version 1

The first dialog box you will create is shown in Figure 11.2. It has a text display line, two Change buttons, and an OK button and Cancel button. This is a basic dialog box that you will use for the first few examples. The dialog box in Figure 11.2 was created with the DCL definition in Listing 11.1.

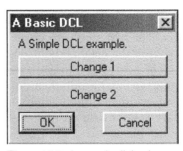

Starting at the top, the primary tile is a dialog type. You usually start with a dialog tile and then define other tiles inside it. In this case, three tiles (text and two button tiles) are defined along with the named object ok_cancel. The named object is a cluster of two buttons in a row showing the text OK and Cancel. When writing DCL files, you should consider named objects to be single tiles. You can create you own named objects, such as

Figure 11.2 A sample dialog box, version 1.

ok_cancel in the DCL file, but the primary ones you will want are already provided in AutoCAD. ok_cancel is a common one that provides two familiar exits from the dialog box. Next, you turn your attention to the text and button tiles in the example listing.

Listing 11.1 Creating a dialog box, version 1.

```
HELLO1 : dialog {
   label = "A Basic DCL";
   : text {
       key = "T1";
       value="A Simple DCL example.";
   }
   : button {
       key = "B1";
       label = "Change 1";
   }
   : button {
       key = "B2";
       label = "Change 2";
   }
   ok_cancel;
}
```

Every tile in the dialog box has a common attribute, named key, which is the name by which your program will reference or recognize a specific tile. Note that key names are case sensitive and must be unique within the dialog definition. I tend to use a simple standard when first laying out a dialog box to see what it looks like on the screen. I name the tiles in sequence, using only a few characters. As I arrange the dialog box and establish the locations for the various elements, I often assign more meaningful key names.

The label attribute contains the text displayed on the tile in the dialog box. This is another common attribute found in all tiles except picture, or image, tiles. Although a label is not mandatory, the lack of one will affect the readability of your dialog box.

To create the dialog box, follow these steps:

1. In the Visual LISP IDE, load the example DCL file from the CD or type the code in Listing 11.1.

2. Set the focus to the DCL file's edit window and then choose Tools > Interface tools.

3. Select the Preview DCL in Editor option. The names of the dialog boxes are displayed in a pull-down list.

4. Select HELLO1 and then click OK. You should see the dialog box shown in Figure 11.2.

The dialog box in Figure 11.2 is a rectangle that contains several rectangles. The buttons are obviously rectangles, but so is the text. Note the space on either side of the text inside the buttons. The extra space was added so that the ok_cancel grouping could fit properly in the dialog box window. Visual LISP adds spaces automatically to fill in the extra room.

The ok_cancel group is a style of dialog box design. It is arranged in a row. Dialog boxes are divided into rows and columns of rectangular shapes, and the sequence of their appearance in the DCL controls how the dialog box looks on the graphics screen. It is up to you whether you want to use other styles, such as rows and columns of toggles or list boxes and edit boxes, when you create dialog boxes. However, Visual LISP dialog boxes should appear the same as AutoCAD dialog boxes to provide operators with a consistent interface.

Version 2

A dialog box is a column by default. You can change the dialog box so that it looks like the one in Figure 11.3 by adding the tile description for row around the two button tiles, as in Listing 11.2. (Look for the two lines marked //New. (The double slash is a comment in a DCL source file.) Tiles like the buttons seen here can be put in a row by inserting the definition of the button tiles inside the brackets for the row tile.

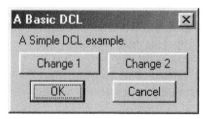

Figure 11.3 A sample dialog box, version 2.

By adding the row tile around the two buttons, you drastically change the shape of the dialog box. The buttons are smaller (so that two fit in a row) and there is more space to the right of the text in the text tile containing the string "A Simple DCL example."

The buttons are contained in row because they appear between the braces for the row tile. You can nest row and column tiles as deep as needed to split up the screen in any fashion you want.

Listing 11.2 Creating a dialog box, version 2.

```
HELLO1 : dialog {
  label = "A Basic DCL";
  : text {
      key = "T1";
      value="A Simple DCL example.";
  }
  : row { //New
    : button {
        key = "B1";
        label = "Change 1";
    }
    : button {
        key = "B2";
        label = "Change 2";
     }
  }   //New
  ok_cancel;
}
```

Version 3

Consider version 3 of the dialog, which is shown in Figure 11.4. In this version, the majority of the dialog box is a row. The buttons are arranged in a column at the end of the row.

The source code is in Listing 11.3. Note the addition of the width attribute for the row, which forces the row to be big enough to hold 60

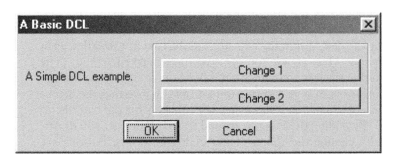

Figure 11.4 A sample dialog box, version 3.

characters (more than enough). Note too the box around the buttons. Both row and column tiles can also be labeled as boxed_row or boxed_column. When boxed is added to the front of the group tile name, a thin line is drawn around the tile. This helps to offset important elements or groups of input in a dialog box.

Listing 11.3 Creating a dialog box, version 3.

```
HELLO3 : dialog {
  label = "A Basic DCL";
  : row {
    width = 60;
    : text { key = "T1"; value="A Simple DCL example."; }
    : boxed_column {
      : button { key = "B1"; label = "Change 1";}
      : button { key = "B2"; label = "Change 2";}
    }
  }
  ok_cancel;
}
```

Inserting row and column adjusts the shape your dialog box. Adding boxes make the dialog box look better organized. You can also add labels to boxed rows and columns to provide a title for the entire grouping. With practice, you will be able to create a variety of dialog box layouts.

Standard Tile Types

The basic tiles defined in Visual LISP are presented in Table 11.1. All of these tiles have attributes. Some attributes are common for all tile and others are unique for a particular tile or have a special meaning for only some tiles.

Table 11.1 Dialog box tiles.

Tile	Description
boxed_column	Rectangular column grouping with a border.
boxed_radio_column	Rectangular column area for radio buttons with a border.
boxed_radio_row	Rectangular row grouping for radio buttons with a border.
boxed_row	Rectangular row grouping with a border.
button	Pushbutton, such as OK.
column	Rectangular column grouping.
edit_box	Text entry box.
errtile	Error-reporting box area at the bottom of the dialog box.
image	Graphic.

Table 11.1 Dialog box tiles. (Continued)

image_button	Graphic that behaves like a button.
list_box	List of text choices.
paragraph	Grouping of text_parts and concatenation.
popup_list	List of text choices that is pulled down to display the list; normally displays only the selected item.
radio_button	Button associated with other radio buttons in a radio_row or radio_column that can be selected to indicate a unique choice. Only one radio button can be selected at one time in a radio row or column. If another is already selected, it will be automatically deselected.
radio_column	Rectangular column grouping for radio buttons.
radio_row	Rectangular row grouping for radio buttons.
row	Rectangular row grouping.
slider	Vertical or horizontal sliding bar used to indicate a value within a range.
spacer	Empty space between tiles.
text	Text display only; no editing.
text_part	Text display only; part of a paragraph. Allows for the insertion of partial text based on the application. Used with the paragraph and concatenation tiles.
toggle	Button that indicates an on-or-off state. It has a checkmark or a box with an X in it.

The attributes you will use most frequently are listed in Table 11.2. Virtually all tiles have these attributes available for use. The label and value attributes, however, are not used with all tiles. For example, value does not make sense in the case of a row. If you do not want to change or modify a tile, it does not need a key.

Some of the attributes can be changed during the evaluation of your Visual LISP programs using the subrs mentioned in the table. You look at those subrs later in this chapter, after you learn about some of the attributes used with specific tiles.

Button tiles

A button tile is an area that the user clicks. You can use buttons to allow the operator to exit the dialog box permanently (such as the OK and Cancel buttons), to exit the dialog box for graphics selection, to change values in other tiles in the current dialog box, or to display another dialog box.

Most programmers follow certain conventions when using buttons. If a button will be used for a graphics selection, the less-than character (<) is often placed at the end of the label. When a button is used to display another dialog box, three periods (...) are displayed at the end of the label.

Table 11.2 Common tile attributes.

Attribute	Type	Description
action	String	Visual LISP expression to evaluate when the tile is selected or changed. This is one of two places where you can establish the callback function reference. To overwrite the callback reference setting, use the (ACTION_TILE) subr.
alignment	Left, Right, Centered	Alignment of a tile within a group.
height	Integer	Count in dialog units (characters) of the height of the tile.
key	String	Name of tile for external references.
is_enabled	True, False	Can the tile be selected and manipulated? The default, which is TRUE, can be overwritten using the (MODE_TILE) subr.
is_tab_stop	True, False	Is the tile a stopping point when tabbing through the dialog box?
label	String	String to be displayed with the tile.
mnemomic	String	Character that can be used for quickly reaching the tile (hot key).
width	Integer	Count in dialog units (characters) of the width of the tile.
value	String	Initial value of the tile. To overwrite it, use (SET_TILE).

In addition, you should clearly mark the function of buttons that exit or change values in the current dialog box.

The IS_DEFAULT and IS_CANCEL attributes are specific to the button tile. Both are Boolean values, so they are true or false. Only one button per dialog box can have either of these values set to true, and no one button tile can have both. When IS_DEFAULT is true for a button, that button is activated (its action called forth) when the user presses the Enter key. When IS_CANCEL is true, that button is activated when the user presses the Escape key.

IMAGE_BUTTON tiles are a variation of button tiles that also supply information as to where on the button the selection was made. An image button can display an AutoCAD slide (SLD or SLB) image to provide a graphic description for operator input. When the operator selects a location in the button, the location (relative to a corner) is available for use in your program.

Text tiles

Text tiles display text data inside the dialog box. The text tiles are text and TEXT_PART, as well as PARAGRAPH to glue the parts together. You can change the text value and use the box to keep the operator informed as to the status of your program while it is running. For example, a message could tell the operator how many objects are currently selected based on the search criteria supplied in the dialog box.

The only attribute unique to text tiles is the Boolean IS_BOLD attribute. When set to true, it forces the displayed text to appear in a bold font.

The data entry tile

The only data entry tile in Visual LISP is the edit_box tile. This tile can be used for entering and editing string data, allowing it to hold numbers, words, and sentences. Your program determines what is allowed in this tile. Should the operator supply something that is not proper, your program must detect that fact and inform the operator of the problem. The ALERT subr is useful for informing the operator of a problem in the midst of a dialog box.

Several attributes are designed for the data entry tile. edit_width sets the width of the display field. EDIT_LIMIT sets the maximum number of characters to be accepted. PASSWORD_CHAR, which is used for password entry, is a replacement character that masks the display of what the operator has typed.

When programming a data entry tile, you should include a default value. If it is something that can be turned on and off, use the toggle or radio buttons with the data entry tile. When the associated toggle is on, enable the edit box so that the operator can see that it is associated with the button. When off, disable the edit box so that the operator can see immediately that data is no longer applicable. To enable and disable tiles, you use the MODE_TILE subr, which is covered in a later section.

Data-entry-tile callbacks occur after the data has been entered and the operator is attempting to leave the tile. A reason code supplied as an argument to the callback function can be tested to determine whether the operator pressed the Enter key (accept the input as provided) or moved to another tile. In either case, the input should be verified for validity by retrieving and checking the stored value.

Toggles and radio buttons

A toggle is something that has one of two values, such as yes or no. Toggles appear as check boxes in a dialog box. The operator clicks the toggle to change its state between on and off. Toggles can be used to turn on and off other sections of the dialog box or as the input device for flags or settings having only two possible values.

For flags and settings with more than two possible values, you can use radio buttons. Radio buttons are like toggles except they are always used in a group. Instead of answering a yes-or-no type question, radio buttons answer a "which of the following" question. Radio buttons can be arranged in a row or a column .

Every time the button or toggle is changed, its associated callback functions are called. A value of 0 or 1 is passed to the callback function as an argument. The value 1 indicates a true, or on, state. A value of 0 is for false, or off.

Toggles and radio buttons appeal to a broad majority of operators — if the default values are right. When using toggles and radio button options, you should not reset the default each time the dialog box is displayed. Instead, maintain the previous default when possible.

List tiles

The two types of list tiles in Visual LISP are boxes and pop-ups. A boxed list has a boundary and scrolling bars on the right for moving through the list of options. Boxed lists may have one or multiple items selected, depending on the application and how the DCL is defined. The MULTIPLE_SELECT attribute controls that aspect of list boxes. Pop-up lists can have only one item selected, and that item is displayed in a single line in the dialog box. When selected, the list pops up for the selection of a single item. Scrolling bars are presented if the content of the list exceeds the number of lines displayed.

For both types of lists, horizontal scrolling is not supported. You must allocate enough space in your dialog box to display the data you want or provide a mechanism of your own design for that purpose. You can use the TABS attribute to establish columns in the list. Then, in the string, insert the tab character (ASCII 9) where you want column breaks.

Although pop-up lists resemble a control known as combo boxes, they do not support the same features. That is, you cannot have a pop-up list and edit box combination in Visual LISP. Perhaps that support will be provided in a future update of the language, one with a next-generation dialog box manager.

The Art of Dialog Box Design

The art of dialog box design is a study in how people use computers. After you have created your interface, it is best to seek feedback from as many users as is reasonable. Each will have an opinion as to how the dialog box should look or act, and you will gain insight about how people view the dialog boxes they use.

The dialog box should be arranged in a readable format. For most users of AutoCAD, that means having neat columns of data with related elements grouped together. Depending on the needs of the operators, your dialog box might range from one that is direct and simple to one with many options.

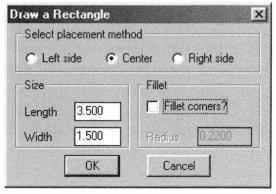

Figure 11.5 Fillet option not selected.

Suppose that you have a dialog box for drawing rectangles that includes an option for adding corners. If operators want rounded corners, they select a toggle and the current fillet radius is presented as the default in an edit box. Figures 11.5 and 11.6 show a dialog box based on that concept. The fillet option is off in Figure 11.5 and on in Figure 11.6.

The dialog box retained the settings from previous runs of the program so that operators could rapidly repeat the same command. Listing 11.4 contains the DCL source code for the dialog box. Note that it has radio options on the top and two columns below, one labeled Size and the other labeled Fillet.

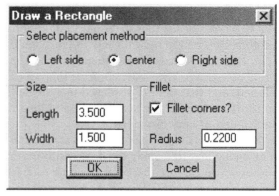

Figure 11.6 Fillet option selected.

Listing 11.4 Creating a dialog box with radio buttons and toggles.

```
RECT : dialog {
  label = "Draw a Rectangle";
  : boxed_radio_row {
    label  = "Select placement method";
    : radio_button {
      key = "LS";
      label = "Left side";}
    : radio_button {
      key = "CE";
      label = "Center";}
    : radio_button {
      key = "RS";
      label = "Right side";}
  }
  : row {
    : boxed_column {
      label = "Size";
      : edit_box {
        key="X";
```

Listing 11.4 Creating a dialog box with radio buttons and toggles. (Continued)

```
            label = "Length";
            edit_width=6;}
        : edit_box {
        key="Y";
        label = "Width";
        edit_width=6;}
    }
    : boxed_column {
    label = "Fillet";
        : toggle {
        key = "FF";
        label = "Fillet corners?";}
        : edit_box {
        key="FR";
        label = "Radius";}
    }
    }
    ok_cancel;
}
```

Reading DCL files can be difficult when columns are inside rows inside columns. That's why Visual LISP has the DCL preview feature. As you create a DCL, start simple. Then improve it step-by-step, reviewing your work in the preview editor. When creating a DCL in the editor, I usually start with everything in the main column, and then I turn things into rows to improve readability and organize the data. A better approach is to design your dialog box on paper and then divide it into rows and columns. After you determine the rows and columns, you know where to place the individual tiles.

The RECT dialog box in Listing 11.4 contains four primary areas:

- The radio box at the top, which has three radio button tiles
- The Size input area, which contains a pair of edit box tiles
- The Fillet input area, which houses a toggle with an edit box
- The OK and Cancel buttons area at the bottom

DCL files define dialog boxes starting at the top. If you want a wide dialog box with multiple columns, you need to define a row at the start. If the entire design fits into a single column, you can just start with the topmost tile because the default shape of a dialog box is as a column. The example in this section is a single column — you can tell because the radio button set stretches from one side to the other. Thus, the first tile in the dialog box is the radio row grouping.

Groupings can have labels, which appear at the top of the group's rectangular area. The label for the radio row sets off the row and provides something of a prompt for the operator.

A row follows the closing brace for boxed_radio_row. The row has no other attributes because it only divides the column into multiple tiles — in this case, two column tiles. The first column tile is for choosing the size of the rectangle, and the second one is for the fillet inputs. The edit boxes and toggle tile definitions sit inside each tile.

Several format options are available for tiles, including setting the width and height. For an edit box, that means not only setting the width of the tile, but also setting the width of the edit window, or the number of characters that can be typed, or both. When I began designing the dialog box, the difference in the width of the characters in the words Length and Width caused the edit boxes to appear out of alignment. By setting the edit_width attribute to the same number, the edit boxes for data entry were the same size.

DCL files are just a written description of the layout of a dialog box. Although difficult to read and comprehend at a glance (just like any programming language), they are easy to maintain and modify. The hardest part is the initial layout, which is why I recommend starting with a pencil and a piece of paper.

Program Manipulation of Dialog Boxes

In this section, you turn your attention to the Visual LISP programming aspects of a dialog box. You must take several steps before a dialog box can even appear on the screen.

The first step in using a dialog box is to load the DCL file into memory. DCL files are read into AutoCAD's memory space for reference by your programs and are assigned a handle. A handle is a number that is used to reference a particular file or dialog library. You use the LOAD_DIALOG subr to obtain a dialog box handle. You give LOAD_DIALOG the file name of the DCL source, including the folder name, as a string. The subr returns a dialog handle after successfully loading the DCL file.

Any errors in the DCL file are reported to an error file, and an alert appears during the loading process. If there are errors, the DCL is not available. That means any other dialog box DCL files expecting to use named parts of the malfunctioned DCL will find them unavailable. This is true even if these parts are fine and the error is in a later dialog definition within the file.

When programming a dialog box, the normal starting sequence is to test the return from LOAD_DIALOG to see whether there are any problems. If everything is okay, LOAD_DIALOG returns a positive value and the program can continue to process the dialog box. Otherwise, you should post an error to the display because you can usually assume that your DCL file is okay and the loading error is the result of a missing file. (You find out more about this in a later chapter about directory management.

If your program will be opening dialog boxes from the same DCL multiple times, you should establish the dialog box handle as a global symbol. At the start of your dialog box functions, check to see whether the symbol is bound to NIL. If so, open the DCL and set the handle into a global symbol so that the next time it is found to be non-NIL.

After obtaining a good dialog box handle, the next step is to display the dialog box on the screen using the NEW_DIALOG subr. NEW_DIALOG has two arguments: the name (case sensitive) of the dialog box to be displayed and the dialog handle obtained when the DCL file was opened.

At the completion of the NEW_DIALOG subr, the dialog is visible on the screen. It is not ready for the user to interact with yet and restrictions now come into play in the programming. One of the restrictions is that you cannot issue command prompts and commands until the dialog box is no longer displayed (and no other dialog boxes are open).

NEW_DIALOG returns NIL if the DCL file is not open or if the dialog box requested was not found in the DCL definition. Names and keys are case sensitive. If your dialog box does not appear after you have created it and written the Visual LISP code to load and display it, check the spelling and case of the dialog box name.

After the dialog box is on the screen, you can display the data to be used as defaults. The SET_TILE subr establishes these values. SET_TILE works with the currently displayed dialog box only. You cannot use SET_TILE to establish values in nested dialog boxes until the target dialog box is the topmost. The data supplied to SET_TILE consists of the key name (case sensitive) for the tile along with the value to be placed in the tile. Data for the tiles is always a string. If you send a non-string value to a tile, an error results or the dialog box freezes on the screen and AutoCAD will seem locked up.

SET_TILE is used to establish the value of tile types that need a single value. These tile types include edit boxes, radio buttons, text, toggles, and sliders. SET_TILE sets the value attribute of a tile. You can also adjust the mode and action settings for a tile, allowing you to change the way a tile appears (enabled or disabled) and what callback function will be used when the tile is manipulated.

To enable and disable a tile, use the MODE_TILE subr, which accepts a key name (case sensitive) and an integer value between 0 and 4 as follows:

- 0 enables the tile if it is not currently enabled.
- 1 disables the tile for input.
- 2 places the focus at a specific tile.
- 3 used only for edit boxes, sets the focus to an edit box and highlights the value
- 4 toggles the highlight status of image tiles

Dialog boxes are intended to give users the ability to move freely through the input system, so be prudent when navigating for the user automatically.

To change the action or callback function for a tile, use the ACTION_TILE subr. Supply a case-sensitive key name to indicate the tile and a string that represents a complete expression in Visual LISP. The string must have surrounding parentheses and a valid LISP expression between the double quotes. If quotes are needed in the string, use the backslash-quote control character. For example, suppose that you want to set the AA symbol to the value "100". The string expression would be

"(setq AA \"100\")"

Visual LISP translates the string to the (setq AA "100") expression. You cover callback functions more thoroughly later in this chapter.

After all the data and actions are established for the dialog box and you are ready to let the operator have at it, invoke the START_DIALOG subr. This subr has no arguments. It starts the interaction with the operator and your program waits until that is finished. Your callback functions are called while the operator manipulates the tiles you've designed for that purpose. When a retirement option is taken (such as the OK or Cancel button), the START_DIALOG subr returns control to the main routine that set up the dialog box in the first place. The dialog box is removed from the screen and you get an integer result.

The integer returned from START_DIALOG is based on the operator's action. If the operator clicked the OK button, a value of 1 is returned. Clicking the Cancel button returns 0. You can use DONE_DIALOG to force other returning options in the callback functions.

Generally, the result of START_DIALOG is stored in a local symbol and then tested in a COND expression. You decide the response that each retirement option will cause, but in general you should save values from the dialog box when OK is clicked and just return with no change data when Cancel is clicked. This is easier if you use temporary symbols for all dialog box manipulations. When processing an OK-return, place the temporary symbol values in global symbols. A Cancel is then processed by not doing anything.

When you have finished using a dialog box, unload it from memory. If you plan to use multiple dialog boxes from the same DCL file or if you expect to return to this dialog box in your application, leave the DCL file loaded. But if the dialog box is a one-shot deal or your application is wrapping up, release memory by using the UNLOAD_DIALOG subr. Supply the dialog handle, and Visual LISP takes care of the rest.

Programming Callback Functions

The actions involved in setting up a dialog box for display and the placement of data is culminated with the user interaction that takes place when the START_DIALOG subr runs. Your program is still running and in control, but the program is running in an event-driven environment rather than in a linear fashion. The operator triggers events by manipulating tiles. When an event takes place, your associated callback function is evaluated.

A callback function can be a simple expression or a call to a complex function of your design. When your function takes over, the operator's interaction is halted. After the callback function is completed, the operator may resume the manipulation of the tiles in that dialog box.

Callback functions can do a lot but there are restrictions. The primary restriction is that callback functions cannot do anything that involves the AutoCAD command line, so data cannot be output through the PROMPT subr and COMMAND activities cannot take place. You can send data to the command line using the WRITE-LINE subr, but you should avoid doing this except when debugging your program because you do not want to cause the operator concern by displaying text that may scroll off quickly.

You can send data from the tile causing the callback directly to the callback function. In the action attribute, the "$key" and "$value" keywords are substituted with the values from the tile. For example, if you set up an edit box tile named AA with an action string of "(My_Function $key $value)", the MY_FUNCTION function is called with the key name and value at the time the tile is manipulated. If the tile has a value of "123" while running and the operator presses the Enter key, the function call is (My_Function "AA" "123").

Another item of information that you can supply is the reason why the callback function is being called. The "$reason" keyword is substituted with an integer code. Most of the time, the reason code has a value of 1, indicating a normal request. The meaning of a normal request depends on the type of tile. An edit box returns code 1 when the Enter key has been pressed. Code 2 results if the operator moved to the next field with the Tab key or a pointing device. Code 3 is associated with sliders and indicates a change in value without a final change setting. List boxes may return code 4 if the operator double-clicks a selection, allowing your callback function to react differently under that circumstance.

After your callback function starts, you can retrieve data from other tiles in the active dialog box. You can also use the SET_TILE and MODE_TILE subrs to set the attributes of other tiles in the active display. Callback functions can even start into another dialog box sequence, resulting in a nested dialog box interface.

You can use the GET_TILE subr to retrieve the current value of a tile, which is returned as a string. The value of an edit box is the text content. The value of a radio button or a toggle is an integer string ("1" for on and "0" for off). The string value for a list box contains an integer indicating the NTH position in the list (list boxes are discussed in more detail shortly).

To retrieve the attributes for a tile, use the GET_ATTR subr. If you want to check against a value stored in the DCL file, the name of the attribute and the tile are presented to GET_ATTR, which returns a string value containing the setting. This setting is the original DCL value, not the current value if that has changed due to SET_TILE or MODE_TILE. You can use GET_ATTR to reestablish the default setting, and you can include custom attributes for a tile. You can use GET_ATTR also to obtain local, language-specific terms to be used in messages related to the tile. If the user changes the DCL file to match local terms or language requirements, the Visual LISP program will adapt accordingly.

Using Lists in Dialog Boxes

Because LISP is a list processing language, it makes sense that dialog boxes will contain lists of data. Special subrs manipulate list tiles (these include regular and pop-up styles of lists). Because you may want to do several things with a list, such as add an item to the end of a list or insert an item in the middle of a list, Visual LISP provides a powerful set of list manipulate subrs.

List boxes are set up one at a time in a dialog box. If the dialog box contains more than one list box, each must be set up using the following sequence. Use START_LIST to open the list tile, use ADD_LIST to add members to the list, and use CLOSE_LIST to indicate that you are finished.

Listing 11.5 shows a sample list box being populated. This sample shows the code associated with the "MYLIST" list box tile in a DCL file that is already opened and displayed on the screen. Note the use of MAPCAR to apply the ADD_LIST subr to each member of the MyDataList list. MyDataList must be a single-level list of strings for this code snippet to work properly. To use nested list structures, just expand the MAPCAR expression with a LAMBDA to manipulate the sublists.

It is important to keep a copy of the list internal to your program. When a list item is selected, the only information that Visual LISP returns is the NTH position selected in the list. It is up to your

Listing 11.5 Populating a list box tile.

```
; … Partial program listing

(START_LIST "MYLIST")
(MAPCAR 'add_list MyDataList)
(CLOSE_LIST)

; … program continues
```

program to equate that position to a value. In the example, the NTH position in the MyDataList list reveals the text that the operator selected in a callback.

Normally, the value of a list tile is a string with the offset position number. You use ATOI to convert the string to an integer, and then use NTH to retrieve the list member. This works fine in the default mode of single selection for a list tile. If you have turned on the MULTIPLE_SELECT attribute for the tile, however, the value for the list box tile is a string of numbers. Suppose that the operator has selected the first, third, and fourth list items on the screen. The list offset positions are returned in the "0 2 3" string. To get the individual offsets in a format that you can use to quickly access the data list, concatenate parentheses characters on each side of the return string and use READ to convert the string to a list of numbers. Now you can loop through that list and retrieve the values.

It takes practice to effectively use list boxes — as well as most tile types in DCL files. Each has specific nuances that you need to learn and experiment with for any given interface requirement. For more information on tiles and attributes, look in the Visual LISP online help files. There is a lot to be found, almost enough for a complete book on just that subject.

Rules and Suggestions for Programming Dialog Boxes

Following are some rules and suggestions regarding the programming of dialog boxes. If your program violates any of the rules, the dialog box will not work properly.

Rule 1: Do not use the command line

When the dialog box is visible, do not attempt to run any AutoCAD commands or send data to the command line using the PROMPT subr. The primary reasons for this is to keep things under control. When Visual LISP is running a dialog box, there is no reason for AutoCAD to perform commands that the operator cannot see. This does not mean that you cannot access the AutoCAD database but it does mean that you cannot interact properly with the command line. An attempt to do so will result in an error in your program.

Rule 2: Use strings in SET_TILE

When you send a non-string value to SET_TILE, the dialog box locks up. And because AutoCAD is waiting on the dialog box, AutoCAD locks up as well. The only way around this is to cancel tasks (with Task Manager), but this could leave a mess (and the loss of unsaved work) in system memory and even the disk system. To prevent this, always double-check your values for SET_TILE to make sure that they are strings.

Rule 3: Use unique names

Dialog box names, key names, and custom attributes should be unique. When the same name is used in a conflicting manner, the dialog box system in Visual LISP generates an error message and then the dialog box is displayed. You can avoid a lot of problems by adopting a standard, such as always using uppercase letters.

Suggestion 1: Do not use abbreviations

Abbreviations can confuse for some applications. Dialog boxes are supposed to be easy-to-use input forms. The use of abbreviations, except when the abbreviation is the accepted standard of communication, makes the dialog box harder to read and understand.

Suggestion 2: Provide shortcuts

Users or your program develop from novices to experts. And expert users look for shortcuts when running a program.

Suggestion 3: Display default values

An empty dialog box entry looks incomplete, whether it is an empty text field or a radio button group without one of the values selected. From a user's perspective, the ultimate dialog box has all the data filled in correctly and simply requires a click of the OK button.

Suggestion 4: Remember changes

Users find it frustrating to change something and then see that it has undone itself. When a value is changed in a dialog box, that change should be remembered when the dialog box is displayed the next time in the same drawing edit session.

Suggestion 5: Report input problems

The adage that there is no time like the present applies to dialog box programming. If an operator supplies incorrect input, tell him or her as soon as possible. The best opportunity for informing the operator about a mistake is in the callback function associated with the input tile. You can tell the operator what went wrong in the error tile or by using the ALERT pop-up dialog box. Then refocus on the tile so that the operator can correct the entry or revert to a previous good value.

Suggestion 6: Provide an escape

A dialog box should have a Cancel button or some other way for the operator to escape from the dialog box without suffering a consequence. When using software, users often explore the interface and select things at random just to see what happens. If they want to back up to a higher level, the interface should allow it.

Suggestion 7: Program fast callback functions

Callback functions should be fast. They should perform basic error checks and then return control to the dialog box manager as soon as possible. Users quickly become impatient if a button or action is taking too long. When a long delay cannot be avoided, give operators a message, letting them know that things are proceeding. The dialog box error tile can be a useful messaging center for this purpose.

Dialog Box to AutoCAD and Back

A common requirement in a dialog box is to leave the box, perform some AutoCAD operation under the guidance of the operator, and then return to the dialog box with new values. For example, you might click a button to jump back to the AutoCAD screen to locate two points representing a distance value to be placed in an associated edit box, which is redisplayed after the selections are completed.

If you want a dialog box to appear, go away, and then come back again, program the dialog box in a loop. The processing of the dialog box remains the same. First you load it, and then you display it, fill it in, and start it. But now the contents from the "display it" task onwards are in a loop. That way, the dialog is redisplayed each time but loaded only once.

In the loop, use the current value of whatever variables the operator may have changed. For example, suppose that you have a dialog box that asks for a distance and a count. Additionally, a button locates the distance graphically. Even though you might think that operators will supply the distance before the count, do not expect them to do that. They may want to choose the count first and then click the distance button. The changed count value must be preserved when the dialog box reappears after the distance input.

Related to this is that your program should not exit with an error from the dialog box when a bad input is received. Instead, you should inform the operator and then return to the dialog box if possible. The only exception is when the Escape is pressed during graphics input, in which case, control is usually returned to the command line as soon as possible.

The remaining piece of the puzzle to discuss is the DONE_DIALOG subr. This subr allows you to describe an integer to be returned as the result of the START_DIALOG subr. START_DIALOG then returns as soon as your callback function is finished. Normally, DONE_DIALOG is the last step (or only step) in a callback function associated with a button from which you retire (close) the dialog box. After the dialog box is retired, it is up to your program to decide what happens next. You can use DONE_DIALOG to return from the dialog box like a modified OK or Cancel. Or you can use DONE_DIALOG to return from the dialog box so that your program can accept graphical input and then loop back to display the data.

Example: Creating the Final Dialog Box

In this section, you improve the dialog box introduced previously (Figures 11.5 and 11.6) for the rectangle generator. A new dialog box layout with buttons for graphics selection is shown in Figure 11.7. The Visual LISP code is provided in Listing 11.6, and the DCL code is shown in Listing 11.7. The RECT2 dialog box is similar to the one introduced previously, but this one contains the action attribute for many of the tiles. action establishes the Visual LISP code that is evaluated when the tile is manipulated. For this example, the only actions defined in the DCL relate directly to the setting of symbols that are part of the source code in Listing 11.6.

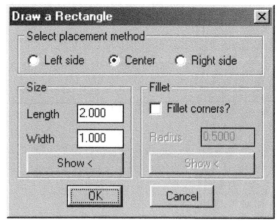

Figure 11.7 A sample dialog box, final version.

Listing 11.6 LSP source code for the final version.

```
(defun C:RE ( / DH FR FF SI XS YS TMP P1 P2)
 (RE_RESTORE_VARS)
 (setq DH (load_dialog "CHAP11.DCL"))
 (while (and (> DH 0) (new_dialog "RECT2" DH))
     (set_tile "FF" (if FF "1" "0"))
     (mode_tile "FR" (if FF 0 1))
     (mode_tile "PFR" (if FF 0 1))
     (set_tile "FR" (rtos FR))
     (set_tile "X" (rtos XS 2 3))
     (set_tile "Y" (rtos YS 2 3))
     (cond
         ((zerop SI) (set_tile "CE" "1"))
         ((= SI 2) (set_tile "LS" "1"))
         ((= SI 4) (set_tile "RS" "1"))
         )
     (action_tile "FF" "(RE_FILLET_FLIP $value)")
     (action_tile "PXY" "(done_dialog 100)")
     (action_tile "PFR" "(done_dialog 200)")
```

Listing 11.6 LSP source code for the final version. (Continued)

```lisp
        (setq TMP (start_dialog))
        (cond
            ((= TMP 0) ;cancel
             (setq DH (unload_dialog DH))
             )
            ((= TMP 1) ;ok
             (while (RE_DRAW_IT))
             (setq RE_SAVED_STATE_P (list XS YS FR)
                   RE_SAVED_STATE (+ SI (IF FF 1 0))
                   )
             )
            ((= TMP 100) ;show size rectangle
             (setq P1 (getpoint "\nCorner point: "))
             (if P1 (progn
                    (setq P2 (getcorner P1 " other corner: "))
                    (if P2
                       (setq XS (abs (- (car P2) (car P1)))
                             YS (abs (- (cadr P2) (cadr P1)))))))))
            ((= TMP 200) ;show fillet size
             (setq P1 (GETDIST "\nFillet size: "))
             (if P1 (setq FR P1)))
           )
         )
    (prin1)
  )
```

The source code for the LISP and DCL files is on the CD. This is the type of example that you could expand into something more application specific. It could evolve into a window generator, a mill plate generator, an electric pad, and much more. The structure of the program is essentially the standard for this sort of dialog box, where the operator may select a variety of input, show it graphically, and then quickly repeat the drawing task with the given parameters.

The first step in the C:RE function is to restore its internal variables. The RE_RESTORE_VARS function on the CD sets initial default values to the local symbols used in the dialog box. By isolating the setup activity in a subroutine, it is easy to append new logic to the initialization sequence if necessary.

Listing 11.7 DCL source code for the final version.

```
RECT2 : dialog { label = "Draw a Rectangle";
  : boxed_radio_row {
    label = "Select placement method";
    : radio_button {
      key = "LS";
      label = "Left side";
      action="(SETQ SI 2)";
      }
    : radio_button {
      key = "CE";
      label = "Center";
      action="(SETQ SI 0)";
      }
    : radio_button {
      key = "RS";
      label = "Right side";
      action="(SETQ SI 4)";
      }
    }
  : row {
    : boxed_column { label = "Size";
      : edit_box {
        key="X";
        label = "Length";
        edit_width=6;
        action="(SETQ XS (ATOF $VALUE))";
        }
      : edit_box {
        key="Y";
        label = "Width";
        edit_width=6;
        action="(SETQ YS (ATOF $VALUE))";
```

Listing 11.7 DCL source code for the final version. (Continued)

```
            }
      : button {
        key="PXY";
        label = "Show <";
        }
    }


    : boxed_column { label = "Fillet";
      : toggle {
        key = "FF";
        label = "Fillet corners?";
        }
      : edit_box {
        key="FR";
        label = "Radius";
        action="(SETQ FR (ATOF $VALUE))";
        }
      : button {
        key="PFR";
        label = "Show <";
        }
      }
    }
  ok_cancel;
}
```

The next step is to load the dialog box stored in the CHAPT11.DCL file on the CD. Copy the DCL file to your local working directory so that Visual LISP can locate it before running the example function. When programming a real-world application, you will want to establish a standard location for support files in your custom applications. If you have only a few, the AutoCAD Support directory is a good location.

A WHILE loop is started and iterates as long as the DH symbol has a value and the RECT2 dialog box can be loaded from the dialog source. LOAD_DIALOG returns a negative integer if it cannot load the dialog box, and NEW_DIALOG returns NIL if it cannot display the dialog box requested. The combination makes an excellent predicate (conditional test) in this type of program structure.

Inside the WHILE loop, SET_TILE and MODE_TILE establish the values of the tiles. Additionally, the ACTION_TILE subr defines several callback actions. These actions can be placed in the DCL or in the Visual LISP source code. This example demonstrates both approaches and also demonstrates my preference for placing in the code the code-based actions, such as the return values set by DONE_DIALOG and function calls. If I ever need to change these, they are in one place and I do not have to access the DCL file.

After the tiles have been prepared, the START_DIALOG subr is called so that the operator can interact with the dialog box. As values are changed, the symbols in Visual LISP are updated. When the buttons are clicked to show the data graphically, DONE_DIALOG is evaluated as the callback action. The values 100 and 200 are used in this example, but you can use any numbers as long as they are unique and do not interfere with the standard return values for OK and others. My preference is to use a larger number than I think Autodesk will ever need.

The START_DIALOG return value is placed in the TMP symbol. A COND then checks to see what was returned so that the appropriate action can take place. If the returning value in TMP is 0, the operator has indicated that he or she has finished drawing rectangles and wants to exit. DH is set to the value returned from the UNLOAD_DIALOG subr. That value is always NIL, so you are in essence setting up the DH symbol for an exit from the main WHILE loop.

When the values 100 and 200 are intercepted in CONS, the user is asked to locate the input. Note that the symbols holding the values destined for the dialog box are updated only after a successful input. For the sizes, two points are requested, and the differences in X and Y are calculated. For the corner fillet, all you need is a simple distance.

When the operator clicks OK, the program starts a tight WHILE loop containing a single function call that serves as a predicate and an operation. The RE_DRAW_IT function requests an input point and draws the rectangular figure described by the parameters. That makes this function set an example of a parametric drawing program. The source code for the RE_DRAW_IT function is on the CD.

Summary

Users are critical of the input and output of a program because this is where they interact with the software. Dialog boxes represent a Windows approach to a user interface that most AutoCAD operators are comfortable with for a number of reasons. Windows provides a standard that operators can learn with ease and then apply to new input. Dialog boxes are Visual LISP's way of carrying that into AutoCAD.

Working with the dialog box system takes practice in order to achieve the proficiency needed to design and build effective interfaces using Visual LISP. But it is not difficult to program despite the lack of a graphical dialog box design tool. Dialog box files are ASCII text descriptions of the layout of the dialog box. A dialog box is defined as a nested set of rectangles displayed for the purpose of user input.

Many types of input can be performed using a dialog box. Text, numbers, and easy selections make up the majority of dialog box input. Each of these (and other) input types has different attributes suited to the application of the item. Attributes give the dialog box character because they are used to define labels and sizes. The order in which something appears in the dialog box definition file is where it will appear in the dialog box.

All dialog boxes are referenced using a case-sensitive name. The components inside dialog boxes, called tiles, are also referenced using a case-sensitive name called a key. After the dialog box is displayed on the screen, Visual LISP modules that interface with dialog boxes do so through the keys.

Dialog boxes come to life using the various subrs in the callback functions that manipulate tiles. You can turn tiles on and off using the MODE_TILE and reset the value at any time using SET_TILE. During run time, values stored in the DCL can be retrieved using GET_ATTR and the current value of a tile using GET_TILE.

This chapter introduced just a few aspects of dialog boxes. You are strongly encouraged to seek out more examples and to learn how the various tiles and attributes can work for you. Visual LISP's online help system contains a comprehensive list of all aspects of tiles and dialog boxes.

CHAPTER 12

Working with AutoCAD Drawings

AutoCAD drawings contain entities that you can manipulate using Visual LISP. Due to the legacy of Visual LISP, you can access these entity objects using two different strategies. These strategies differ based on how you address drawing objects such as lines and arcs. The older but still effective approach uses entity data types first introduced in AutoLISP. The newer approach uses the same object-oriented programming techniques as Visual BASIC and Visual C++ when interfacing with AutoCAD. You can use these approaches separately or can combine them in your programs.

This chapter introduces the Visual LISP subrs for entity manipulations. The subrs require either an entity name or an entity object ID that points to an entity in the drawing. The name or ID is obtained directly from the drawing, so the first topic in the chapter is how data is stored in a drawing.

Entities, Selections, and Tables

You can access objects in a drawing database from three levels: entities, selections, and tables. Entity access involves entity names or object IDs obtained from the drawing as the result of a user selection on the screen, a sequential read of the drawing file, or a pointer stored in a selection or table entry.

A table is a collection of similar or related data. In the case of an AutoCAD drawing, a table is used to store layer specifics, line type details, and viewport data. Tables are used also to store block names, and block definitions are tables of entity objects. In Chapter 13, you explore several table-accessing subrs provided in Visual LISP. For now, it is important to understand that tables are used to store similar data in a drawing and that entity objects are stored in tables. A table of entities exists for the model space, for each layout space, and for each block defined in the drawing.

A selection is a picked or selected collection of entity objects. Selections are used frequently when working with a group of entity objects or interfacing with AutoCAD commands that contain the `Select objects` prompt, such as `ERASE`, `COPY`, and `MOVE`. In Chapter 13, you learn more about the special subrs for handling selections. I mention them here because selection sets are a source of entity names.

Selections and tables are the source of most of the entity names you will be using in your programs. User input and external databases may provide additional sources. When you use entity names stored in an external database, you use a form of the entity name called the entity handle.

Entity names, object IDs, entity handles, and more may seem overwhelming at first. But the concept is well structured, and after you see how it works, you will rarely get lost in the hierarchy.

Defining Entities in AutoCAD

The AutoCAD database contains variable-length table entries for entity objects. Each table entry contains an entity-type code defining what the entity object is and what data is expected from the entity itself. From the Visual LISP perspective, entity-type codes are descriptive strings, such as `LINE` or `ARC`. Database manipulations are handled inside AutoCAD, shielding Visual LISP programmers from the details.

When written to a file, a drawing database contains tables of entity objects. The table entries vary in length depending on what you store in them. Each contains coded links to relevant tables elsewhere in the database, such as the layer table and the styles table. Each table entry also contains additional data based on the type of entity. For example, a `LINE` entity has a from-point and a to-point, whereas an `ARC` entity has a center point, a radius, a start angle, and an end angle. The parameters in the file are converted to entity objects when you load the drawing into the editor. Basically, they become the properties of the entity objects and are used to calculate additional properties as needed by AutoCAD or your programs.

To access an entity object using Visual LISP, you must first load the drawing. Loading a drawing into the editor creates a table of entity names and object IDs. The table values point to the various entity details as stored on the disk or in memory. Each time you load a drawing, a new entity name or object ID sequence is assigned to the entities. As a result, there is a third member of the entity-object ID table called the entity handle. Entity handles are unique for each entity in a drawing and remain unique (and unchanged) in the drawing over time. External databases use entity handles to reference specific entity objects in the drawing database. When a drawing is opened in the drawing editor, a table is created that contains the entity handle, an entity name just created but assigned to a specific entity, and an object ID also assigned to the specific handle.

Given an entity name, you can now open and access details of the entity. You can retrieve what is known as an entity data list, which contains the basic parameters of the entity in an easy-to-access format for your programs. It does not contain the extra methods and properties associated with a given entity object. In other words, an entity data list does not allow you to take advantage of the object-oriented-programming features in Visual LISP, but it does permit access to the raw data for an entity object.

You can use an entity name also to get an object ID. Given an object ID, you can access the various properties and methods associated with the object. When you convert an entity name to an object ID, you are opening the object for access by your functions. If that same object is changed elsewhere, your program must retrieve the latest data. This is where accessing the object ID differs most from accessing the entity data list. Object access through the object ID always retrieves the latest data. On the other hand, an entity data list is created at the time you access the entity, and subsequent changes to the entity do not automatically change the contents of the entity data list. For most applications, this is not a critical situation.

The other difference between programming based on object IDs versus entity data lists is that the object methods and properties available to your program greatly exceed the basic raw parameter data found in the entity data list. As a result, most new applications for Visual LISP utilize object IDs.

Accessing Entities

Most Visual LISP subrs for handling entities start with the ENT characters. For example, the ENTLAST subr returns the entity name of the last object added to the drawing database. ENTLAST is frequently used to get the entity name of an entity just created using the COMMAND subr.

To obtain the first element in the drawing database, you use the ENTNEXT subr. When evaluated without parameters, ENTNEXT returns the first entity name in the active drawing. When evaluated with a single entity name parameter, ENTNEXT returns the next object in the database.

For example, Listing 12.1 shows a template for a function that reads every entity object in an AutoCAD drawing. The ENTNEXT subr is used twice: before the WHILE loop when it gets the first drawing entry and again at the end of the WHILE loop when the next entity is retrieved. ENTNEXT returns an entity name for the next entity object in the drawing or NIL when the last entity is encountered.

Listing 12.1 Reading entities in a drawing.

```
(DEFUN READ_DRAWING ( / EN)
    (SETQ EN (ENTNEXT)) ;get first drawing database entry
    (WHILE EN ;loop while EN has binding
        ; process entity name EN
        (SETQ EN (ENTNEXT EN)) ;get the next database entry
    ) ;end WHILE loop
)
```

Given an entity-handle string, the HANDENT subr returns an entity name that can be used to retrieve the specifics for the entity object. Handles are created at the same time that entities are created. They are strings that are unique in a given drawing. That is, no handle is repeated in a drawing, even if the entity object that was originally given the handle is erased. This makes handles well suited to point to entities in a drawing from an external database. Handles are obtained from entity data lists or as an object property after an entity object has been created.

To retrieve an entity data list, you use the ENTGET subr. Given an entity name, ENTGET returns a data list containing all the parameters for the entity. Entity data lists have a specific structure that makes accessing the parameters simple, although the structure may appear cryptic to someone just learning LISP. Entity data lists are stored as nested association lists, in which the first member of each sublist is an integer code number.

Entity Data Lists

As mentioned, ENTGET returns an entity data list, which contains the basic parameters of the individual entity object. To retrieve these items, you pull them out of the association list using a list-accessing subr called ASSOC. Entity lists are always association lists that use an integer key code as the first member of the sublists. To get a value from the list, you need to know the code number value for use with ASSOC.

The code numbers are the same as those found in the DXF (Drawing Exchange Format) file generated by AutoCAD. DXF files predate Visual LISP and even AutoLISP. When entity access was introduced in AutoLISP, it was a logical choice because the use of integers saved memory space in the computer and the coding system was well documented. Today, we have objects and little concern about memory restrictions, but the integer code system survives because of its succinct elegance.

Table 12.1 Common group codes.

Group code	Meaning
-1	Entity name
0	Entity type string
1, 2	Text strings, such as block names and dimensions
5	Entity handle string
6	Line type name string
7	Text style name
8	Layer name string
10	Primary point list
11 to 15	Additional point lists
38	Elevation
39	Thickness
40 to 48	Floating-point scalars such as text height and circle radius
50 to 58	Floating-point angular values, such as the start and end angle of an arc or the rotation of a block insert
62	Color code
67	Paper or model space indicator
70 to 78	Integer values for flags and counters
210	Entity coordinate system vector

The online DXF Reference Help library provides an easy way to learn about the DXF codes used in entity data lists. The code numbers are called group codes because they signify the beginning of a new grouping of data. Group codes are consistent from one entity object to the next. For example, the group codes 0, 8, and 10 signify the entity type, layer name, and primary point, respectively. To find out what type of entity is in the entity list, test the value associated with the 0 group code. Table 12.1 lists the group codes you will most likely encounter when working with entity data lists.

An example might make the entity list concept clearer. Listing 12.2 contains a command sequence with AutoCAD, with the operator's input in boldface. The entity data list has been spread out in the listing for readability; it appears as a single list sequence in AutoCAD when you duplicate the command sequence.

Listing 12.2 Generating an entity list.

```
Command: LINE
Specify first point: 1,1
Specify next point or [Undo]: 2,5
Specify next point or [Undo]:
Command: (entget (entlast))
((-1 . <Entity name: 4005fd58>)
 (0 . "LINE")
 (330 . <Entity name: 4005fcf8>)
 (5 . "2B")
 (100 . "AcDbEntity")
 (67 . 0)
 (410 . "Model")
 (8 . "0")
 (100 . "AcDbLine")
 (10 1.0 1.0 0.0)
 (11 2.0 5.0 0.0)
 (210 0.0 0.0 1.0))
```

All the details about the line-entity object just created are contained in the entity data list. Group code -1 is the entity name, 0 is the entity type, 10 is the starting point, 11 is the ending point, and so forth. (Refer to Table 12.1 and the online help to learn the details about the various group codes shown.) You might want to try the same thing with other entities in AutoCAD to learn how they are stored in the database.

Normally, you use ENTGET with a SETQ expression so that the entity data list is preserved for access in your program. After all, the entity data list exists mainly so that you can retrieve data from the AutoCAD database directly.

In Listing 12.2, note that the association list contains nested lists that are dotted pairs when they contain only two elements. The reason for this is twofold. First, the use of a dotted pair conserves memory space, which was a great concern in the earlier days of AutoLISP and that legacy has carried forward. Second, this allows programmers to use CDR to retrieve data associated with the sublist extracted through ASSOC. Thus, the (CDR (ASSOC)) expression is seen frequently in code that involves entity data lists. For example, the (CDR (ASSOC 0 EL)) expression returns the entity-type string from an entity list referenced by the EL symbol.

Entity lists can be modified and sent back to the AutoCAD drawing database. If the entity list is still valid and the base parameters have changed, the list is changed in the drawing. The ENTMOD subr takes an entity list as its sole argument and attempts to apply the modifications to the drawing database. To change an entity list and keep it valid, you use the list substitute subr, SUBST. By just substituting the elements you want to change, you can keep the list structure intact and not worry about rebuilding it from the individual pieces. Listing 12.3 contains an example function demonstrating this basic sequence of operations. In this listing, all data elements not found on layer 0 are changed to layer 0. The layer group code is 8. Note how the CONS expression is used to build the (8 . "0") dotted pair list inside the substitution expression. You could also use the quoted list, as in '(8 . "0"), for the same result.

Listing 12.3 Converting entities to layer 0.

```
(DEFUN LAYER0 ( / EN EL)
    (SETQ EN (ENTNEXT)) ;get first entity in drawing
    (WHILE EN
        (SETQ EL (ENTGET EN))
        (IF (/= (CDR (ASSOC 8 EL)) "0") ;not on layer zero
            (ENTMOD
                (SUBST (CONS 8 "0") (ASSOC 8 EL) EL)))
        (SETQ EN (ENTNEXT EN))
    )
)
```

Listing 12.3 is a nested programming example as well. The ENTMOD expression uses the modified entity data list returned from the SUBST expression. SUBST is substituting the result of the CONS expression with the value found using the ASSOC expression in the entity list. This happens in an IF expression that tests to see whether the layer name is not equal to 0.

ENTMOD is used to update an entity's internal storage. It updates the display of the object only if the entity is not part of a complex object such as a polyline. Thus, your program can update the various parts of a complex polyline and then update the display when all the changes have been completed. When you are ready to regenerate the display for an entity, use the ENTUPD subr with an entity name from the collection of entities that make up the complex object.

You use ENTUPD when you are changing complex, three-dimensional polyline objects or when updating attributes attached to a block insertion. Other entity objects in AutoCAD require only a single object definition and are updated in both the drawing database and the display with ENTMOD alone.

The ENTMAKE subr creates a new instance of an entity object. Given the majority of an entity data list, ENTMAKE attempts to create the entity described. When successful, a completed entity data list is returned. Should ENTMAKE fail, the result is NIL. Entity data lists are specific, and sometimes ENTMAKE needs more information than you think it needs. As a result, many programmers avoid using ENTMAKE and prefer to stick with COMMAND. The main advantages to using ENTMAKE are speed and control. ENTMAKE processes entities faster that COMMAND. In addition, ENTMAKE lets you know whether there was a problem, whereas COMMAND does not.

The easiest way I've found to use ENTMAKE is to copy the data list directly from AutoCAD. The process is somewhat backhanded, but it saves time. First, create a sample entity in an empty drawing using the normal AutoCAD operator commands. Then get the entity data list from the object, as in Listing 12.2. Using the Edit feature of the AutoCAD text window (press F2 to display the text window), copy that text to the Clipboard. Then paste the text in the VLIDE text editor window. Remove the parts you do not want (such as the entity name) and place a single quote at the beginning — and you have a template ENTMAKE entity data list ready to use.

Entity data lists provide the parameters that drive entity objects in AutoCAD, and you can write robust applications that involve these data elements. If you find entity lists confusing and bulky, however, you can use an alternative: entity objects.

Entity Objects

Starting in AutoCAD Release 13, Autodesk began converting all the entities in the drawing database to objects. By AutoCAD 2000, the entire system was object-oriented, which enabled a greatly expanded set of programming interfaces. Visual BASIC, Visual C++, and other languages could tie into the AutoCAD 2000 system through the ActiveX Automation tool kit.

ActiveX Automation is a program-to-program communications protocol defined by Microsoft that allows one program to serve as a host to another program and share internal components. These components are called objects and contain both properties (data) and methods (functions). Because Visual LISP can make use of ActiveX Automation, it can use the same automation tools.

Objects are defined in computer programming as containers of properties and methods. In Visual LISP, objects are typically represented as functions. All ActiveX Automation subrs are not initially loaded in Visual LISP. To make them available, your application must make a specific request using the VL-LOAD-COM subr. (Any additional calls to the subr return immediately.) After VL-LOAD-COM loads the additional utility routines, you can begin to take advantage of the VLAX (Visual LISP ActiveX) library of functions in Visual LISP.

A typical VLAX function includes an object reference of some type. You create an object reference from an entity name by using the VLAX-ENAME->VLA-OBJECT subr. For example, Listing 12.4

is a pair of utility functions that convert entity names and VLAX object references after testing to see whether the data type is proper.

Listing 12.4 Converting object references.

```
(DEFUN ENAME-OBJ (EN)
   (V1-LOAD-COM)
   (IF (= (TYPE EN) 'ename)
      (VLAX-ENAME->VLA-OBJECT EN)
   )
)
(DEFUN OBJ-ENAME (OBJ)
   (VL-LOAD-COM)
   (IF (= (TYPE OBJ) 'VLA-OBJECT)
     (VLAX-VLA-OBJECT->ENAME OBJ)
   )
)
```

You can use the VLAX-GET-PROPERTY, VLAX-PUT-PROPERTY, and VLAX-INVOKE-METHOD subrs to access the properties and methods associated with all ActiveX Automation objects, both outside and inside AutoCAD. But for objects inside AutoCAD, there is a good chance that a VLAX routine already exists. For example, consider a circle that has been opened as an object. You can use the VLA-GET-RADIUS subr instead of VLAX-GET-PROPERTY with RADIUS as an argument. The same is true for most methods in Visual LISP. In fact, Visual LISP has hundreds of VLAX functions. The best way to learn about them is to simply try them out as you encounter the requirement in an application.

When you look up objects in the help system, you are presented with Visual Basic terminology and examples. Simply use the name preceded by VLA-GET or VLA-PUT, depending on whether you are retrieving or storing the property. When working with the VLIDE, the entry changes color as you complete the typing of the property name. For example, if you type VLA-GET-RADIUS in the Console window, the entry changes color as you type VLA-GET and again as you complete the entire subr name. (If the text did not change color, VLIDE did not recognize the subr, which means you need to run VL-LOAD-COM.)

You might also want to use the reserved-word searching feature of the VLIDE. Type VLA-GET and a hyphen followed by the first one or two characters of the property name. To have the VLIDE assist in filling out the name, perform the name search. (After typing the first several characters of the subr you want, press Ctrl+Shift+spacebar. The Apropos window is displayed with matching names that you can then select.)

You can also test to see whether a property is available in your program. This may be useful when performing a task in which you cannot be certain about the type of entity. The

VLAX-PROPERTY-AVAILABLE-P subr returns NIL if the property name does not exist for a given object ID reference. A True result is returned if the property is available.

Object methods are equally simple to use, after you understand how to translate the Basic-oriented online help to Visual LISP. To use VLAX-INVOKE-METHOD, you supply the object ID reference and the name of the method, followed by any arguments that the method is expecting. And like properties, most common methods already have many subrs defined. Add the characters VLA to the front of the method name and provide the parameters as required, as in VLA-ADDCIRCLE or VLA-COPY.

Remember that when your program is communicating with the ActiveX Automation side of AutoCAD, you are communicating between two different programming environments. This difference is most visible when sending nonstandard data types such as point lists. ActiveX Automation understands real (floating-point) numbers, integers, and so on, but it does not understand the list type of data used in LISP. Consequently, you must convert the data from the list storage scheme to variants and arrays that can be recognized by the ActiveX interface.

The VLA functions that convert data from one type to another are shown in Table 12.2. Two data types in the ActiveX interface are different than in Visual LISP: the safe array and the variant. A safe array is like a list but it is a fixed size and contains only a single data type. A variant is a general-purpose storage container for holding data and can be made up of numbers, strings, pointers, safe arrays, and so on.

Table 12.2 VLA conversions.

Function	Description
VLAX-3D-POINT	Converts a list of numbers into a variant, safe array data type
VLAX-ENAME->VLA-OBJECT	Converts an entity name into an ActiveX object reference
VLAX-MAKE-SAFEARRAY	Creates a fixed array to be passed to an ActiveX method
VLAX-MAKE-VARIANT	Creates a variant data type to be passed to an ActiveX method
VLAX-SAFEARRAY->LIST	Converts a safe array to a list of data
VLAX-VARIANT-TYPE	Gets the type code number of a variant variable
VLAX-VARIANT-VALUE	Gets the value of a variant and places it in a LISP symbol reference
VLAX-VLA-OBJECT->ENAME	Converts the object reference to an entity name

In most cases, you will be using the conversion utilities only before and after you send data to one of the many subrs that utilize these data types. The simplest course to follow is to create a library of utility routines that solve the conversion and call problem, thereby shielding your primary application flow from excess code. The utility routines also improve the readability of your program by providing you with the ability to create names that best fit the application. For example, instead of having a utility routine named INSERT-BLOCK, you could use something meaningful such as PLACE-CLAMP or ADD-WINDOW.

So why go through all the troubles of converting entity information into object references? If you have not had the opportunity to explore the object library provided with AutoCAD's ActiveX Automation interface, you will be surprised and pleased to see all that is available to you. Powerful methods such as `IntersectWith` and valuable properties such as the area or length of an object are already calculated and available for your use.

Most of the improvements for programming AutoCAD, such as the Mechanical Desktop and Architectural Desktop tools, involve objects. Although VLA shortcut names may not be available for these objects, everything that is exposed can be accessed using the more generic `VLAX-GET-PROPERTY` and `VLAX-INVOKE-METHOD` subrs.

Examples: Accessing and Manipulating Entities

The two functions in this section are examples of accessing and manipulating entities. Both accomplish the same thing but use a different style. The first function uses an entity data list, and the second uses object references. The functions loop through the entire drawing model space and retrieve each entity. The text entities are tested to see whether the string contains a match to an input string (case specific). If a match is found, the object's color is changed to mark the text.

At the end of the examples, you can decide which you prefer and which you find less cryptic. Both examples represent the basic structure for navigating through an entire drawing and performing an edit or testing operation on a global basis.

Listing 12.5 contains the version of our text test and color mark function that uses entity names and entity lists. The function starts by having the operator enter the text string to be located. If the text entry in the `TXT` symbol is not an empty string, the operator is asked to supply a color code number. This number is used for entities that have text that matches `TXT`, the input string. A default value of 2 is presented with `GETINT` for the input. If `CLR` is `NIL`, nothing was input, indicating that the value 2 should be used.

Group code 62 signifies the color code in an entity data list. Using `CONS` to stick 62 to the front of the `CLR` color number builds a dotted pair that can be used in the entity data list. `TXT` is then updated for wildcard matching by adding asterisks on either side.

You are now ready to begin looping through the database, starting with the `ENTNEXT` subr (with no parameters). A `WHILE` loop iterates as long as `EN` has a value indicating that another object has been found in the drawing database.

Inside the `WHILE` loop, you start by using `ENTGET` to obtain the entity data list, which you then place in the `EL` symbol. `EL` now points to an entity data list, and you can test that to see the type of data you have just retrieved. Group code 0 holds the type of entity, and group code 1 holds the text data itself. After testing to see whether the entity data list contains a text entity and whether the text string matches the search string, the program moves on by using `ENTNEXT` again to get the next object in the database. `ENTNEXT` returns `NIL` when it is has exhausted the database.

Take a look at the `ENTMOD` expression in the middle of the code. This expression expects a modified entity list. I point out this expression because it shows how to add a new member to the entity data list if one does not already exist. The color code entry is optional, so it may not appear in an entity data list. This function tests to see whether it does by using the `ASSOC` subr. If `ASSOC` finds something with a 62 group code, the color code already exists. In that case, `SUBST` substitutes the

Listing 12.5 Locating text in a drawing.

```
(DEFUN C:TEXTFIND ( / TXT CLR EN EL)
  (SETQ TXT (GETSTRING 'T "\nText to locate: "))
  (IF (/= TXT "")
    (PROGN
      (SETQ CLR (GETINT "\nColor code <2>: "))
      (IF (NULL CLR) (SETQ CLR 2))
      (SETQ CLR (CONS 62 CLR)
            TXT (STRCAT "*" TXT "*")
            EN (ENTNEXT)
      )
      (WHILE EN
        (SETQ EL (ENTGET EN))
        (IF (AND (= (CDR (ASSOC 0 EL)) "TEXT")
                 (WCMATCH (CDR (ASSOC 1 EL)) TXT))
          (ENTMOD
            (IF (ASSOC 62 EL)
              (SUBST CLR (ASSOC 62 EL) EL)
              (APPEND EL (LIST CLR)))))
        (SETQ EN (ENTNEXT EN))
      ) ;End While EN
  )) ;End IF PROGN
  (PRINC)
)
```

CLR value with the current group code 62 data. If ASSOC finds nothing, the CLR value is appended to the list after being nested another level deeper in the list so that the APPEND list is proper.

The frequent use of CDR and ASSOC in the code makes the entity name and data list version of this example look complex and forbidding for the beginning Visual LISP programmer. The good news is that the template remains the same for most similar programs — all you change are the group code numbers. And those values can be obtained from the online help references provided in the VLIDE.

The next listing is similar, but you process objects instead of entities one at a time. Listing 12.6 contains the C:OTF (object text find) function. It starts in the same basic way as Listing 12.5, by asking for the text to locate and the color number to assign to that text. The similarities stop when the VL-LOAD-COM expression is evaluated.

Listing 12.6 Changing text, object version.

```
(DEFUN C:OTF ( / TXT CLR)
  (SETQ TXT (GETSTRING 1 "\nText to locate: "))
  (IF (/= TXT "")
    (PROGN
      (SETQ CLR (GETINT "\nColor to change to <2>: "))
      (IF (NULL CLR) (SETQ CLR 2))
      (SETQ TXT (STRCAT "*" TXT "*"))
      (VL-LOAD-COM)
      (VLAX-MAP-COLLECTION
        (VLA-GET-MODELSPACE
          (VLAX-GET-ACTIVEDOCUMENT
            (VLAX-GET-ACAD-OBJECT)))
        'OTF-TEXT)
  )) ;end IF progn
  (PRINC)
)
;
(DEFUN OTF-TEXT (OBJREF)
  (IF (VLAX-PROPERTY-AVAILABLE-P
        OBJREF 'Textstring T)
    (IF
      (WCMATCH
        (VLA-GET-TEXTSTRING OBJREF)
        TXT)
      (VLA-PUT-COLOR OBJREF CLR)
    ) ;end IF wcmatch
  ) ;end IF property
)
```

The next expression, VLAX-MAP-COLLECTION, is a looping expression that works very much like the MAPCAR subr. That is, it allows you to process a collection of data, such as all the entities in model space. Each entity is processed one at a time. The function in Listing 12.6 gets the entities in model space from the current document in the current AutoCAD application session. Each entity is in turn passed as a parameter to the OTF-TEXT function, which is also shown in Listing 12.6. This function simply tests the object reference to see whether the property named TEXTSTRING exists for the object. If so, the text string is compared to the input test string; if there is a match, the color is set for the object.

For the most part, the object-oriented version is a lot easier to describe, although the VLAX and deeper hierarchy tracings make it more difficult to digest at first. You may find it easier to work with object-oriented concepts after you get accustomed to testing only whether something is available. Some day, Autodesk might improve Visual LISP by exposing the function or property you were missing. If you program the object-oriented interfaces properly, the code you write should run for many future releases of AutoCAD (unless they make drastic changes).

Summary

Entity manipulation is an important aspect of AutoCAD productivity programming. This introduction scratched the surface of object-based programming and showed the basics behind both that style and processing based on entity data lists. Visual LISP has a long legacy, so you will probably encounter examples that use entity data lists and names. Therefore, having a firm grasp on how they work is important. Newer code most likely takes advantage of the more recent object-oriented style of programming because it provides a more elegant way to express problems to the computer.

Execution speed is rarely an issue these days because the speed and capacity of desktop machines far exceed the requirements of this style of programming. The only real difference in speed is when you use the VL-LOAD-COM expression, because the computer slows down for a few moments while it loads the support modules. And that happens only once — future calls to VL-LOAD-COM do not require any processing time.

You also looked at how entity names and object IDs are related to the drawing system. The entity handle was presented as a solution for external file interfaces because an entity retains that value when saved and reloaded in a later editing session. Handles are strings and must be converted to entity names and then object IDs before they can be used in additional subrs.

In the next chapter, you look at selection sets, which are groups of entity objects. The entity processing methods introduced here work also with the entity name values obtained from selection sets.

CHAPTER 13

Using Selection Sets and Tables

In this chapter, you explore groups of entities or related information. There are basically two kinds of data in this regard: data that you want to use temporarily and discard when finished, and data that must stay so that it can be referenced from other locations in the drawing database. A selection set is a temporary grouping of entity objects. A block, which is defined in the block table, is a more permanent grouping of entity objects.

Using Selection Sets

A selection set is a specific data type in Visual LISP known as a PICKSET. AutoCAD operators use selection sets all the time in commands such as MOVE, COPY, and ROTATE. Whenever AutoCAD prompts to Select objects, you are building a selection set.

You can create a selection-set object in Visual LISP in several ways. You can use the SSADD subr by itself and create an empty selection set. For example, the (SETQ SS1 (SSADD)) expression creates a new, empty selection set referenced by the SS1 symbol. You can use SSADD also to add entities one at a time to a selection set by providing the entity name values as parameters along with the existing selection-set reference.

Listing 13.1 is a simple function that builds a selection set by reading through a drawing looking for specific entities. (Note that this task can be performed using a better approach; this listing is provided only as a simple example.)

The first step is to create a new selection set by calling SSADD with no parameters. In the WHILE loop that reads through the drawing, SSADD is used again but this time with the entity name and the selection-set reference.

The result returned from SSADD is the selection set, and thus the second occurrence could have been used in a SETQ but that would have been redundant. SSADD and the other selection-set edit tools are unique in Visual LISP in that they pass the reference, not the value. Therefore, changes made to the reference are global. If both SS1 and SS2 point to the same selection set and a new

Listing 13.1 Searching for circles.

```
(DEFUN LOOK_FOR_CIRCLES ( )
  (SETQ SS1 (SSADD) ;emtpy selection start
        EN (ENTNEXT) ;first entity
)
  (WHILE EN
    (SETQ EL (ENTGET EN))
    (IF (= (CDR (ASSOC 0 EL)) "CIRCLE")
      (SSADD EN SS1)
      )
    (SETQ EN (ENTNEXT EN))
    )
  (IF (> (SSLENGTH SS1) 0) SS1)
  )
```

entity is added using the reference for SS1, accessing SS2 would also reflect the change. This is unusual for LISP programmers, but the situation exists because of the special nature of selection sets. Selection sets are AutoCAD objects, and Visual LISP is merely referencing a gateway to them. When the contents of the selection set are altered at the AutoCAD level, all accesses through the gateway show the same contents.

Another way to create a selection set is to use the SSGET subr. With no parameters, SSGET prompts the user to Select objects. The operator is then free to select as many or as few objects as desired using any valid object-selection mechanism in AutoCAD. SSGET returns a new selection set every time unless there was a problem or the operator selected nothing.

SSGET has many options, such as filters for controlling what objects the operator selects. You can also run SSGET in automatic mode, in which object selection is made using a wide range of parameters supplied by your program. I only touch on a few of the aspects of SSGET in the examples and in this chapter. I strongly recommend that you refer to the online help to learn more about this powerful tool.

Accessing a selection set

In addition to adding an entity object to a selection set, you need be able to retrieve entities, remove them, and test them to see whether they are already included in the set. The SSNAME subr extracts entity names given the offset as an integer. The SSDEL subr removes an entity object from a selection set. SSMEMB determines whether a given entity object is already part of an existing set. The syntax for SSMEMB and SSDEL resembles the SSADD subr. The entity name is supplied before the selection set in the parameter list. For example, if you have an entity name in the EN symbol and a selection set in the SS1 symbol, the (SSMEMB EN SS1) expression returns true (T) if the EN entity is part of the selection set. If EN is not in SS1, the SSMEMB expression returns NIL.

The (SSDEL EN SS1) expression removes the EN entity from the SS1 selection set. Note that SSDEL removes the entity from the selection set, not from the drawing. Also, if the entity was highlighted at some point in the editing process, it is not regenerated. Highlighting and regeneration are specific tasks performed by the AutoCAD editor under your guidance.

SSNAME retrieves entities from a selection set one at a time using an integer offset into the set. The offset starts at 0 and increments by 1 for each object. The second element in the selection set is at offset 1, the third element is at offset 2, and so on until the last element in the list, which is at an offset determined by subtracting 1 from the total number of items in the selection set. Thus, to use the SSNAME subr effectively, you need to know how many elements are in a given selection set. That information is obtained from SSLENGTH, which returns an integer count of the total number of entity objects in a set. Subtracting 1 from the result of SSLENGTH gives you the offset of the last element in the set for the purpose of SSNAME.

Listing 13.2 shows the SSLENGTH, SSNAME, SSMEMB, and SSDEL subrs in use. This function filters entity objects out of an existing selection set. When the routine is finished, only entity-object types identified in the KEEPTHESE list remain in the selection set. For example, to clean the SS1 selection set of everything but lines, arcs, and circles, you might call the function as follows:

```
(SS_CLEAN SS1 ("LINE" "ARC" "CIRCLE"))
```

Listing 13.2 Filtering entity objects from a selection set.

```
(DEFUN SS_CLEAN (SS1 KEEPTHESE / CNT1 EL)
  (SETQ CNT1 (SSLENGTH SS1))
  (IF (NOT (LISTP KEEPTHESE))
    (SETQ KEEPTHESE (LIST KEEPTHESE)))
  (REPEAT CNT1
    (SETQ EL
      (ENTGET
        (SSNAME SS1
              (SETQ CNT1 (1- CNT1)))))))
    (IF (NOT (MEMBER (CDR (ASSOC 0 EL)) KEEPTHESE))
      (SSDEL (SSNAME SS1 CNT1) SS1)))
  (IF (> (SSLENGTH SS1) 0) SS1)
  )
```

The function starts by getting the length of the selection set and storing it in CNT1. The KEEPTHESE parameter is tested to see whether it is a list. If not, it is converted to one. You are now ready to process the contents of the selection set. You already know the total number of members, and the total number to be processed will not change during the operation of this function, even though you may change the total number of entity objects in the selection set. As a result, the REPEAT loop is perfect for your needs.

When processing a selection set with an operation that will result in the removal of entities from the set, you should always start at the end of the set and work towards the front. Remember that selection sets are global and that you use an offset into the set when processing. If you started at the beginning and then removed an entity, the counter would skip the next entry, requiring additional logic to maintain the counter. However, if you start at the end and remove one, the next one down is still there. It didn't move; all the ones on top that are already processed moved instead. The SS_CLEAN function in Listing 13.2 does just this. It starts at the end of the selection set and works its way to the front.

In the REPEAT loop, the EL entity list is filled from the entity information stored at the location indicated by CNT1 minus 1. To understand these expressions, go to the middle parentheses, where CNT1 is decreased. CNT1 starts as the number of entity objects in the SS1 selection set. It is decreased by 1 because it will now be an offset into the SS1 selection set. SSNAME retrieves the entity name for ENTGET to use. ENTGET returns the entity data list to place in EL.

Given the entity list, the entity type (group code 0) is tested to see whether it is a member of the KEEPTHESE list. If not, the entity object at position CNT1 is removed from the SS1 selection set. This process is repeated for the entire selection set. At the end of the REPEAT loop, SS1 is returned as a result of the function.

Listing 13.2 is just an example; there are much better ways to produce a purified selection set using filters with SSGET. Next, you look at the power of SSGET.

Getting a selection set

The SSGET subr is a versatile tool. When used with any parameters, it displays the Select objects: prompt and allows the operator to choose objects from the display in the same manner as the COPY or MOVE command.

If the first parameter to SSGET is a filter list, the rules of the filter list are applied to the selection process. This allows you to construct an input function that accepts only a particular entity type. Listing 13.3, for example, allows for the input of only LINE objects. A filter looks just like a partial entity data list. In this simple example, the function builds a filter list consisting of only the entry for a LINE entity type.

Listing 13.3 Selecting only lines.

```
(DEFUN SEL_LINES (PRMPT / SS1 FLTR)
  (SETQ FLTR '((0 . "LINE")))
  (PROMPT PRMPT)
  (SSGET FLTR)
  )
```

Listing 13.3 also demonstrates a type of utility routine that can be created to make controlled object selection easier. If your application calls the operator to select only certain types of objects, this sort of utility function can greatly improve the readability of your program code.

When the function inListing 13.3 is evaluated, the PRMPT string is displayed followed by the Select objects: command prompt. But instead of allowing operators to select anything, they can select only lines. Anything else is rejected during the selection process.

You can use SSGET also to select objects in the drawing automatically, without operator control. If the first parameter to SSGET is a character string, the selection process is by parameter control only. Table 13.1 lists the most frequently used characters supported by SSGET.

Table 13.1 Common SSGET character-string options.

Character string	Meaning
C	Crossing
CP	Crossing polygon
F	Fence selection
I	Implied selection
L	Last entity
P	Previous selection set
W	Window
WP	Window polygon
X	Use filter

The parameters that follow the character string depend on the character string used. In the case of C or W, two point lists are needed to define the limits of the window. Use the online help system to learn more about all the character-string options and parameters for SSGET.

The most powerful feature of the SSGET subr is the filter option. With filters, you can build well-defined selection sets from a drawing. For example, suppose that you need to find all the circles on the POSTS layer that are 12 inches (drawing units) in diameter. The key to creating a filter fitting these criteria is to construct a partial entity data list. For the type of entity and the layer, the group codes are 0 and 8, respectively. The group code for the radius is 40. The filter list would appear as follows:

```
((0 . "CIRCLE")(8 . "POSTS")(40 . 6.0))
```

This can be read as a logical AND sequence. For an object to be included in the selection process, it must meet all these specifics. If any one of the specifics is not matched, the object is not added to the selection set.

If you want to obtain all the circles on the POSTS layer that are 12 inches or greater in diameter, the filter just described will not work because it returns only circles with an exact size match. You need to add some logic to the filter for testing the parameters, and that is provided with the -4 group code. The -4 group code options are special parts of a filter intended to make the SSGET function more precise. Specifically, the -4 group code provides a mechanism for comparison testing in the selection process. The following filter searches for all circles on the POSTS layer that are 8 inches or greater in diameter:

```
((0 . "CIRCLE")(8 . "POSTS")(-4 . ">=")(40 . 6.0))
```

Logic options in the -4 group code include all the basic numeric-relation tests, such as less than, greater than, equal, and bit testing.

You can combine tests using Boolean combinations such as OR and AND with the -4 group code. Suppose that you want to obtain all the circle objects as before, but this time within a range of 6 to 12 inches in diameter. The filter would be as follows:

```
((0 . "CIRCLE")(8 . "POSTS")(-4 . "<AND")(-4 . ">=")(40 . 3.0)(-4 . "<=")(40
. 6.0)(-4 . "AND>"))
```

The AND conjunction is used with two -4 tests of the radius settings.

To build complex filters, start by writing down the logic you want to apply to the search. For example, you would start the circle search by saying that you want CIRCLE objects on the POSTS layer. Those two are easy because you only need to add the group codes 0 and 8. The more difficult part is the radius description. You want circles with a diameter of 6 inches to 12 inches, which means you want a radius between 3 and 6. Expressed in logical terms, you seek circles with a radius greater than or equal to 4 and less than or equal to 6. In pseudocode, you would write (Radius >= 3.0) AND (Radius <= 6.0). Then, in typical LISP fashion, you move the AND to the front, followed by the tests. Another AND appears at the end as well to balance the code and allow for nesting of tests.

Filters are evaluated differently than LISP code itself. If the format is wrong, the entire expression is invalid. For easy testing and subsequent maintenance, I suggest that you isolate functions involving filters. Filters are one of the more powerful tools in tasks related to automated editing, data importing, and data exporting.

A simple filter that uses a combination test is shown in Listing 13.4, in which the operator is asked to select arcs or circles. The example listing shows how the combination tests look using the -4 group code. Another way to set up the filter shown in Listing 13.4 is to use a comma, as in the following:

```
'((0 . "ARC,CIRCLE"))
```

This filter accomplishes the same thing but with fewer lines of code. It is nice to know that Visual LISP often has more than one way to solve a problem.

To free selection-set memory when you are finished with it, set all references to NIL. This does not automatically free the memory, but it does orphan the set. Orphaned sets are cleaned up when the Visual LISP memory manager determines that it needs more memory for something. The operation of cleaning up memory, called garbage collection, is automatic. You can force a garbage collection using the GC subr, but this practice is discouraged. Visual LISP cleans up after itself on a regular basis and programs that invoke GC just slow things down.

Listing 13.5 demonstrates most of the selection-set subrs discussed in this chapter. This utility routine merges two selection sets. The SS2 selection set is merged into the SS1 selection set, and any objects not merged are retained in SS2. The routine operates the same as most selection-set-based functions. SSLENGTH gets the length of the merging selection set because that is the one we need to operate on. A REPEAT loop is started to go through each member in SS2.

Listing 13.4 Selecting with a filter.

```
(DEFUN SEL_ARCS-N-CIRCLES (PRMPT / SS1 FLTR)
  (SETQ FLTR
    '((-4 . "<OR")
      (0 . "ARC")
      (0 . "CIRCLE")
      (-4 . "OR>"))
  )
  (PROMPT PRMPT)
  (SSGET FLTR)
  )
```

Listing 13.5 Merging selection sets.

```
(DEFUN SS_MERGE (SS1 SS2 / CNT2)
  (SETQ CNT2 (SSLENGTH SS2))
  (REPEAT CNT2
    (IF (NOT
          (SSMEMB
            (SSNAME
              (SETQ CNT2 (1- CNT2))
              SS2)
            SS1))
      (PROGN
        (SSADD (SSNAME SS2 CNT2) SS1)
        (SSDEL (SSNAME SS2 CNT2) SS2)
    )) ;end if progn
  ) ;end repeat
  (LIST SS1 SS2)
  )
```

Inside the REPEAT loop, SSNAME extracts the entity name of a member of the selection set. Because you are using an offset to access the list (base 0), 1 is subtracted from the counter. The nesting of SETQ inside the SSNAME subr is a feature of Visual LISP, although some would argue that it makes the code appear cryptic.

SSMEMB tests the entity name extracted with SSNAME against the SS1 selection set. If the entity is not already a member of SS1, the SSADD subr adds the entity object to the SS1 selection set and SSDEL removes it from the SS2 selection set.

The result of this function is a list containing the new SS1 and SS2 selection sets. As you can see, selection-set manipulation is quite easy, which makes sense because it is such an important aspect of Visual LISP programming.

The data in a selection set consists solely of entity names. You then use the entity name to obtain the entity list, which contains the parameters of the entity. Some of the parameters, such as the layer name, are just a name and do not contain any other information. For those details, such as color and line type, you must turn to the tables in AutoCAD.

Using Tables

A table is a collection of similar items that are referenced more than once in the drawing. Layer properties, line type descriptions, text styles, dimensions, and blocks are some of the tables in the AutoCAD system. Table definitions exist for anything that has a one-to-many relationship. Changing the description of that one item will result in multiple graphics objects changing. If you change the color of a layer, the objects on that layer change color because each object by default references the table for that type of information. (You can set an object's color code for an override value, however, in which case the layer change would not change the object's color.)

Like entity data lists, table data is manipulated using an association list structure. When you access a table entry, it is formatted as an association list, with the primary data available by group code. You retrieve these entries using the TBLSEARCH and TBLNEXT subrs. TBLSEARCH searches a table for a given entry. The table name must be specified, such as "LAYER" or "BLOCK", along with a string containing the name of the entry, such as the layer name or block insert name. TBLSEARCH returns NIL if it does not find a match or the association list of the entry if a match is found.

TBLNEXT steps through a table sequentially. The table name is the first parameter to the function. With an additional non-NIL parameter, TBLNEXT resets the sequential read of the table to the beginning of the table. Subsequent TBLNEXT subr calls without the extra parameter (just the table name) return each table entry one at a time in the order in which they were originally defined to the drawing. Thus, (TBLNEXT "LAYER" T) returns the first table entry in the layer table. (TBLNEXT "LAYER") returns the next entry in the table or has a value of NIL when the last table entry has been processed.

TBLSEARCH and TBLNEXT access table entries. To update the data list back into the table, use ENTMOD. To construct new entries, use ENTMAKE, although you must be precise, just as you are when using ENTMAKE to create entities.

The contents of the AutoCAD drawing database tables can be found in the online help in the DXF section for the tables. As in the entity data lists, group codes are associated with the names and parameters that make up the table entry. For example, consider the layer table entries in Table 13.2. The layer table data list does not have nearly as many entries as a typical entity data list.

Table 13.2 Entries for the layer table.

Group Code	Contents
0	Constant string value of "LAYER"
2	String value of the layer name; must be unique
70	Layer generation flags as a bitmap, as follows: Bit 1: Layer is currently frozen Bit 2: Layer will be frozen in all new viewports Bit 4: Layer is locked Bit 16: Layer defined due to XREF binding Bit 32: XREF binding resolved properly if bit 16 also set Bit 64: Layer is in use by at least one entity in drawing
62	Color code number for the layer
6	Line type name associated with the layer; this name must appear in the line type table before being referenced in a layer table entry

Example: Finding Points in a Block Definition

The block table is of particular importance in the creation of many applications. A block is a collection of graphics that you can reuse in a drawing. In the drawing, a block is referenced as an insert entity object. Insert entity objects contain insertion parameters, including the insert point, layer, rotation angle, scaling factors, and name of the block. You use the block name to retrieve the block definition from the block table. The block definition contains the graphics used to define the block. Thus, if you need to locate a point inside a block, you must go through a series of references to obtain the specific point.

Given a block name, you can use TBLSEARCH with the block table to find the table-record entry for the block. The block-table record contains a -2 group code attached to an entity name. Use ENTNEXT with this entity name to begin reading the entity names of the block-definition geometry. When ENTNEXT returns NIL, you have reached the end of the definition for that block.

An example of accessing entities inside a block is provided in Listing 13.6 with the DRILL_POINTS function. This function has one argument, the name of the block in which you want to search. The search routine looks for circle entity objects inside the block definition and returns a list containing the center point and radius of all circles found.

TBLSEARCH retrieves a block-table record containing the block name. If the search of the block table is not successful, the value in EL is NIL and the function ends. Otherwise, EL references a data list as returned from the table search activity, and in that data list is the -2 group code entry containing the first entity name of the block definition. The EN symbol is set to the value of the -2 group code and is then used in a WHILE loop to iterate through the entire collection of entities for the block. While EN has a value, the loop repeats.

Listing 13.6 Finding points inside a block.

```
(DEFUN DRILL_POINTS (BLKNAM / EN EL PTS)
  (SETQ EL (TBLSEARCH "BLOCK" BLKNAM))
  (IF EL
    (PROGN
      (SETQ EN (CDR (ASSOC -2 EL)))
      (WHILE EN
        (SETQ EL (ENTGET EN)
              EN (ENTNEXT EN))
        (IF (= (CDR (ASSOC 0 EL)) "CIRCLE")
          (SETQ PTS
            (CONS
              (LIST
                (CDR (ASSOC 10 EL)) ;center
                (CDR (ASSOC 40 EL)) ;radius
              )
              PTS))))
      PTS
  )) ;end IF PROGN
)
```

In the loop, ENTGET retrieves the entity details, and ENTNEXT positions EN to the next entity object in the block definition. Note that the values of point lists in entity data lists are relative to the base point of the block. This is important if you are using the points to define locations in the drawing after the block has been inserted. I return to this in the next example.

Given the entity list in EL, the type of object is checked to see whether it is a circle. If it is, the center point (group code 10) and radius (group code 40) are saved in a list. These two data elements are merged into a single list that is added to the PTS master list. The resulting PTS list has the following structure:

```
(((point-n) radius-n) ... ((point-2) radius-2) ((point-1) radius-1))
```

The first point and radius pair is added at the end of the list due to the use of the CONS subr to construct the data list. The WHILE loop then continues in this fashion until it encounters the last entity object in the block definition.

Example: Converting Block Points

When working with blocks and points inside blocks, you need to convert the data points stored in the block to the coordinates inside the drawing where the block is inserted. The utility program in Listing 13.7 is one possible solution for solving two-dimensional point conversions. Given an entity name of a block insert and a list of data points, the function applies the rotation, scaling, and translation needed to convert the points to match the insert point of the block.

A point is a list of two or three real numbers. You can rotate a point about some other point (normally the origin), scale the axes of the point, or move the point to a new relative position through translation. Performing each operation is a matter of applying some basic math.

The translation is the easiest. Just add the point ordinate values to the offset values. For example, shift point (10 15 0) by (5 –5 0), and you have (15 10 0). This is the same as the following expression:

```
(MAPCAR '+ '(10 15 0) '(5 -5 0))
```

Scaling is only a matter of multiplying the value by the scale factor before applying the translation or rotation.

Rotation causes the most confusion. If you want to rotate a coordinate about the origin and you know the angle from the positive x-axis direction (measured counterclockwise), it is a simple formula series. To compute the new X-ordinate value, you multiply the cosine of the rotation angle by the scaled X-ordinate. Then you subtract the value resulting from the multiplication of the sine of the rotation angle by the scaled Y-ordinate. The Y-ordinate is computed in much the same manner. Multiply the sine of the rotation angle by the scaled X-ordinate and then add to that the result of multiplying the cosine by the scaled Y-ordinate. These equations can be expressed mathematically as follows:

```
New_X = (Cosine(Rotation) * X-scale * Old_X) - (Sine(Rotation) * Y-scale *
Old_Y) + Insert_X
    New_Y = (Sine(Rotation) * X-scale * Old_X) + (Cosine(Rotation) * Y-scale *
Old_Y) + Insert_Y
```

Listing 13.7 applies the preceding transformation to a list of points in PTS after obtaining the parameters from the insert-block-entity object. EN is either an entity name or the entity data list of a block insert; the first section of code checks the data type of EN. If EN is an entity name, ENTGET retrieves the entity data list and places it in EL. If EN is a list, it is set to EL. Otherwise, EL does not have a binding because it is a local symbol with respect to the function and thus has an initial value of NIL.

The program tests the EL value to see whether it contains an entity data list. First it checks to see whether the EL symbol evaluates to something other than NIL. Next it checks to see whether an association group 0 is in the list. If the list is not an association list, this test fails and the AND expression fails immediately. Finally, the association group 0 is tested to see whether it contains the string "INSERT", indicating a block-insert object. If all these tests pass, the function proceeds to transform the coordinates.

With a valid insert-object-entity data list in EL, the parameters for the insert point (code 10), rotation angle (code 50), and scaling factors (codes 41, 42, and 43) can be retrieved and placed in

Listing 13.7 Converting block-definition points to insert parameters.

```
(DEFUN INS_TRANS (EN PTS / EL RT XS YS ZS IP COSRT SINRT)
 (COND
   ((= (TYPE EN) 'ENAME)
    (SETQ EL (ENTGET EN)))
   ((LISTP EN)
    (SETQ EL EN)))
 (IF (AND EL
          (ASSOC 0 EL)
          (= (CDR (ASSOC 0 EL)) "INSERT"))
   (SETQ IP (CDR (ASSOC 10 EL))
         RT (CDR (ASSOC 50 EL))
         XS (CDR (ASSOC 41 EL))
         YS (CDR (ASSOC 42 EL))
         ZS (CDR (ASSOC 43 EL))
         COSRT (COS RT)
         SINRT (SIN RT)
         PTS (MAPCAR
               '(LAMBDA (PT)
                  (LIST
                    (+ (CAR IP)
                       (* (CAR PT) XS COSRT)
                       (* (CADR PT) YS SINRT -1.0))
                    (+ (CADR IP)
                       (* (CAR PT) XS SINRT)
                       (* (CADR PT) YS COSRT))
                    0.0))
               PTS)
   ) ;end SETQ
 ) ;end IF
 PTS ;return modified data list
)
```

local symbols. To save a little time during the next operation of the program, the cosine and sine of the rotation angle are also computed and saved in local symbols.

The next step is the transformation of all the data points. MAPCAR loops through each point and then applies the code in the LAMBDA expression. LAMBDA receives each data point in PT and then performs the calculations described previously. The result of each calculation set is returned as a result of MAPCAR to the PTS variable, which is returned as the result of the function.

This function converts a series of data points from the block definition (as in Listing 13.6) to points that relate to where a given instance of the block is inserted. You can use this to create you own intelligent object snaps for specialized blocks.

Summary

Selection sets and tables are collections of related information. You use selection sets to group entity objects for common manipulation. Tables, on the other hand, store information referenced elsewhere in the drawing. Both are equally important when working with AutoCAD applications that involve entities.

The operator or a program can create selection sets. When created by the operator, the SSGET subr allows for any style of object selection, including individual entities or polygon borders. You can also apply a filter to SSGET to force the operator to select only specific entity types. Filters are a powerful tool in selection-set building because they permit applications to dig out specific data from a drawing automatically or with an operator's assistance. You can use filters also with parameter-driven selection-set methods by using a coded character, followed by the parameters needed to fulfill the command requirements and an optional filter.

The SSDEL, SSNAME, and SSADD subrs are used to manipulate selection sets. These subrs remove from, retrieve from, and add to a selection set, respectively. Selection sets only store entity-object names; you must use the ENTGET subr to get the data for each under program control.

Tables are a little easier to manage. You use the TBLSEARCH and TBLNEXT subrs to retrieve data from them. You use the ENTMOD and ENTMAKE subrs to update a table's contents from within a program, just as you use them to manipulate entity-object data in the drawing database. Table entries, like entity data lists, are group-code-based association lists that use dotted pairs for non-list data. Generally, table data lists are much shorter because they contain only common information referenced by name elsewhere in the database.

The last topic you explored was the block table and how it points to entity data objects that define the block. A few utility functions were presented to show you how to utilize the tables; you can expand these functions to suit your application requirements.

Selection-set and table manipulations are frequently required when programming advanced AutoCAD applications. Sometimes, you will need to be creative when saving selection-set information and other data related to your program. Blocks and expanded data dictionaries (Chapter 14) offer two possible ways you can save data in a drawing for use in multiple edit sessions.

Saving and Sharing Data

Your applications will probably require data that extends beyond the basic geometry available in AutoCAD drawings. In addition, you will probably need to preserve some data between multiple drawing edit sessions. The normal operation of a Visual LISP program is to be loaded and then evaluated. When the evaluation is finished, data may be left in global variables that can be accessed immediately when the program is restarted.

But what happens to global data when a drawing is closed? In this chapter, you look at that situation and learn ways in which you can preserve data in a drawing to use in a later run of the same program with the same drawing. Data can be stashed away in several different places in a drawing, and each has its advantages and disadvantages.

Application Exposure

An application tied to a drawing most likely needs to store data associated with the drawing. For example, suppose that you have an application involving components with parameters. In many cases, you can use blocks with attributes to carry the parameters.

But what are your options when a block is not suitable, such as when you are using polylines to define a path. As is typical of Visual LISP, you have several options. The option you choose depends on how exposed you want your application to other applications and AutoCAD operators. An application is considered exposed if entities and data can be manipulated outside the program using other tools.

Most Visual LISP applications that rely on or create AutoCAD entity objects are exposed to AutoCAD command edits. That means an AutoCAD operator can change or remove entity objects, possibly compromising the application's integrity. Leaving global variables on the heap in hopes that they will be proper when restarting the program later in the same edit session is another area of exposure. Suppose that the operator runs a different macro that uses the same variable names and is equally sloppy in leaving symbol references on the stack. The results will most likely be erroneous.

Saving Data in User Variables

One method of saving data has the highest level of exposure but is the simplest: using specific AutoCAD system variables provided for programmers. These system variables all start with the letters USER followed by a letter indicating the type of data (I for integer, R for real, and S for string) and a digit from 1 to 5. Thus, you can have five integers, five real numbers, and five strings saved as system variables. Integer and real number variables are saved with the drawing.

String variables are not saved with the drawing, so you should use string variables (USERS1 to USERS5) for temporary data during the program run. If you need to preserve data values for a later edit session, use the USERI1 to USERI5 (integers) variables and the USERR1 to USERR5 (real numbers) variables. Of course, this leaves your data open to editing by the operator and other applications that may want to utilize the same variables. If your application is the only one being run by the operator, however, you can get away with using these system variables. In that case, simply use SETVAR and GETVAR to set up and later retrieve the values of the system variables used.

Saving Data in Attributes

Another place to store data is in attributes attached to blocks. An AutoCAD operator can easily modify or erase a block to which you have attached variables that need saving, but it is less likely that another program is using the same block name. Thus, the level of exposure for your data remains high, but is not as random as using system variables alone.

When you want an operator to have direct access to these variables, an elegant solution is to use an attribute sequence in a block. If you do not want an operator to have easy access, create the attributes as invisible with a small text height and do not add graphics to the block definition. Another solution is to use dictionary data objects, which you look at later in this chapter.

The manipulation of blocks and attributes is simplified by the use of utility routines that read and write groups of attributes for a block. Then it is easy to use attributes for saving and retrieving data.

Attributes are attached to block inserts as independent entity objects. When viewed in the drawing database by Visual LISP, an INSERT entity object contains a 66 group code entry. If the value associated with the 66 group code is 1, attributes follow the INSERT object in the drawing database. ENTNEXT steps through the attributes until it encounters a SEQEND entity. Each ATTRIB object contains a key (group code 2) and a data string (group code 1) that can be updated or retrieved as called for by the function.

To update an ATTRIB object, the ENTMOD subr writes the modified entity data list to the database. But the new text is not displayed until an ENTUPD or REGEN has been performed for the insert object itself. That way, you can make many changes to the attributes and not be slowed waiting for the display to update for each modification.

You can modify the location of an ATTRIB as well. And that location remains in the drawing even after the drawing is regenerated or loaded from a file. ATTRIB is an entity object, and if the location or other geometry properties are changed (text size, rotation, and so forth), the object is stored in the drawing with those changes. This means your program can move an attribute to a new location to make a drawing more presentable. The effect is the same as the operator changing the attribute object using grips or the property list.

Examples: Handling Attributes

The use of utility routines to handle the grunt work of manipulating attributes has a significant effect on your programming and the use of these data objects. Two example functions are presented in this section, and several more are provided on the CD for you to study and use. The first example returns a list of attribute data associated with an inserted block object. The second example updates one attribute attached to an inserted block object.

Listing 14.1 contains a function that gets all the attributes attached to a block given the entity name of an INSERT object in the EN argument. An association list is returned with dotted pairs for each attribute located. The resulting list format is (("tag" . "value") ...), which allows you to pull attributes out of the list using a (CDR (ASSOC)) expression, just as you do with an entity data list.

The function starts by getting the entity data list for the first attribute, which follows the insert object. ENTNEXT skips past the INSERT, and then ENTGET reads the entity data list. A WHILE loop then starts and iterates until the entity type is no longer ATTRIB.

In the WHILE loop, the tag name and attribute values are extracted from group codes 2 and 1, respectively. CONS combines these values in a dotted pair, and then another CONS adds them to the front of the RES result list. The process is repeated with the next attribute entity list, until all ATTRIB objects have been read. At the end of the function, the contents of RES are reversed (CONS builds lists by adding new members to the front) to serve as the returning value.

To use this function, supply the entity name of an inserted block. A list of attribute tags and values are returned. Some variations of this function are supplied on the CD as companions to Listing 14.1. Attributes can serve as a good storage medium for data that you want to preserve from one drawing edit session to another.

Because the operator is still empowered to edit the objects directly, erasing and purging the blocks can reset the entire system. This is a good compromise for many AutoCAD applications in which the operator needs to be able to start over or try something different without recreating the entire drawing. Blocks with attributes are easy for operators to manipulate, and with utility functions, they are simple for the programmer as well.

The second utility, shown in Listing 14.2, updates an attribute entry in the drawing. The arguments supplied to the function are the entity name of the base block, the tag string, and the string value to place in the attribute object. The processing for attributes is basically the same from one function to the next. Given the insert object, use ENTNEXT to move to the first attribute, and then use ENTNEXT again to step through the sequence of ATTRIB objects. Attribute objects always follow an insert object and have no other entity object types in between. A SEQEND object appears after the last attribute object.

In ATT:UPDATE, you want to update just one attribute, so the WHILE loop is used to read the entity data lists of the attribute objects and then test for a match with the TAG value. If a match is not found, EN is moved to the next entity object (another attribute or the end of the chain). The WHILE loop continues until the last attribute object has been processed or the tag is located.

Listing 14.1 Retrieving block attributes.

```
(DEFUN ATT:GETS (EN / EL RES)
  (SETQ EN (ENTNEXT EN) ;;skip INSERT
        EL (ENTGET EN)  ;;get ATTRIB
  )
  (WHILE (= (CDR (ASSOC 0 EL))
            "ATTRIB")
    (SETQ RES
      (CONS ;;add to front of result list
        (CONS  ;;build dotted pair
          (CDR (ASSOC 2 EL))  ;;tag
          (CDR (ASSOC 1 EL))  ;;value
        )
        RES ;;result list
      )
        EN (entnext EN) ;;next ATTRIB
        EL (entget EN)
    )
  )
  (REVERSE RES) ;;reverse result list
)
```

After the WHILE loop, the value in EL is tested to see whether it equals an ATTRIB object, which indicates that an attribute with a matching tag name was located. ENTMOD modifies the contents of the attribute data list given the new data to substitute into the entity data list. ENTUPD forces a regeneration of the entity on the screen so that the attribute update appears immediately in the drawing.

You can optimize the program in Listing 14.2 for your application. Because most applications update only one or a few attributes after they are stored, I used a single tag update example.

Attributes work well if you are willing to expose your data to the operator for editing as well as possible deletion. If you want to shield your data from external edits but not from deletion, use extended data, the topic of the next section.

Listing 14.2 Updating an attribute by tag name.

```
(DEFUN ATT:UPDATE (EN TAG NEW / EL)
   (SETQ EN (ENTNEXT EN) ;;skip INSERT
         EL (ENTGET EN)  ;;get ATTRIB
   )
   ;; Search attribs for match of tag name
   (WHILE (AND (= (CDR (ASSOC 0 EL))
                  "ATTRIB")
               (/= (CDR (ASSOC 2 EL))
                   TAG)
          )
      (SETQ EN (ENTNEXT EN) ;;next ATTRIB
            EL (ENTGET EN)
      )
   )
   (IF (= (CDR (ASSOC 0 EL)) "ATTRIB")
      (PROGN
         (ENTMOD ;;modify entity data
            (SUBST ;;substitute in list
              (CONS 1 NEW) ;;new data
              (ASSOC 1 EL) ;;old data
              EL            ;;list
            )
         )
         (ENTUPD EN) ;;force regen of entity
      )
   )
)
```

Saving with Extended Data

Extended data is programmer-defined data attached to an entity object and accessible only in a programming environment such as Visual LISP. Operators cannot view or edit the extended data unless they write a program as well. Operators can, however, move or erase an object with extended data, so your data still has a high degree of exposure. Do note that certain online utilities allow operators to view and edit extended data, so the exposure is higher when the operator is well versed in tools available online.

Extended data is nested in an entity data list in Visual LISP. But to have it present in the entity data list, you must request the data by name. This name is called the application ID, or APPID. Application IDs are maintained in a table and must be declared before they can be used. To register or declare an application ID in the APPID table, use REGAPP with the name of the application to register. If the application is already in the table, REGAPP returns immediately. Otherwise, the name is appended to the list and you can use it when appending application data to entity data lists. The APPID table contains only the names provided by applications and a bit-coded flag that indicates whether the application came from an external reference or whether any entities are known to contain this application ID as extended data.

Adding extended data to an object requires that you have the entity data list. Extended data is found nested in a -3 group code structure. The first member of each list in the -3 sublist is the name of the application ID. Following the application ID is the data associated with the application. The lists are deeply nested so that multiple applications can apply extended data to an object.

Listing 14.3 shows a general description of extended data in an entity list. This example contains two application ID entries called NAME1 and NAME2. Note how the -3 group can be accessed using ASSOC in the entity data list, just like all other members. Removing -3 from the front of the list and using an ASSOC with the name of the application ID provides access to the extended data. If you remove the name of the application ID from the front of that list, the extended data can be accessed using the group codes you defined for that purpose. This might seem complicated, but it is basic list processing, which is easy for LISP.

Listing 14.3 General format of extended data.

```
(  ...entity data list...
   (-3   ;start of extended data
      ("NAME1"  ;start of extended data for application ID "NAME1"
         ...extended data...
      )
      ("NAME2" ;start of extended data for application ID "NAME2"
         ...extended data...
      )
   )
)
```

The group codes used in extended data all number 1000 or greater. The group code number indicates the type of data involved, such as an integer, a string, or a real number. The standard group codes used in extended data are 1000 for strings, 1010 for points, 1040 for real numbers, and 1070 for integer numbers. You may want to investigate other 1000-series group codes in the online help; the ones just mentioned are the principle codes your application will need.

For example, the following extended data list for an application named "TEST" contains a string ("ABC"), a real number (1.25), and an integer (25):

```
(-3 ("TEST" (1001 . "TEST") (1000 . "ABC") (1040 . 1.25) (1070 . 25)))
```

Note that the data appears just like an entity data list consisting of dotted pairs with group codes. Should you need to use more of a particular data type, repeat the group code. For example, multiple 1040 list groups would be found for each real number to be stored. Your program has to keep track of where a particular value resides in extended data, which can cause problems when you are first developing a sophisticated program.

You are limited in the amount of extended data that you can attach to an entity object. That limit, which is about 16 kilobytes of data, helps keep the database streamlined when used in an interactive environment. Most applications come nowhere near the limit. Two subrs determine whether data can fit in an entity object. XDROOM and XDSIZE report the amount of space available in an entity and the amount of space consumed by an extended data list, respectively. To find out whether there is enough room to spare, you generally test to see whether XDSIZE is less than XDROOM. To use XDSIZE, the extended data list must be created first and it must be of the proper format. Otherwise, an error results.

Extended data might seem difficult to use at first glance. You can greatly simplify things by using utility routines. Remember that the purpose of extended data is to provide a place to store data in the drawing. This does not mean the data should be manipulated in the same format. For most applications, you should write a utility set that converts between the extended data stored in the drawing and the data in your program. Next, you look at some example functions that do just that. These functions also demonstrate how extended data is attached to objects as well as retrieved from them.

Listing 14.4 contains the X_DATA_ADD function, which is a general-purpose utility for appending extended data to an entity. It has three arguments: the entity name of the object to append the data, the application ID string, and a data list populated with 1000 group codes ready to be used. The -3 and application ID should not be part of the 1000 group code list. For example, the function could be called using the following expression, with EN containing an entity name:

```
(x_data_add EN "MYAPP" '((1000 . "Testing")(1040 . 37.5)))
```

Listing 14.4 demonstrates all the basic extended data handling performed in Visual LISP. The first step is to register the application ID using REGAPP. If the application ID is already registered, REGAPP returns immediately. Otherwise, it registers the ID in the APPID table for the drawing. The next step is to use ENTGET to get the entity data list and then construct the extended data entry. To construct the extended data component of the entity data list, you add the name of the application to the front of the data list and then add -3 to the front of the resulting list. This creates the nested structure needed for extended data entry.

Before adding the data to the entity, the function tests to see whether there is sufficient room. XDSIZE is used against the extended data list, and XDROOM is used with the entity name. If XDSIZE results in a smaller value, the data can be added. Your extended data list in TMP1 is appended as a

Listing 14.4 Adding extended data.

```
(DEFUN X_DATA_ADD (EN APID DLST / EL TMP1)
   (REGAPP APID)
   (SETQ EL (ENTGET EN)
         TMP1 (LIST -3 (CONS APID DLST))
   )
   (IF (< (XDSIZE TMP1) (XDROOM EN))
       (ENTMOD (APPEND EL (LIST TMP1))))
)
```

list to EL, the existing entity data list. That list is then supplied to ENTMOD to make the change in the drawing database.

Retrieving extended data is even easier than writing it to the database. Because Visual LISP excels at handling lists, the code is brief, as you can see in Listing 14.5. Given the entity name and application ID string, the function uses ENTGET to retrieve the entity list plus the extended data. The purpose of this function is to get the extended data as a list of 1,000 group codes. If the entity contains extended data for the application ID supplied, EL has a -3 group code entry. Using CDADR with the result returned from the ASSOC of the -3 group code results in only the 1000 group code list.

Listing 14.5 Getting extended data.

```
(DEFUN X_DATA_GET (EN APID / EL)
   (SETQ EL (ENTGET EN (LIST APID)))
   (IF (ASSOC -3 EL)
      (CDADR (ASSOC -3 EL))) ;;return only data items
)
```

CDADR is a composite primitive created by combining CDR and CAR, as in (CDR (CAR (CDR. Thus, the first CDR removes the -3 group code. Extended data is nested in another association list based on the application ID and, because you supplied only one application ID, CAR returns the first and only member. Last, CDR removes the name of the application ID from the front of the list, resulting in just the 1,000 group code list.

Again, remember that the purpose of these utilities is to demonstrate how to access data and simplify your coding efforts. Using utilities can greatly enhance your ability to take advantage of features such as extended data in the AutoCAD system.

You can use the companion utilities on the CD for extended data manipulations. For the most part, extended data provides a good way to store data that is only marginally exposed to the operator. Because the data is attached to actual objects in the drawing, it is easy for the operator to reset the application by simply erasing these objects. Your application should be aware that this could happen and react appropriately.

Saving Data in a Dictionary

To protect your data in a drawing from the majority of AutoCAD users, the object holding the data cannot be visible for editing by the operator. This means you should store data in non-graphical objects called XRECORD entity objects. These objects work best when you organize them in dictionaries.

You can retrieve and add data using a variety of dictionary subrs. All subrs for dictionary manipulation contain the characters DICT. For example, NEWDICT creates a dictionary, DICTADD adds a member to an existing dictionary, and DICTSEARCH searches a dictionary for an entry.

An XRECORD object has significant advantages over extended data. First, an XRECORD object does not have associated graphics for the operator to manipulate, thereby making your data reasonably safe. Second, there are no restrictions as to the amount of memory that the XRECORD object can consumes. If you need to store a lot of data and want to do it in the drawing, XRECORD is the best solution. Third, normal group codes are used for housing the data in XRECORD. It is up to your program to know what the group codes signify.

Power users, however, can use certain utilities to search dictionaries and make edits. If you want protection from power users, use an encryption system to shield the data from all but the most persistent users, from whom nothing can be considered entirely secure.

Creating and using a dictionary with XRECORDs involves more steps than all the other data storage mechanisms, but you can accomplish the primary tasks using utility subroutines. In this section, you go through the process of creating and accessing dictionary objects, and then you look at a solution provided in Visual LISP that makes this much easier.

To use a dictionary, you must first create it. This is accomplished by defining a dictionary entity object as an entity data list of the following form and then sending that list to the ENTMAKEX subr:

```
((0 . "DICTIONARY") (100 . "AcDbDictionary"))
```

ENTMAKEX is a special version of ENTMAKE for creating non-graphics objects such as dictionaries. ENTMAKEX is different in that it does not define an owner for the object, thereby preventing the object from being written to the output file when the drawing is saved. Only owned objects are written to the file.

To provide proper ownership for the dictionary, it must be given a name and added to the named object dictionary list for the drawing using NAMEDOBJDICT and DICTADD, respectively. The resulting entity object name returned is used to reference the dictionary in subsequent DICTADD calls while adding members to the dictionary. After the dictionary is added to the list, it is owned by the named object dictionary and resides with the drawing.

You add XRECORD objects to dictionaries by creating XRECORD entity data lists, by using ENTMAKEX to append them to the drawing, and by then adding the resulting entity to the dictionary. For the object to remain in the drawing after it is saved, you must add the entry to the dictionary to establish ownership. Be aware that if the name you use to add something to a dictionary already exists in the dictionary, the value for that name is overwritten. Thus, you need to devise a way to make names unique in your application as you add dictionary and XRECORD objects.

Several steps are involved in creating and accessing dictionary and XRECORD objects in the drawing. You must follow these steps in the proper order to achieve the desired results. Following are the steps for the primary functions you would perform involving dictionaries.

To create a dictionary:

1. Create a dictionary entity list.

2. Use ENTMAKEX to add the dictionary entity list to the drawing.

3. Use DICTADD to add the new dictionary entity object to the named object dictionary of AutoCAD accessed using NAMEDOJBDICT. Supply a unique name for your dictionary.

To add an item to a dictionary:

1. Create a non-graphics object entity list.

2. Use ENTMAKEX to add the non-graphics object entity list to the drawing.

3. Use DICTADD to add the new object to the dictionary. Supply a unique name for your new entry in the dictionary. This name is used to retrieve the associated entity name pointing back to the non-graphics object.

To access an existing dictionary:

1. Use DICTSEARCH and NAMEDOBJDICT to access the named object dictionary so you can get the object reference to your dictionary.

2. Access the dictionary object to get the entry of interest using DICTSEARCH.

To remove an entry from an existing dictionary:

1. Use DICTSEARCH and NAMEDOBJDICT to access the named object dictionary so you can get the object reference to your dictionary.

2. se DICTREMOVE to remove the object in question from the dictionary. The ownerless object is returned as a result of the DICTREMOVE subr. It is deleted from the drawing when the drawing is saved and reloaded from the disk.

Dictionaries provide a powerful tool for storing data, but they do require some manipulations as shown. Utility functions would assist greatly in this regard, and they are already provided in Visual LISP. Run the VL-LOAD-COM subr to load more subrs that can be used for working with dictionaries, as you will see next.

You can use VLAX-LDATA-PUT and VLAX-LDATA-GET to put data in and get data from, respectively, a dictionary or an entity object. You usually use them with a named dictionary object, but you can also establish a dictionary owned by an entity. If you use VLAX-LDATA-PUT with an entity object, the data sent is attached as a dictionary owned by the object.

You can write any type of Visual LISP data to the dictionary, but remember that entity names change between sessions, and using them in this manner is not acceptable. If you want to simply keep track of another entity within a dictionary entry, use handles.

The beauty of using the VLAX-LDATA functions is that you don't have to hassle with dictionary objects. That work is performed inside the utility function. Simply supply a dictionary name, a key name for the object you want stored, and the value to be stored when saving the data. To retrieve the data value later, you need only the dictionary name and the key name. You do not have to open the dictionary or do any other programming because that is accomplished in the VLAX-LDATA functions.

Two subrs complement VLAX-LDATA-PUT and VLAX-LDATA-GET. VLAX-LDATA-DELETE deletes entries from a dictionary when the data is no longer useful or needed by your application. VLAX-LDATA-LIST returns a list of the data saved to a dictionary or attached to an entity object. Each entry saved is returned as a sublist in the resulting list so that it appears as an association list.

As an example of the LDATA subrs, Listing 14.6 presents two functions that write and read Visual LISP symbol data. SAVE_SYMBOLS accepts a list of symbol names and a string for the name of the dictionary to use. The symbols in the list are evaluated and written to the dictionary one at a time in a FOREACH loop. The VL-SYMBOL-NAME subr converts the name of the symbol to a string to be used as a key. The second function, GET_SYMBOLS, uses the same dictionary name to read back the list of symbols. Each element in the resulting list is processed in MAPCAR to convert the name to a symbol name and then set the value to the data stored with the key.

With the LDATA feature of Visual LISP, the programmer can save data in a simple yet reasonably secure manner. And if more advanced data storage requirements are encountered, you can use the dictionary objects.

Summary

Storing data in a drawing is part of any advanced application, and this chapter presented a set of mechanisms for accomplishing the task. Which one you should use is based on the level of exposure you are willing to provide to the operator.

At the highest levels of exposure are blocks with attributes and USER system variables. These options allow the operator to view and edit values.

Dictionaries and extended data, which are at the lower levels of exposure, protect the data from most AutoCAD operators but not from sophisticated programmers. If you have written something so special that it deserves protection at the highest levels, consider using C++ instead of Visual LISP, which goes only so far in protecting your data in a drawing environment.

Listing 14.6 Saving symbol values.

```
(DEFUN SAVE_SYMBOLS (SYMLIST DNAME / SYM)
  (VL-LOAD-COM)
  (FOREACH SYM SYMLIST
    (VLAX-LDATA-PUT
      DNAME
      (VL-SYMBOL-NAME SYM)
      (VL-SYMBOL-VALUE SYM)))
)
(DEFUN GET_SYMBOLS (DNAME / TMP)
  (VL-LOAD-COM)
  (SETQ TMP
    (VLAX-LDATA-LIST DNAME))
  (MAPCAR
    '(LAMBDA (SYM)
       (SET
         (READ (CAR SYM))
         (CDR SYM)))
     TMP)
  TMP
)
```

CHAPTER 15

AutoCAD Interface Programming

The input system discussed thus far is based on the operator selecting objects from the drawing, typing data, or interacting with a dialog box. But AutoCAD has much more: menus across the top, sidebar menus, pop-up menus, toolbar icons, the text screen, and the graphics display. Each can be controlled by Visual LISP programs. In addition, operating-system-level interfaces are provided because AutoCAD runs in a Windows environment. Visual LISP programmers can exploit ActiveX automation tools from other environments. This provides plenty of power for even the most demanding applications.

In this chapter, you look at the AutoCAD menu system as seen from the Visual LISP programming perspective and learn how to interface Visual LISP to ActiveX server systems. By controlling the display system and menu contents, you provide operators with guidance that is less intrusive than a dialog box.

Manipulating AutoCAD Menus

Most operators begin customizing AutoCAD through the menu system. By changing the layout of the menu system, you can have a significant effect on productivity. And because Visual LISP integrates well with the menu system, advanced control of the interface is possible.

When looking at menus in relation to Visual LISP, the first place to start is with the loading functions. You can initiate your functions with a simple expression structure. Use a ^C sequence to cancel any existing commands followed by ^P to turn off the echo of the menu to the command line. Then use an IF expression to test the function name for a binding. If no binding exists, the value of the function is NIL.

You can use the following to test the binding and then load the function library when needed:

```
(IF (NULL <FUNCTION_NAME>)(LOAD "<function_file>"))
```

Following the closing parentheses, add a semicolon (which is the same as pressing the Enter key in a menu) and then the name of your function. The semicolon forces the evaluation of the previous IF expression, thereby ensuring that your function is loaded. Although the semicolon is not needed when using normal LISP functions, its use is highly recommended when you use a command function (a symbol name starting with C:).

For example, suppose you have a function named C:COOL in the COOLTOOL.LSP source file, which is located in the support directory of AutoCAD. The menu macro appears as follows:

```
^C^C^P(if (NULL C:COOL) (LOAD "COOLTOOL.LSP"));COOL
```

This expression tests to see whether C:COOL has a non-NIL binding. If the value of the symbol is null, the function is loaded from the COOLTOOL.LSP source file located somewhere in the AutoCAD program search paths. After the IF expression, a semicolon forces the evaluation before the COOL command function is started.

When your Visual LISP programs are running, the operator can provide input to your prompts through the menu system. Menu input is treated the same as keyboard input. In most cases, the transparent commands of ZOOM and PAN operate from the menu without causing any problems for your programs. You can use the menu system to your advantage in this regard by controlling the content of pull-downs, icons, and even toolbars.

You control the menu system by using the MENUCMD subr with the same basic syntax used in multiple-page menu programming. The (MENUCMD "P5=*") expression forces the current pull-down menu at POP5 to unfurl. String command sequences are presented one at a time through MENUCMD.

If you want to change the contents and unfurl a menu, you need to use two MENUCMD expressions. For example, suppose that your application wants to display the MYMENU menu at POP2 and then unfurl it to point the operator towards those selections. Use the following expressions:

```
(MENUCMD "P2=MYMENU")
(MENUCMD "P2=*")
```

Menu groups can also be referenced in MENUCMD after the group is loaded. The MENUGROUP subr verifies that a group has been loaded into memory before attempting any manipulation of the group contents. If MENUGROUP returns NIL when given the group name, use the COMMAND subr to issue the commands needed to load the menu group for your application.

After the group is available, you can reference it using the group name and name tag as in normal menu programming in AutoCAD. For example, if the MYGROUP menu group contains the ME menu and you want to unfurl it, the menu command string is "MYGROUP.ME=*".

The MENUCMD subr can be used also to run DIESEL macros and to test the contents of menus. If your application relies on a menu-based interface, MENUCMD will be an important tool.

Exploring AutoCAD Objects

Although you can write complex applications in Visual LISP without ever using objects, it is still helpful to know what they can do for you. When looking at AutoCAD from an object-oriented programming point of view, there are many objects — and not just the entity objects you have already looked at in this book. The entire AutoCAD system is defined as an inverted object tree rooted at the application object.

Visual LISP is fully capable of exploiting AutoCAD objects, but you must understand some concepts to successfully navigate the object tree. First, VL-LOAD-COM is required before any object handling can be enabled. The object tree is serviced through ActiveX, so the extended objects module of Visual LISP must be loaded before any internal subrs are available.

Second, an application starts at the root and works its way down the tree to the data or function of interest. For the best performance, object links into the tree should be established only one time in a program and then referenced from that point forward. A program that is adding entities to the model space should establish a link to the model space at the beginning and use it instead of rebuilding the link each time.

The VLAX-GET-PROPERTY and VLAX-PUT-PROPERTY functions retrieve properties and update properties, respectively, for any object in the tree. In many cases in AutoCAD, the property name already exists as a defined subr when concatenated to the end of the VLA-GET- or VLA-PUT- subr, as in VLA-GET-MODELSPACE. To find out whether that is the case for a given property, type VLA-GET- followed by the property name. The VLIDE identifies the subr as you type it. If the subr does not exist, use the generic VLAX-GET-PROPERTY and VLAX-PUT-PROPERTY functions.

Access to the root of AutoCAD is provided with the VLAX-GET-ACAD-OBJECT subr. This subr has no parameters and returns only the object reference for the root of the AutoCAD application. The root is then used to navigate to any point in the drawing database and the AutoCAD system. Where you go next depends on what you are looking for. All the details of the AutoCAD object model are in the online help, but it is somewhat imposing. To help you understand the online help, you look at a few objects here. Explore the rest in the online help when the interest strikes and time is available.

First you should learn about a tool for exploring objects with Visual LISP called the VLAX-DUMP-OBJECT subr. With VLAX-DUMP-OBJECT, you get a listing of an object's properties and their current values. Use VLAX-GET-PROPERTY to retrieve the values associated with a given property, such as getting the path name from the AutoCAD application object:

```
(VLAX-GET-PROPERTY (VLAX-GET-ACAD-OBJECT) "Path")
```

Remember that if you will be getting a lot of data from an object, it is best to use SETQ to establish a reference to the object. While there is a binding from a symbol to an object, the object remains open in AutoCAD. I recommend that your application free memory when it has finished using VLAX-RELEASE-OBJECT. This is not required, but it does improve the overall performance of AutoCAD when a lot of object manipulations are involved.

The most commonly used object links can be built using a utility function as in Listing 15.1. You can then use the utility in Listing 15.2 to clear these links when the main program is terminating. Global symbols defined in these two functions can be part of the main program's local symbol list (recommended) or remain on the heap.

The LINKS2ACAD function in Listing 15.1 demonstrates the VLAX-GET-PROPERTY subr in action retrieving properties from the Preferences object. The properties being accessed are objects themselves, containing the User, Display, and Files objects. The VLA-GET- subrs are used to retrieve properties directly for the model space, Preferences base object, and active document

Listing 15.1 Building links to AutoCAD's object mode.

```
(DEFUN LINKS2ACAD ()
  (VL-LOAD-COM)
  (SETQ ACADAPPOBJ (VLAX-GET-ACAD-OBJECT)
        ACADDOCUMENT (VLA-GET-ACTIVEDOCUMENT ACADAPPOBJ)
        MODELSPACE (VLA-GET-MODELSPACE ACADDOCUMENT)
        OBJPREFS (VLA-GET-PREFERENCES ACADAPPOBJ)
        USERPREFS (VLAX-GET-PROPERTY OBJPREFS "User")
        DISPPREFS (VLAX-GET-PROPERTY OBJPREFS "Display")
        FILEPREFS (VLAX-GET-PROPERTY OBJPREFS "Files")
  )
)
```

Listing 15.2 Releasing object links.

```
(DEFUN FREELINKS2ACAD ()
  (VLAX-RELEASE-OBJECT FILEPREFS)
  (VLAX-RELEASE-OBJECT DISPPREFS)
  (VLAX-RELEASE-OBJECT USERPREFS)
  (VLAX-RELEASE-OBJECT OBJPREFS)
  (VLAX-RELEASE-OBJECT MODELSPACE)
  (VLAX-RELEASE-OBJECT ACADDOCUMENT)
  (VLAX-RELEASE-OBJECT ACADAPPOBJ)
  (SETQ FILEPREFS NIL
        DISPPREFS NIL
        USERPREFS NIL
        OBJPREFS NIL
        MODELSPACE NIL
        ACADDOCUMENT NIL
        ACADAPPOBJ NIL
  )
)
```

object. If given the choice, it is generally better to use the VLA-GET- style subrs instead of the generic VLAX-GET-PROPERTY subr because they are a bit faster at retrieving the data requested.

At the end of a main program that used the links to AutoCAD established by (Links2Acad), you can use the (FreeLinks2Acad) function (in Listing 15.2) to release the memory that housed the object links. This function further sets the symbols to NIL, but this step may not be required if the symbols are local to a function of higher scope than FREELINKS2ACAD (that is, if they appear somewhere in the parameter list of a function that calls FREELINKS2ACAD).

In a new drawing in AutoCAD, load and run the LINKS2ACAD function in Listing 15.1. The source code is on the CD provided with this book. At the VLIDE console ($ prompt) or the AutoCAD command line, type the following expression:

(VLAX-DUMP-OBJECT FILEPREFS)

The result is a listing of file preferences for the current system. Here is a partial listing:

```
$ (vlax-dump-object fileprefs)
; IAcadPreferencesFiles: AutoCAD PreferencesFiles Interface
; Property values:
;   AltFontFile = "simplex.shx"
;   AltTabletMenuFile = ""
;   Application (RO) = #<VLA-OBJECT IAcadApplication 00a7b334>
;   AutoSavePath = "C:\\windows\\TEMP\\"
...
;   TemplateDwgPath = "C:\\PROGRAM FILES\\AUTOCAD 2000I\\template"
;   TempXrefPath = "C:\\windows\\TEMP\\"
;   TextEditor = "Internal"
;   TextureMapPath = "C:\\PROGRAM FILES\\AUTOCAD 2000I\\textures"
;   WorkspacePath = "C:\\PROGRAM FILES\\AUTOCAD 2000I\\Data Links"
T
```

Note that the names of the properties are not case sensitive, but it improves readability to use the mixed case shown in the object dump.

If your program needs to retrieve one of these values, use the name to the left of the equal sign. For example, to learn the value of the automatic save path, use the following expression:

(VLAX-GET-PROPERTY FILEPREFS "AutoSavePath")

As you explore the object map of AutoCAD, you will encounter a new type of object called a collection. A collection is a table of similar things such as layer or dimension-style table. The block definitions, model, space, and layout space are collections of entity objects.

Collections are used in ActiveX for referencing groups of similar objects. Because Visual LISP provides other tools to access tables and entity objects, you probably won't need to work with collections in those regards, but other collections may be of interest. For those, Visual LISP has VLA-ITEM, VLA-GET-COUNT, VLAX-MAP-COLLECTION, and VLAX-FOR.

VLA-GET-COUNT gets the number of items in a collection object. VLA-ITEM retrieves individual members of a collection object, using an offset index starting at 0 for the first item. VLAX-FOR and VLAX-MAP-COLLECTION are like FOREACH and MAPCAR, except they are applied to each member of a collection instead of a list. The subrs iterate through a collection, supplying the members one at a time to the mapped function or expressions.

Listing 15.3 contains an example of VLAX-FOR handling a collection of data. In this case, the collection is the set of open documents in the AutoCAD editor. The DOCUMENTS property returns a collection of drawing or document objects. The function loops through each document and compares the drawing name provided as an argument against the drawing name (along with the full path name). If a match is found, the FLAG symbol is set to NIL. FLAG is returned as a result of the function by being the last thing evaluated. Thus, the function returns T if a matching drawing name was found or NIL otherwise.

Listing 15.3 Collection handling.

```
(DEFUN ISITOPEN (DWGNAME / DWGS DWG FLAG)
  (VL-LOAD-COM)
  (SETQ DWGS (VLAX-GET-DOCUMENTS (VLAX-GET-ACAD-OBJECT))
        DWGNAME (STRCASE DWGNAME))
  (VLAX-FOR DWG DWGS
    (IF (OR
          (= (STRCASE (VLAX-GET-PROPERTY DWG "Name"))
             DWGNAME)
          (= (STRCASE (VLAX-GET-PROPERTY DWG "FullName"))
             DWGNAME))
      (SETQ FLAG T)
    )
  )
  FLAG
)
```

ActiveX Automation

The AutoCAD object model demonstrates just one ActiveX automation server system. Others may be stored in your computer, such as the integrated Microsoft Office software set (Word, Excel, and Access). ActiveX is a Windows standard for interprocess communications in a computer (that is, one program talking to another program), similar to a pipeline between two applications. ActiveX provides everything needed for one program to run another program or borrow some of the capabilities of the other program.

The use of ActiveX automation in Visual LISP is almost identical to interfacing with the AutoCAD object model just described. The first step is to establish a link to the application object. From there, you follow the structure of the application to get where you want to go. If the application is document based, the first route to follow is to the documents collection and then to a specific document. Be aware that different terms may be used. For example, Excel uses the term worksheet instead of document.

A primary difference between interfacing with another ActiveX server and AutoCAD's server is that you know AutoCAD is up and running when your Visual LISP program is running. (Otherwise, your program would not work.) But you may not always be sure of that situation with other programs in the system, so Visual LISP provides object link routines.

VLAX-GET-OBJECT attempts to link with a running program. You use this subr when you expect the operator to have already started an associated program and have a file loaded. VLAX-GET-OBJECT returns NIL if the object cannot be located in the active memory of the computer. Use the application name to tie into another program's object server. The application name is typically found in the online help of the server program.

After the application object is attached, use the VLAX-DUMP-OBJECT subr to explore the details of the objects exposed for use by your program. Remember that VLAX-GET-OBJECT returns the root of an object tree. You may have to climb up a few branches before finding the necessary details.

VLAX-CREATE-OBJECT creates a new instance of the running program or object. This subr is used when you need to initiate the application being interfaced from a fresh starting point. As in getting a running application object, the program ID indicates which application you want to load. Windows stores information about applications in the system registry. It uses the program ID to locate the name of the object server, which can then be used to start a new run.

Use VLAX-GET-OR-CREATE-OBJECT when you want to only attach to the application, running or not. If an existing instance is running, this subr attaches to the root of that object. Otherwise, the subr creates a new instance of the object as if you had used VLAX-CREATE-OBJECT. The VLAX-GET-OR-CREATE-OBJECT subr is often used when you want the other application to solve a problem using the objects it defines, or when multiple users are sharing a common application server (such as in a database environment). If you are the first user for the day, the object is created. If you log on later, you are sharing the object already loaded.

After you get your hands on the root object of a system, such as Access, Excel, or Word, the VLAX-DUMP-OBJECT subr reveals all the details that your application can exploit. If you do not already know the application you are interfacing with or are learning the object system it supports, plan to spend some time finding out how to navigate the object tree.

ActiveX interfaces are typically documented for the Visual Basic programmer — that is, the examples and syntax are all in Visual Basic. Visual LISP can use the same methods and properties but in a slightly different format. To help the Visual LISP programmer decipher the syntax, special tools are provided.

The VLAX-PUT-PROPERTY and VLAX-GET-PROPERTY subrs retrieve and update properties for objects. VLAX-INVOKE-METHOD runs a method attached to an object. The parameters to the subrs include the object reference followed by the name of the property or method as a string. When setting a property value or invoking a method, there are usually additional parameters, which follow in the same order as documented. On the way into an ActiveX method or property, be sure to convert the data types to the proper format for ActiveX.

Before you look at a data-type conversion, note that some methods return values in parameters that mean a call-by-reference approach is needed instead of the normal call-by-value approach. In Visual LISP, call by reference is accomplished using a quoted symbol. For methods that return more than one data element through parameter references, include a quoted symbol where needed. An example is the bounding box method, in which two points are returned given an entity object reference:

```
(VLAX-INVOKE-METHOD MYOBJ "GETBOUNDINGBOX" 'MINP 'MAXP)
```

The GETBOUNDINGBOX method returns a point in MINP and another in MAXP for the bounding points around the object referenced by MYOBJ. The GETBOUNDINGBOX method is accessed through ActiveX, so the data returned for the points is not a data list. Instead, the data is returned in a safe array (described in Chapter 12). Use the VLAX-SAFEARRAY->LIST subr to convert a safe array variable type to a list that can be manipulated in Visual LISP.

Other conversion subrs include VLAX-3D-POINT to convert a three-dimensional point list into a variant safe array for sending to one of the methods, VLAX-MAKE-SAFEARRAY to create a multidimensional array, and VLAX-SAFEARRAY-PUT-ELEMENT to populate it. There are conversions for safe arrays and variants so that you can convert the data types in Visual LISP to and from those supporting the ActiveX interface.

A couple of constants that bear mention are :VLAX-FALSE and :VLAX-TRUE, which are used as arguments to and from Boolean methods and properties. They stand for FALSE and TRUE in the ActiveX system. NIL and non-NIL are used in LISP programming and will not operate correctly with ActiveX.

Another way to work with an ActiveX server system is to import the library. The VLAX-IMPORT-TYPE-LIBRARY subr reads in the method and properties library for an object family and creates VLA functions for use in your programs for the entire group. When you import a type library, you must provide a prefix string to apply to all the methods and another for the properties. You can then use the apropos feature in the VLIDE to view information about the various methods and properties imported. A subr such as VLA-ADDLINE or VLA-GETBOUNDINGBOX is the result of a type library import in AutoCAD. (The AutoCAD type library is imported when VL-LOAD-COM is issued.)

Summary

This chapter introduced interfacing with the operator and computer in ways that go beyond the keyboard and dialog boxes. Menus are the first place where most users begin customizing AutoCAD. If you are a commercial developer, you should use menus sparingly so as not to interfere with user menus. That doesn't mean that commercial applications should do away with any form of menu interface. Menus are still the easiest way for users to launch applications. But developers should strive to use an isolated menu system and not replace the user's interface. In this case, developers include anyone writing code for use by other people, not just commercial developers.

Menus are part of the AutoCAD object tree, an extensive structure of data that includes the application as well as the drawing data. The chapter covered several Visual LISP subrs for manipulating objects in the tree. You also saw how to navigate the tree efficiently through the use of global variables pointing to various levels in the tree. The object system in AutoCAD is powerful and opens the door for many things that you may need to have happen in an advanced application.

The discussion of objects led to a more general discussion of objects in the Windows environment and how Visual LISP programs can use ActiveX. Due to the diversity of potential applications, nothing was covered in detail or with examples.

The goal of this chapter was to open doors to other ideas and ways of doing things in Visual LISP. Programming is an art that uses tools, and the objects in ActiveX are just some of the wonderful tools provided in the AutoCAD Visual LISP programming environment.

CHAPTER 16

Event Programming

After you are comfortable writing Visual LISP functions based on command type structures and dialog boxes, you are ready to begin exploring the next level of interactive programming: event-based programming. Event-driven programs respond to things as they happen in the computer and thereby represent a high degree of integration between the application and AutoCAD. Event-driven programs consist of a set of reactor functions. Each function will react to a particular event in the system.

Event programming is not well suited for all applications and can be difficult to pull off correctly using Visual LISP. So, although you explore the concepts behind events and writing programs for them in this chapter, keep in mind that the best strategy is to start with simple concepts and be pleasantly surprised as they evolve into a deeply integrated application.

What Are Events?

An event is something noteworthy that is happening in the computer, such as opening a new file or adding an entity object to a drawing. Some applications may want to know about these sorts of things going on in the computer, and it is through events that an application learns of them.

The supplier of the environment determines exactly what events are considered noteworthy. In Visual LISP, the environment is AutoCAD, so Autodesk has determined which the events you can be notified about. Events occurring at the Windows level are not exposed to Visual LISP because they are generally not important to AutoCAD-based applications. (If they are important, you must use C++ and either set up an ActiveX server to communicate with Visual LISP or utilize the ObjectARX library.)

AutoCAD events are divided into groups, such as database, editor, and command reactors, as shown in Table 16.1. Reactor names all start with the :VLR- character sequence followed by the reactor group name. In some cases, the reactor groups overlap. For example, the insert reactor and the database reactor are both available when a block is inserted. Variations are provided so that your applications can have access to AutoCAD at various levels, focusing access to the location of critical interest.

Table 16.1 Categories of events.

Reactor name	Reactor group	Trigger event(s)
:VLR-ACDB-Reactor	Database reactor	Adding, removing, or modifying objects in the drawing
:VLR-Command-Reactor	Command system reactor	Starting and either terminating (due to an error) or completing an AutoCAD command
:VLR-DeepClone-Reactor	Custom objects reactor	Cloning (copying) a custom object; used not in Visual LISP but in ARX-type development work
:VLR-DocManager-Reactor	Document manager reactor	Opening or closing a drawing
:VLR-DWG-Reactor	Drawing reactor	Saving, closing, or loading the current drawing
:VLR-DXF-Reactor	DXF reactor	Starting or ending DXF (Drawing eXchange Format) file transfer operations (importing or exporting)
:VLR-Editor-Reactor	Editor reactor	Combination of the command, drawing, and other reactors as used by the editor system in AutoCAD
:VLR-Insert-Reactor	Block reactor	Inserting a block into a drawing, and whether or not that was successful
:VLR-Linker-Reactor	ARX reactor	Loading or unloading an ARX module
:VLR-LISP-Reactor	LISP reactor	Starting or stopping LISP evaluation
:VLR-Mouse-Reactor	Mouse reactor	Clicking (right button) or double-clicking the mouse
:VLR-Object-Reactor	Object-level reactor	Changing or erasing a particular object; can be tied to any individual object in the database
:VLR-SysVar-Reactor	System variable reactor	Changing system variables in AutoCAD
:VLR-Toolbar-Reactor	Toolbar reactors	Changing a toolbar in AutoCAD; this notification allows your program to update related display information
:VLR-Undo-Reactor	Undo system reactor	Activating the UNDO mechanism in AutoCAD
:VLR-Wblock-Reactor	WBLOCK reactor	Writing block definitions to a new drawing
:VLR-Window-Reactor	Window reactor	Changing the size of the AutoCAD window
:VLR-XREF-Reactor	External references reactor	Manipulating an external reference block or inserting it into the drawing

You use the VLR-REACTION-NAMES subr to find out what events are available in a group. Type the subr name followed by the reactor group name (be sure to include the colon). For example, the following displays the database reactor events. Your programs can be notified whenever any one or more of these events takes place in AutoCAD:

```
Command: (vlr-reaction-names :VLR-ACDB-REACTOR)
(:VLR-objectAppended
 :VLR-objectUnAppended
 :VLR-objectReAppended
 :VLR-objectOpenedForModify
 :VLR-objectModified
 :VLR-objectErased
 :VLR-objectUnErased
)
```

Figuring out exactly when an event happens is easy when you become familiar with the terminology. Understanding the basic structure of the AutoCAD database also helps. Using the database events in the preceding as an example, an object is appended to the database when it is added for the first time. If an UNDO operation removes the object, it is UnAppended. But if the object is removed as a result of the ERASE command, the objectErased reaction takes place. If REDO is used after an UNDO when an object was unappended, it is ReAppended. But if you UNDO an erase operation, the object is UnErased. This means the same function might have to service multiple reactions to achieve predictable results.

To use reactors, you must consider exactly what your application will react to, when it will react, and why it will react. Suppose you have an application that makes use of certain entity objects. Would it be best to attach entity-object-level reactors to just those objects, or should you use database-level reactors? The answer depends on what you want to be able to accomplish with the objects. If you need to only keep track of them, entity object reactors are fine because you don't need to slow the process by reacting to any and all database changes. You want to react only if one of the critical objects is touched. On the other hand, if you are keeping track of a certain type of object, such as lines on a particular layer, a database reactor is the easiest to implement.

Setting Up a Reactor

Programming a reactor is a lot like programming dialog boxes. In both cases, you prepare callback functions. Callback functions are called by the event-handling system, not by your program. In the case of a dialog box, the callback functions are invoked when one of the tiles or controls is manipulated. Reactor callback functions are invoked when an event takes place. Thus, before you can use a reactor, it must be defined and announced to the event-handling system.

A reactor callback is defined by creating a function and setting up an association of that function with an event in the handling system. The function must be created with the correct number of arguments. Each reactor sends a specific number of parameters to the callback function, including the symbolic name of the reactor or the owner of the reactor. Additional data includes related parameters. For example, in a command-level reactor, the names of active commands are supplied. In an object-level reactor, the object reference is included in the parameters.

To learn what parameters will be passed to a callback function, see the online help provided in Visual LISP. Go to the AutoLISP Reference, select the V function list, and then page down to the VLR functions. Now select the reactor group of interest, such as VLR-OBJECT-REACTOR, VLR-COMMAND-REACTOR, or VLR-ACDB-REACTOR. In the paragraphs detailing the callback functions, you will find information about the types of parameters passed to each callback function.

In this section, you work with a simple example by setting up a reactor that keeps track of how many times a new command is started. The callback function increments a counter each time a command is started. Therefore, it is attached to the command notification reactor set using the VLR-COMMAND-REACTOR subr. Two parameters are supplied for the reactor setup: a string of your own design that identifies that reactor as one of yours and a list of dotted pairs. Each dotted pair contains the name of an event (such as :VLR-CommandWillStart) and the name of the function to evaluate when the event occurs.

Listing 16.1 contains two functions. The first, CMD-COUNTER, is the callback function. The REFOBJ and CMDLIST arguments contain the reference object and a list of commands. Normally, the command list has one member. In this example, that one member is the command just started because this callback function is associated with the "command will start" event. You are not using the parameters, but they are still required. You instead use a global symbol named CMD-COUNT-VALUE. The function first tests to see whether this symbol has a binding. If not, it is set to 0. Then the function increments the counter and ends. The best callback functions are short and quick like this one. They are called into action, take care of business as quickly as possible, and finish.

Listing 16.1 Counting commands with a reactor.

```
(DEFUN CMD-COUNTER (REFOBJ CMDLIST)
  (IF (NULL CMD-COUNT-VALUE)
    (SETQ CMD-COUNT-VALUE 0))
  (SETQ CMD-COUNT-VALUE
    (1+ CMD-COUNT-VALUE))
)


(DEFUN C:CMDCNT1 ()
  (VL-LOAD-COM)
  (VLR-COMMAND-REACTOR
    NIL
    '((:VLR-COMMANDWILLSTART . CMD-COUNTER))))
```

The second function in Listing 16.1 sets up the callback reactor association with the command notification system. Note that VL-LOAD-COM loads the component object manager. The callback system works through the ActiveX interface, so the extended Visual LISP function set must be in memory. The next expression, VLR-COMMAND-REACTOR, attaches the CMD-COUNTER function to the "command will start" event notification list in the command reactor set. After CMDCNT1 is activated, the CMD-COUNTER function counts every command that is started .

Events are specified using a colon before the VLR name. When the colon is present, the value is actually a constant that signifies a particular standard value in AutoCAD. (Like :VLAX-TRUE, the VLR constants begin with a colon.) The :VLR and function name are symbols, not strings. The single quote mark at the start of the nested list definition allows for the use of the names directly without further notations.

To disable reactors, you use the VLR-REMOVE subr. Given the reactor reference, this subr shuts off the specific reactor. You can turn it back on using the procedure in the previous example. To disable all reactors for a given category, use the VLR-REMOVE-ALL subr. If you use VLR-REMOVE-ALL without parameters, all reactors in the system are disabled.

Within a callback function, do not modify the reactor system that called the function because this can confuse both you and the operator. All reactor-based activities should be defined while your application is loading or getting started. It cannot be emphasized enough that you must be careful when developing reactor-based programs. You can change the way AutoCAD is expected to work at a fundamental level, resulting in problems in the system. Autodesk has taken precautions to ensure that a crash resulting from Visual LISP does no permanent damage to the AutoCAD system. In the worst case, you will have to restart the Windows system and then restart AutoCAD. If your program is tied into an automatic startup feature or suite, remove it until you have corrected all the problems causing the crash.

Although your program should ideally know whether it has a reactor present and running, that may not always be the case. The reactor may be something that comes and goes or is loaded on demand. Or you may need to know about reactors currently programmed in the system. Whatever the reason, you can use several subrs to find out about active reactors in the system. Start with VLR-REACTORS, which returns a list of all the reactors active for a category. Use the colon-starting-name of the group, such as :VLR-COMMAND-REACTOR, to obtain a list of all reactors currently attached to that notification group. Given the group of reactors (which are dotted pairs consisting of the event name and the function symbol), you can now interrogate each one separately for a match.

Listing 16.2 contains an example function that checks the command reactors to see whether the callback function from Listing 16.1is defined as part of a reactor. The function starts by using VLR-REACTORS to obtain all the command reactors in the system. CRL is a list, the first member of which is the category code, such as :VLR-COMMAND-REACTOR. Each member in CRL is put into CR in the outermost FOREACH loop. The reactors are supplied as a list; the first member is the code type (as in :VLR-COMMAND-REACTOR) followed by the command reactor objects. There could be one or many command reactors in this list, so CDR is used to supply a list to the inner FOREACH loop.

The VLR-REACTIONS subr returns a list containing groups of events and callback function links given a valid reactor object. This function streams through the list using the third FOREACH loop.

Listing 16.2 Determining whether a reactor is attached

```
(DEFUN CMDCNTACTIVE ( / CRL CR RL RE FND)
  (SETQ CRL (VLR-REACTORS :VLR-COMMAND-REACTOR))
  (FOREACH CR CRL
    (FOREACH RE (CDR CR)
      (FOREACH RL (VLR-REACTIONS RE)
        (IF (EQ (CDR RL) 'CMD-COUNTER)
          (SETQ FND T)))))
  FND
)
```

The CDR of the reactor linkage data is checked for a match to the CMD-COUNTER function. If a match is made, the FND symbol is set to True.

Keeping track of reactors is the responsibility of your application. It is easy to have multiple reactor definitions for the same thing cluttering your system and causing "interesting" results. As such, I strongly recommended that you create housekeeping utilities such as the one shown in Listing 16.2.

One way to keep track of an application full of reactors is to use the data option when defining reactors to the system. The first parameter sent to the VLR-*-REACTOR subrs is the data option. This can be NIL if you don't need to keep track of the reactor, or it can be any LISP data item such as a string. The VLR-DATA subr then retrieves this data after you have the reactor object. Listing 16.3 demonstrates the use of VLR-DATA for housecleaning. Any reactors with data matching the parameter are disabled.

Listing 16.3 Disabling reactors by name.

```
(DEFUN CLEANREACTORS (NAM )
  (SETQ CRL (VLR-REACTORS))
  (FOREACH CR CRL
    (IF (= NAM (VLR-DATA (CADR CR)))
      (VLR-REMOVE (CADR CR)))))
```

It is easy to get things muddled in the system if you are not careful. By using data traces and keeping track of running reactors in your program, your reactors can work properly with others and with AutoCAD.

Object-Level Reactors

Object-level reactors are essentially the same as the command and database types of reactors except they are used only when a specific object is manipulated. Database reactors run every time the database is changed and provide a powerful way to keep track of objects on a global level. They also slow things in AutoCAD because they must be serviced every time the database is updated. If you want to keep track of only a few objects, this is not the right way to proceed. Instead, you should set up specific object reactors.

The reactor can be tied to a single object or a set of objects. When called, the object reactor function is passed three parameters: a reference to the object causing the notification, the reactor object link, and a list containing additional parameters. The content of additional parameters varies based on the reactor being serviced. For entity objects, only the VLR-COPIED and VLR-SUBOBJMODIFIED events send parameters, specifically the new entity object references. The other entity object events send an empty list as the last parameter.

When an entity object reactor is notified, the entity object causing the notification is supplied as an argument to the callback function. Properties and methods for the entity object are available immediately. In many cases, objects that cause a notification event are related to other entity objects. The idea is that if one entity object changes, the others must change or at least be aware of the change. An example, which you will program shortly, is to associate text to a property of another object, such as the area.

The act of attaching a notification event and an associated function reactor to an entity object establishes the entity object as an owner of the reactor. Multiple entity objects can share ownership of a reactor. When the reactor object is first defined, a place is provided for a list of VLA entity objects that claim ownership of the reactor object. Following is the syntax for defining an entity object reactor:

```
(VLR-OBJECT-REACTOR owners data callbacks)
```

Owners is a list of VLA entity objects and may be one or many. data is NIL or contains some Visual LISP data that you can use to identify this reactor as yours. callbacks is a nested list of notification events and associated functions to call when the event takes place.

Inside the callback function, the reactor object is provided as the second argument. Several expressions can be used with the reactor object beyond VLR-DATA. VLR-OWNERS returns a list of VLA entity objects that own the reactor. VLR-REACTIONS returns a list of reactions defined for the reactor. VLR-TYPE reports the type of reactor. VLR-DATA-SET allows you to change the data associated with an object.

Next, you focus on the owner concept because that is an important feature of reactors. In a way, the relationship of objects from a reactor is a lot like a relationship of objects from a selection set. When the reactor is established in the system, a set of entities is related to it. These entities own the reactor. That is, when the entity changes, the reactor is told about it. If the reactor is changed, the entities do nothing; it is a one-way street in that regard. Another way that an ownership group is similar to a selection set is that the group exists only in the current drawing edit session (under normal circumstances).

VLR-OWNERS returns a list of owner object references. You can modify the set of owners stored with a reactor by using VLR-OWNER-ADD or VLR-OWNER-REMOVE to add or remove, respectively, entity objects one at a time after the reactor has been established. These subrs are similar to the SSADD and SSDEL subrs for selection set handling. Objects are added and removed one at a time from the ownership group just as they are with a selection set.

When building an ownership group, it is critical to consider what the different owners mean to the callback function. In some cases, you will want to skip the entity objects because changes to them will not modify other entities. And keep in mind how changes to objects in the ownership list will cause the reactor to fire again should the routine modify the entities.

The primary advantage to having an ownership group is that it makes it easy to find objects related to each other as they are changing. As an example of how these concepts work, Listing 16.4 starts the Visual LISP code for a reactor that ties a text string to an entity object. The basic application is that a text entity object houses the area of the attached objects in the text string. As the entity object is modified, the area value updates automatically. On the other hand, as the text is changed, the object with the area property remains untouched by the reactor.

Listing 16.4 Reactor for updating the display of the area.

```
(DEFUN AREALINKFIX (NOBJ ROBJ PLIST
                   / NEWAREA OBJS VOBJ TOBJ)
  (IF (VLAX-PROPERTY-AVAILABLE-P NOBJ "AREA")
    (PROGN
      (SETQ NEWAREA (VLA-GET-AREA NOBJ)
            OBJS (VLR-OWNERS ROBJ))
      (FOREACH VOBJ OBJS
        (IF (VLAX-PROPERTY-AVAILABLE-P
               VOBJ "TEXTSTRING")
          (SETQ TOBJ VOBJ)))
      (IF TOBJ
        (VLA-PUT-TEXTSTRING TOBJ
          (STRCAT "Area = "
              (RTOS NEWAREA))))))))
  )
```

Listing 16.4 contains the callback function for the reactor. The parameters to the callback function are the notification object (NOBJ), the reactor object (ROBJ), and the parameter list (PLIST). The parameter list is empty because this reactor function is called for an object-modified event. Parameters are passed only for copy and submember change events.

The first expression in the reactor function is a conditional expression to see whether the object that caused the notification is the area object. For each area reactor, there are two entity object owners: one owner is the entity from which the area value is derived, and the other is the text displaying the area value. Thus, this test determines whether the object in question is the text or the one with the area. Because text objects do not have area, only the data source object is selected.

If the object supplying the area is the reason for the callback function being started, the code in PROGN is evaluated. The first step is to extract the area value and place it in the NEWAREA local symbol. Next, the list of entities that are considered owners of the reactor object is placed in OBJS. A FOREACH loop is started in which each entity object is placed in VOBJ. This object is checked to see whether it contains a TEXTSTRING property. If so, it must be the text object, and you want to save that link in TOBJ. Each object in the OBJS list is tested in this manner to locate the text object where the area will be displayed.

After the objects have been processed through the loop, the TOBJ symbol is checked to make sure you found a text object that can be updated. If so, the TEXTSTRING property is updated with the new area value.

Listing 16.4 contains the reactor function. Listing 16.5 contains the setup for the reactor. In this function, the operator is asked to select an object that has area. If a successful selection is made, the object's area is used to create a text entity object to be output at an operator-selected location. Both the text and selected objects are then defined as owners of a new reactor.

Next, you walk through the code in Listing 16.5 to see how the reactor is established with the object ownership. The first step is to call the LINKACTIVEX function, defined in Listing 16.6, which sets up the ActiveX interface reference symbols ,such as the one for model space.

Back in Listing 16.5, ENTSEL is then called for the operator to select an object. If a good selection is made, ENP contains a non-NIL binding and the code continues by setting the V_ENP symbol to the VLA object for the entity in ENP. Next, the V_ENP object is tested to see whether the AREA property is available.

With the AREA property available, the next question to the operator is where to locate the text point. The ENT symbol is set to the data point input as a result of GETPOINT. VLA-ADDTEXT adds a new text object to the model space. This subr is one of the automation extensions in Visual LISP, and the parameters are the entity space into which the object will be added, the text string, the location, and the text size. Your new text object is being added to model space, and the object link for that was established in the (linkActiveX) function. The string for the new text entity is the result of combining the "AREA = " string constant with the string representation of the AREA property. To use VLA-ADDTEXT, the point location in ENT must be converted from a three-dimensional point list to a safe array for ActiveX processing. The VLAX-3D-POINT subr does the conversion. Last, the text height is extracted from the system variables and supplied directly to the VLA-ADDTEXT subr.

VLA-ADDTEXT returns an entity object reference, which is saved in V_ENT. This entity object plus the one selected and saved as V_ENP are the owners of the reactor built in the VLR-OBJECT-REACTOR expression. The first parameter to the object reactor build subr is a list containing the two object references, thereby establishing the ownership of the reactor by these two objects right away. The next two parameters passed to VLR-OBJECT-REACTOR are optional data and the list of reactions. This example function uses the "AreaConnect" string as the attached data for identification by other processes or modules. You are programming only one reaction, and

Listing 16.5 Setting up the area reactor.

```
(DEFUN C:AREALINK ( / ENP ENT V_ENP V_ENT)
  (LINKACTIVEX) ; set link to model space
  (SETQ ENP (ENTSEL "\nSelect object "))
  (IF ENP (PROGN
      (SETQ V_ENP
        (VLAX-ENAME->VLA-OBJECT (CAR ENP)))
      (IF (VLAX-PROPERTY-AVAILABLE-P
              V_ENP "AREA")
        (PROGN
         (SETQ ENT
           (GETPOINT "\nText point: "))
         (IF ENT (PROGN
            (SETQ V_ENT
              (VLA-ADDTEXT
                MODELSPACE
                (STRCAT ;Text
                  "Area = "
                  (RTOS
                    (VLA-GET-AREA V_ENP)))
                (VLAX-3D-POINT ENT)
                (GETVAR "TEXTSIZE")))
            ;
            (VLR-OBJECT-REACTOR
              (LIST V_ENP V_ENT)
              "AreaConnect"
              '((:VLR-MODIFIED . AREALINKFIX))
            )))))))
  (PRINC)
)
```

Listing 16.6 Setting up some reference symbols.

```
(DEFUN LINKACTIVEX ()
  (VL-LOAD-COM)
  (IF (NULL MODELSPACE)
    (SETQ
      ACADAPP (VLAX-GET-ACAD-OBJECT)
      DOCOBJ (VLA-GET-ACTIVEDOCUMENT ACADAPP)
      MODELSPACE (VLA-GET-MODELSPACE DOCOBJ))))
```

that is in response to any changes to the objects. If either the text or the area data objects are changed, the (AreaLinkFix) function is called.

That concludes the setup of the reactor. All you did was select one entity, build a second based on information from the selected entity, and then create a reactor owned by the two objects. The reactor launches the (AreaLinkFix) routine when either entity is modified. The next step in the program is to wait for the event just set up to take place.

One thing that amazes me about Visual LISP is how few lines of code are needed to set up such a complex interaction between AutoCAD objects. The power of object manipulation and the language itself combine well in this regard to deliver a succinct and elegant solution.

The Life of a Reactor

After you define a reactor, it remains active until it is removed using VLR-REMOVE or the drawing ends. When you leave that drawing, the reactor is no longer active. If you start a new drawing, load an older drawing, or close the existing drawing and reload it, the reactor is not available and the setup function is missing — unless you take extra steps to preserve it.

Reactors can be either persistent or transient. By default, all reactors are transient, which means they go away at the end of the drawing edit session. The VLR-PERS subr changes a reactor from transient to persistent. Persistent reactor links are stored when the drawing is stored. Note that only the links, not the reactor functions, are stored with the drawing. Should these drawings end up at a workstation that does not have the functions available and loaded, error messages will indicate that the reactors are missing. To work seamlessly with the CAD system, drawings containing persistent reactors must have the functions installed and set up for loading with the drawings.

Callback functions can be loaded as part of the AutoCAD startup suite. I recommend that you compile the program into a VLX file for faster loading and force the VL-LOAD-COM call during the loading. By setting up a VLX file, you can better integrate into the AutoCAD environment and make use of faster processing. (To set up a VLX file, use the Make Application option in the File menu of the VLIDE.)

Rules and Suggestions for Working with Reactors

A reactor is like a dialog box in that it requires some setup work before it is operational. After that, the similarities end. A dialog box is put up on the screen, filled in, and processed. When the operator clicks a retirement button such as OK or Cancel or a DONE_DIALOG is processed, the dialog box completes and the callback functions are no longer part of the application picture. That is not the case in with reactors. A reactor remains active until it is removed using VLR-REMOVE. You may have a command running and the reactor suddenly runs because the command triggers an event. That command may be running inside another Visual LISP function or a VBA macro, and the reactor function suddenly pops in for evaluation. Because of this type of situation, reactors must not interact with the operator or change the flow of command sequence.

Although you might think that reactors give you supreme power over the system, they do not. Instead, you must adhere to a set of rules that help keep things running in good order. These rules and some suggestions follow.

Rule 1: You cannot cancel or overrule the cause of the reaction

A reactor should not try to cancel or overrule the activity that caused the reaction. This is especially true for command-based reactions. Suppose that an object is to be moved, and your reactor moves it back to where it started. By moving the entity object, your reactor causes another move reaction to take place. If you are not careful, this could result in a reactor that keeps running until the system runs out of memory.

Rule 2: You can not access a deleted object

When an object is being deleted, you can no longer access it inside the reactor. Instead, you are told that the object is tagged for deletion. The VBA object reference cannot be converted to an entity name, and attempts to access this object will be futile. There are clever ways to program around this by storing the entity data elsewhere in the system, but the key is that you cannot stop the delete operation from finishing. Ideally, this is the time when your application would clear any related data or update LISP variables based on the changing object.

Rule 3: Do not modify the object causing the event notification

Object-level reactors should not attempt to modify the object that caused the event notification. Doing so presents problems, even if you try to trick the event handler by causing another event with a different object. It is best to simply work with the data as the object is changing, such as in the area example.

Rule 4: Reactors must not interface with the operator

Do not attempt to perform user interface work in a reactor. Subrs such as ENTSEL and GETPOINT should not appear in a reactor callback function because they modify the sequence of input for a command in AutoCAD. Do not display a dialog box because this greatly changes the interface flow from a user's point of view. Reactors should be free of user input. Instead, the object causing the reaction should be considered the input.

Suggestion 1: Do not change objects in a reactor

In a reactor function, try to not trigger the same event by changing an object that also owns the same reactor. If you are not careful, you could trigger an infinite loop in your program as the reactor calls on the reactor and so on.

If you do trigger the same event, use a test to avoid changing things you don't want to change, as in the area link example. Another way to prevent reactor functions from ending up in an infinite loop is to use global flags that indicate whether the reactor is already busy and whether this iteration of the function is due to changes to a related object in the ownership group.

Suggestion 2: Check before defining an event

You should verify that an event is not already defined before defining another instance of one. Otherwise, you could end up cluttering memory and causing delays in the way AutoCAD runs. The other way to keep memory under control is to keep track of reactors in your application.

Suggestion 3: Keep reactors fast and error free

Reactors should be quick and as free of errors as possible. More than one reactor may be attached to an object, so you may have to service more than one reactor in an advanced environment. The reactor that behaves best does the least. Reactors are for data gathering more than graphics manipulation. Although you can do graphics manipulations, as demonstrated in the example functions, that is not a reactor's strong point. Graphics-manipulation-based functions that are completely error-free can be difficult to write, especially if you try to keep the user in mind at all times.

The real power of reactors is in fact gathering and checking. As data is entered, you can check it and monitor the operator's performance. The latter is not of interest unless you time operators to check productivity or bill by the hour for CAD time. The next level up in complexity is the use of reactors to set up an intelligent system by "learning" as you draw. Consider an application that designs bridges. It starts by drawing a polyline representing the centerline of the highway, and then inserts a rectangular polyline representing the bridge limits. The reactors could sense the addition of the bridge limits and suggest a next step or an alternative alignment.

Suggestion 4: Make reactors self-contained

You cannot anticipate the sequence of reactor calls. Just because your computer runs a particular sequence does not mean that my computer will run the same sequence when a complex series of reactors is involved. As such, each reactor should be self-contained and not expect to see data from other reactors in the system. The only exception is reactors tied to the start and stop of related events, such as the LISP command starting and ending events.

Summary

Event-driven programming is becoming more common in interactive environments. You have already seen some event-driven programming in the form of dialog boxes. The preparation steps are roughly the same for dialog boxes and event-driven programs: Define some functions to serve as callback functions, and then link them to the notification management system. After the functions are linked, they are on their own to run whenever a particular event takes place.

This chapter discussed the types of reactors available to the Visual LISP programmer, starting with the global, or general, reactors and leading to the object-level reactors. You looked at a command-level reactor that simply counted the number of commands started by the operator. The example showed what was required to set up a basic reactor function and have AutoCAD make use of it as events take place.

You learned how to manipulate reactor objects using a variety of VLR subrs in Visual LISP. An example utility was presented that demonstrated the use of the optional data attribute for reactor management. You then followed the steps involved in setting up a reactor group and attaching entity objects. An example showed the LISP code required for pulling off some reactor "magic." The reactor example changed text as the area of a linked object was adjusted due to changes caused by operator edits.

Reactors are a powerful tool in the Visual LISP programmer's toolbox. But with this tool comes more responsibility than with other Visual LISP programming tools. Reactors can change the way AutoCAD runs and can have a great effect on operators as a result. Follow the guidelines for programming good reactors as closely as possible to avoid having reactors that go out of control.

CHAPTER 17

Working with the Computer

The traditional place for storing data in a computer is in a file. Files can be on a disk, on backup media (such as a tape or CDR), in the computer's memory, or elsewhere across a network. In most cases, a file is a simple sequence of bytes that means something to a program. That sequence may consist of ASCII characters, binary representations of numbers, or other data types.

A typical integrated application environment gathers data from one source, manipulates it, and then stores it in a file to be processed later by another application that reads the file. That other application may report on the data or use it for something else, such as verifying an external reference. In other words, files are used for communication between processes as well as a place to house data while it is not in active use.

In Visual LISP, programming files are used to read data from other sources and to store data for other applications. Visual LISP file accessing is powerful but also has limitations. This chapter explores the subrs provided in Visual LISP for file processing and also points to where you should go next depending on your interface or integration needs.

Types of Data Files

You have worked with `LSP` and `DCL` files, the source code files for your Visual LISP program modules using the VLIDE. But a computer has many other types of files. Most have a file type, which is considered the file name extension in Windows. For example, an `EXE` file is an executable binary file, a `VLX` file is a compiled Visual LISP project, and a `DLL` file is a dynamic link library. Most file types in Windows have an associated application, such as DWG for AutoCAD drawings and TXT for Notepad. An application can declare a file extension to be associated with the application.

Thus, when you think of a type of data file, you often think of associated data files for applications. But there are only two types of data files, regardless of their extension: ASCII files and binary files. The difference between the two is simply whether or not an elementary text editor can read them. ASCII text file examples include `LSP` and `DCL` files. They can be viewed not only in the

VLIDE but also using a simple text editor such as MS-DOS EDIT or Windows NOTEPAD. DWG files are examples of binary files. You can view them only with AutoCAD or in a program written specifically to read and display DWG files. Visual LISP applications that involve files will most likely use ASCII text files.

Visual LISP has subrs for reading and writing sequential text files. In a sequential file, you start at the beginning and proceed through the file until either the end is reached or the item being sought is located. (With a random access file, you can back up or jump around in a file. The Visual LISP subr library does not support random access because Visual LISP it is not a file manager or database system.) When accessing files, you will be either reading a stream of text or working with an external database system (such as Access).

Database systems in Windows can be programmed through ActiveX automation or by using a driver system. You looked at the basics behind ActiveX automation in Chapter 15 (attach the application object and then use methods and properties), and it should be clear that the tools used to run another program are documented in the other application's help system. Database systems such as Microsoft Access use ActiveX automation for external process interfaces, and Visual LISP works quite well with that tool.

Database system suppliers adopted the SQL standard several years ago. As far back as AutoCAD Release 12 with the ASE (AutoCAD SQL Extension), database access has been available from inside AutoCAD. For more information about attaching a database to AutoCAD, see the DBCONNECT information in the main AutoCAD online help, because the ASE routines are no longer supported.

Disks, Files, and Directories

Files are organized in directories, which are on disks or some other storage device. When accessing a file, the program normally must supply the complete path — unless the file is in the same search path as AutoCAD or in the default current directory. Even if a file is located in a local directory, you may need to supply the complete path, name, and extension so that subrs can locate the file.

In Windows, directories are called folders. A folder name can consist of most characters, including spaces. The name cannot contain colons and slashes because these characters are used to separate the device (drive) and folders so that the system can find a particular file. The "C:\Program Files\Acad2000\test1.txt" file name string means that the file is located on the local C device in a folder named Acad2000, which is in a folder named Program Files. This method of designating files and directories has been used in computer programming for a long time and continues today.

In Visual LISP, the backslash character has another purpose in string handling. Visual LISP interprets the backslash as the first character of a control sequence, as in "\n" for a new line or "\e" for the Escape key. Thus, Visual LISP would send an ASCII 27 (character code for the escape key) instead of "\e" to another device or program. There are two ways to get around this problem with file and external device handling. The first is to use a forward slash in place of the backslash. The file name "C:\TEMP\TEST1.TXT" would be written as "C:/TEMP/TEST1.TXT". The other option is use a double backslash character sequence, as in "C:\\TEMP\\TEST1.TXT". A double backslash tells Visual LISP that the slash is not a control character but rather a slash in the string.

To locate a file using Visual LISP, use the FINDFILE subr. FINDFILE searches the AutoCAD search paths defined in the preferences for a particular user profile. (User profile objects are accessed in the AutoCAD application root object.) FINDFILE returns NIL if it cannot locate the file in question. Otherwise, it results in a string that contains the complete path and file name plus the extension. The string contains double backslash characters for the directory separations and is suitable for use in any Visual LISP subrs that uses file names. FINDFILE has one parameter, the file name to seek. If the file name supplied contains a directory path, that is the only place FINDFILE looks. When the file name contains no path or folder information, the entire AutoCAD search path is checked.

Another way to locate a file is to have the user point it out with a file browser. A file browser is a dialog box that appears for the purposes of navigating devices and folders to locate a file. The GETFILED subr displays a browser dialog box with defaults based on the parameters supplied to the subr. There are four parameters: three strings and an integer flag. The first string is the title for the dialog box, such as Select my file. The second and third strings contain a default file name and default file extension to display, respectively. The last parameter is an integer indicating what kind of file the operator can select.

GETFILED can be used when you want the operator to select new or existing files. When set up for new files, any selection of an existing file results in a message telling the operator that the file will be overwritten. For existing files, you can prohibit the input of a file name, forcing the operator to select an existing file instead. Both GETFILED and FINDFILE return NIL if no file is selected or found. If the file is found, they return a string, which can be used to further process the file.

Processing Files

File processing in Visual LISP is straightforward. The first step is to open the file. When a file is opened, you must declare whether you intend to write a new file, append to an existing file, or read an existing file. After the file is opened, you read it or write to it, but not both at the same time. If you open a file twice at the same time, once for reading and again for writing, the results will most likely not be what you want because the file transactions are buffered in memory.

Because all files processed by Visual LISP are ASCII text files, strings are used to send and receive data. Strings can be handled one character at a time or as a complete set of characters. After the file processing is finished, the file must be closed before it can be used again. Thus, the steps for processing a file are to open it, read it or write to it, and then close it.

The OPEN subr opens a file and returns a file handle, which is a special data type in Visual LISP for communicating with the operating system. The operating system is responsible for handling all file-based transactions between computer memory and the disk system (or network). When a file is opened, a place in the operating system's memory is reserved and assigned an ID. The controlling program uses that ID when referencing the open file.

In Visual LISP, the file handle is used to get file ID information. This is why it is important to close files when you are finished with them. Even though your Visual LISP program may have finished, AutoCAD cannot be sure you are finished with the file. After all, another module may start and expect to find that file open and ready for processing. If the file handle is no longer available but the file is left open, no other programs can access the associated file until the drawing is closed.

OPEN has two arguments: the file name and the processing mode, which are both provided as strings. The file name should include the complete path and extension of the file using either forward slash or double backslash characters for the dividers between the folder (directory) names. The processing mode options are "a" for append, "r" for read, and "w" for write. If OPEN is successful, a file handle is returned; otherwise, the result if NIL. The result returned from OPEN must be saved in a symbol reference using SETQ for further references to the file.

OPEN should always be used with SETQ, as in the following expression:

```
(SETQ FH (OPEN "MYFILE.TXT" "r"))
```

This expression opens the MYFILE.TXT file in read mode. The file is expected to be located in the current directory or search path for AutoCAD. The result of the OPEN expression is saved using the FH symbol for further access to the file just opened. The next step in any program is to test the binding of FH. If NIL, the OPEN did not succeed.

OPEN can fail for a variety of reasons, depending on the open mode used. When reading files, a failed open signifies that the file is missing, the file is not where you told the system to get it, the file name is invalid, the path is invalid, the extension is wrong or missing, or the file is locked by another program. When writing files, errors vary from being out of disk space, an invalid file name, invalid path information, or a locked file. Appending to a file is just like writing to the file. In fact, if the file does not exist and you've requested to append data to the file, a new file is created for output just as if you had requested to write data.

When you have finished processing a file, you use the CLOSE subr to release memory and finish any remaining tasks with the file. Visual LISP files are buffered in memory, so they are not updated every time you write something to them. The act of closing a file that has been opened for writing flushes any unwritten data from memory to the disk file. For example, Listing 17.1 contains a function that records events to the EVENT.LOG text file in the current directory. The function starts by opening the EVENT.LOG file in append mode. This means that if the file exists, new data in the S string is written to the end of the file. If the file is not found, a new one is created in the current directory.

Listing 17.1 Logging an event.

```
(DEFUN EVENTLOg (S / FH)
  (SETQ FH (OPEN "EVENT.LOG" "a"))
  (WRITE-LINE S FH)
  (CLOSE FH)
)
```

WRITE-LINE outputs a string to a file given the file handle. At the end of the string, an Enter keystroke is added. WRITE-LINE is like typing into a text editor and then pressing the Enter key. The characters for a newline are appended to the string, forcing the next output to a new line when displayed in a text viewer. A new line is character code 10 (line feed) or the combination of codes 13 and 10 (carriage return and line feed). Visual LISP uses the latter. These values become important when you process the file in another application.

The last action in the function is to close the file. Closing the file sends the string to the disk so that, when the function returns, the file is not left open and data is not left in memory.

The function in Listing 17.1 represents the sort of routine that you can use in advanced and time consuming applications. An event-logging system assists in tracking down problems in a process or in updates later in the life cycle of the software. Because this function opens and closes the file each time, the processing is slightly slower, but the tradeoff is that the information in the log is always current, containing the last message processed by the function.

Writing Data

You can use the PRINT, PRINC, and PRIN1 expressions along with WRITE-LINE and WRITE-CHAR to output data to files one you use depends on the type of data you are writing to the file. String data is best handled with WRITE-LINE. The newline character sequence is automatically appended to the string with the output. PRINT also outputs a newline sequence but at the front of the string. In addition, it adds a space at the end of the string and outputs the double quotes.

PRIN1 outputs the string with double quotes, but no new line at the beginning and no space at the end. PRINC, on the other hand, removes the double quotes for output and provides no extra characters at the front or back. The choices are varied because your needs are varied.

WRITE-CHAR uses integers representing the ASCII character values of the string to be output. You use this subr when you need exact format control or are outputting exceptionally long strings of data.

In most Visual LISP file output situations, you can use the WRITE-LINE or PRIN subrs. WRITE-CHAR is for situations requiring special characters or control characters from the ASCII set, such as the tab character. Writing ASCII value 9 is the same as a tab in a text file.

Listing 17.2 demonstrates how to write a tab-delimited file, where a tab character (ASCII 9) separates each item of data. The TabFileOut function takes a list and writes it to the file with a tab character between each element. The function starts by opening a file in append mode, and then it writes the first element from the list to the file. To complete the output of the list, a FOREACH loop goes through the remaining items in the list. Inside the FOREACH loop, a tab character is output using WRITE-CHAR and the list item is output using PRIN1. After exhausting the list, an ASCII code 10 is sent to the file. This character causes the carriage return (code 13) to be output as well because a text file under MS-DOS and Windows normally uses the codes 13 and 10 as a pair.

Writing data to a file is easy as long as you don't try to do too much. Visual LISP's file output capabilities are intended for report generation and interfacing to other applications. If you need random access file writing, Visual LISP is not the solution unless the file output can be accomplished using ActiveX-type interfaces or unless an ObjectARX extension can be custom written to interface with the files you need. For most applications involving Visual LISP, sequential file output is sufficient.

Reading Data

Reading data from files also involves working with ASCII text files. You can use only two subrs to read data from a file after it is opened in read mode: READ-LINE for reading a string and

Listing 17.2 Writing to a tab-delimited file.

```
(DEFUN TABFILEOUT (FILENAM ALIST / FH ITEM)
  (SETQ FH (OPEN FILENAM "a"))
  (PRIN1 (CAR ALIST) FH)
  (FOREACH ITEM (CDR ALIST)
    (WRITE-CHAR 9 FH)
    (PRIN1 ITEM FH)
  )
  (WRITE-CHAR 10 FH)
  (SETQ FH (CLOSE FH))
)
```

READ-CHAR for reading a character as an ASCII value. READ-LINE reads the characters of a file until a newline sequence is encountered. In most cases, READ-LINE works fine for reading data from a file. READ-CHAR is required when you are working with very long lines of text or using specially formatted strings in files.

When reading data from a file that is destined for a list, the READ subr can be used to quickly convert everything to numbers and strings. To convert the input to strings, the double quotes and delimiters must be consistent with what Visual LISP normally recognizes. That is, delimiters can be any white space such as the space character, a tab, or a newline. Normally when reading from a text file, the delimiter is a tab or a space. Newline-delimited files are read by simply issuing repeated calls to READ-LINE. (An example of a newline-delimited file is the AutoCAD DXF file.)

You'll frequently encounter comma-delimited files. Although you might be tempted to use the string search-and-replace utilities provided in Visual LISP to replace commas with spaces, keep in mind that those utilities replace legitimate commas in the data strings as well. Thus, a more robust parser that knows when to convert a comma may be required. An example is provided on the CD as part of Listing 17.3. Listing 17.3 contains a function that reads a comma-delimited data file into a list.

READ-LINE pulls each line from the file. The text lines are converted using the (COMMA_PARSE) utility, which is on the CD as part of Chapter 17's example functions. The result from (COMMA_PARSE) is a string with the commas replaced by spaces. This string is passed to STRCAT with an open and closing parentheses pair, making the string suitable for processing by the READ subr. READ converts the string to a data list that is added to the RES result list. After the file is read, it is closed, and the RES result list is reversed to return the list data in the order in which it was encountered in the file.

Although reading a file has fewer options than writing to a file, your applications will often have to do more work to convert the data to something usable. The ideal situation is when you are the programmer of both the output and the input formats. But with increased advances in integration concepts and tools for computers, it is unlikely that such a luxury will exist for all applications that you will write.

Listing 17.3 Reading a comma-delimited file.

```
(DEFUN READCOMMALIST (FILENAME / FH LN LS RES)
  (SETQ FH (OPEN FILENAME "r"))
  (IF FH
    (PROGN
      (WHILE (SETQ LN (READ-LINE FH))
        (SETQ RES
          (CONS
            (READ
             (STRCAT
               "("
               (COMMA_PARSE LN)
               ")"))
          RES)))
      (SETQ FH (CLOSE FH))))
  (REVERSE RES))
```

Visual LISP File Management Tools

Rounding out the file tools in Visual LISP is a set of basic file management subrs. Actions such as renaming and deleting files are accomplished using these utilities, which mimic the original MS-DOS or UNIX commands. Table 17.1 lists only a portion of the subrs supplied in Visual LISP for file manipulation.

Most of these subrs use file name strings of the type that appear in an OPEN expression — folders are separated with double backslashes or a forward slash, and the extension appears after the last period in the file name. For example, VL-FILE-RENAME accepts two strings representing file names. The first is the original file name and the second is the new file name. If you supply path names, they are used. This means you can use VL-FILE-RENAME to move files from one directory to another by simply changing the path name of the destination but keeping the file name the same. Listing 17.4 demonstrates this feature of VL-FILE-RENAME by using several VL-FILE subrs to define a utility function that moves a file from one directory to another.

Listing 17.4 has two arguments: the file name to be moved and the name of the new directory to which the file will be moved. FINDFILE is used to locate the exact position of the source file. If it is successful, the last character from the new directory is extracted for testing. If that character does not equal a slash (either a forward slash or a double backslash), a double backslash is added to the end of the directory string. At this point, VL-FILE-RENAME has everything it needs and can start. The source file name is used along with the result of concatenating the new directory string plus the file base name and extension from the original source file.

Table 17.1 Common file management tools.

Subr	Description
VL-FILE-COPY	Copies a file to a new location
VL-FILE-DELETE	Removes a file from the directory
VL-FILE-RENAME	Renames a file or moves it to a new directory
VL-FILE-SYSTIME	Gets the file creation specifics
VL-FILENAME-BASE	Returns just the base file name from a file string
VL-FILENAME-DIRECTORY	Returns just the path or directory from a file string
VL-FILENAME-EXTENSION	Returns just the extension from a file string
VL-FILENAME-MKTEMP	Creates a temporary file name
VL-FILESIZE	Reports the byte size of a file

Listing 17.4 Moving a file.

```
(DEFUN FILE_MOVE (FILENAME NEWDIR / CH)
  (SETQ FILENAME (FINDFILE FILENAME))
  (IF FILENAME
    (PROGN
      (SETQ CH (SUBSTR NEWDIR (STRLEN NEWDIR)))
      (IF (AND
            (/= CH "/")
            (/= CH "\\"))
        (SETQ NEWDIR (STRCAT NEWDIR "\\")))
      (VL-FILE-RENAME FILENAME
        (STRCAT
          NEWDIR
          (VL-FILENAME-BASE FILENAME)
          (VL-FILENAME-EXTENSION FILENAME))))))
```

You can use the file manipulation tools in Visual LISP to build a variety of utilities to match your application. For example, suppose that you want to insert a line in an existing file. You could use VL-FILENAME-MKTEMP to create a new file name for temporary use, and then rename the old file to this new name. As a result, the original file no longer exists and can be created again. Open the temporary file for processing and copy the lines or records from the original file to the new file until the point where you want to insert the new line(s). Write the new lines, and then continue copying the old file to the new location. When the operation is finished, delete the temporary file. This sort of file and data manipulation takes a long time when dealing with vast amounts of data, but it is fast when working with small data sets.

VL-FILE-DELETE erases a file. The file is removed from the system entirely, and you must use an undelete utility to recover it. Visual LISP does not provide such a utility because that is the realm of the operating system.

Two subrs deal with the creation and listing of directories. VL-MKDIR creates directories, and VL-DIRECTORY-FILES returns a list of file names. The list of directory files is based on wildcard selections defined by the calling routine. For example, you can request that VL-DIRECTORY-FILES return a list of only DWG (drawing) type files. Or you can have the subr return a list of directories instead of file names. This powerful subr can be used to populate a list box in a dialog box to create your own browser, giving you more control over the operator's selections.

An example of the VL-DIRECTORY-FILES subr in action is provided on the CD. The FileSelect function demonstrates a custom browser dialog box from which an operator may select more than one file name. Listing 17.5 shows only a portion of the code; the remainder is on the CD itself.

Listing 17.5 Preparing to browse for files.

```
(SETQ FL (VL-DIRECTORY-FILES
         DIR (NTH IEXT PAT) 1)
     DR (VL-DIRECTORY-FILES
         DIR NIL -1)
     FL (VL-SORT FL 'str_compare)
     DR (VL-SORT DR 'str_compare))
```

The DIR symbol contains a string with a directory name. IEXT is an integer offset into a list of strings named PAT with the file extension patterns from the FILESELECT function on the CD. Thus, the first expression with VL-DIRECTORY-FILES returns a list containing the file names in the DIR directory with an extension as selected from the PAT list. The code value 1 as the last parameter indicates that you are interested only in file names. The list of files matching the pattern string is placed in FL at the end of this expression.

The second time VL-DIRECTORY-FILES is used in the example listing, it obtains a list of directory names to be placed in the DR symbol. NIL is used as the extension name when searching only for directories.

The last two expressions call the Visual LISP sort utility to put the file and directory names in order. The STR_COMPARE function is provided on the CD. VL-SORT accepts a list and a subr name. The subr must be defined in a proper format with two arguments. The function returns T (true) if the value of the first argument appears in front of the value in the second element. The function returns NIL (false) if the first argument's value must be swapped with the second. Because the comparison function is your own design, you can use VL-SORT to work with all types of lists.

See the source code on the CD for the remainder of the multiple-selection dialog box example. Note that a DCL file must accompany the LSP file and must be located in the search directory of AutoCAD.

Summary

Visual LISP provides a robust set of file manipulation and management tools, although they are not as sophisticated as other programming environments for data file control. A basic set of Visual LISP subrs are dedicated to file output and input for string data. Because a wide variety of tools are available for converting data to and from strings, a string-based system serves most applications quite well.

File interfaces are an important way to integrate various tasks and jobs in a computer network. Examples of file interfacing for Visual LISP are reading the input coordinates from a measuring machine and obtaining a list of notes to be placed in a drawing. Output files may be used, for example, in a finite element analysis or downloaded to a machine tool for creation of the part drawn. To perform these tasks, you can use sequential text files.

Visual LISP can also speak with database engines running with an ActiveX automation interface. If the database system has an exposed ActiveX interface, such as Access does, Visual LISP can attach to the database and take advantage of any methods and properties.

Using the Visual LISP file management tools, a program can perform elementary directory operations such as creating new directories and navigating through a hierarchy programmatically. Most of the time, such searches are based on operator directions, but you can write a Visual LISP program to search an entire drive or network system.

Remember that searching through a file takes significantly longer than searching through a list. As such, you should use files for storing information that you read or write once during an application run. If you need random access to a data structure, load it into a large list, process the data in that fashion, and then write it to the disk. Visual LISP and the power of list processing make such applications feasible; you might be surprised to see how large a list Visual LISP handles with ease.

Epilogue

After reading a book like this, you are probably asking, "Where do I turn next?" Technology is always changing, so there will always be more to learn — and exploit. Even after working with LISP for more than 15 years, I continue to learn on a regular basis.

So where do you go next? The best place is the keyboard or your desk to start writing and designing applications. Start small and dream big. Begin with a small part of the project and solve it. You will learn from that experience and be better prepared to solve the next small part of the dream. Do not throw away the dream just because it seems to be something that will take years to achieve at your current skill level.

Caesar would have made a good applications designer. "Divide and conquer" is a good philosophy not only for the deployment of armies but also for the design of a complex application. When confronting a large application, divide it into many pieces by creating a hierarchy of connected modules with some command and communication between them. And then further divide those until you begin to define chunks that you can "see" as program code. This hierarchy of command and logic will allow you to keep your application connected as you create the various modules and utilities that make up the application.

The following are some books that you might find helpful along the way:

- *Visual LISP: A Guide to Artful Programming* by Phil Kreiker (2000, published by Autodesk Press)

- *AutoCAD Database Connectivity* by Scott MacFarlane (1999, published by Autodesk Press)

- *AutoLISP Treasure Chest* by Bill Kramer (1997, published by CMP Books)

- *ObjectARX Primer* by Bill Kramer (2000, published by Autodesk Press)

- *Programming AutoCAD 2000 Using ObjectARX* by Charles McAuley (2000, published by Autodesk Press)

There is no substitute for trying, which is why I end every article I write about programming with the simple message, "Keep on programmin'."

Index

Symbols

A

B

C